Christian -and- Married

How To Be One Without Losing The Other

MARRIAGE LINE DO NOT CROSS

MARRIAGE LINE DO NOT CROSS

Learn. Laugh. Live. And Love Again.

by Tiffany Kameni

CHRISTIAN AND MARRIED: HOW TO BE ONE WITHOUT LOSING THE OTHER

by Tiffany Kameni

Anointed Fire™ Christian Publishing
www.anointedfirecp.com

COPYRIGHT

ISBN-10: 0-9854106-0-4
ISBN-13: 978-0-9854106-0-5

Contributors
Tiffany Buckner-Kameni (Author)
Iris L. Jones (Editor)

Anointed Fire™ Christian Publishing

DISCLAIMER

- Some names and identifying details have been changed to protect the privacy of individuals.

- I have tried to recreate events, locales and conversations from my memories of them. In order to maintain their anonymity in some instances I have changed the names of individuals and places, I may have changed some identifying characteristics and details such as physical properties, occupations and places of residence.

- This book is designed to provide information and motivation to our readers. It is sold with the understanding that the publisher is not engaged to render any type of psychological, legal, or any other kind of professional advice. The content of each article is the sole expression and opinion of its author, and not necessarily that of the publisher. No warranties or guarantees are expressed or implied by the publisher's choice to include any of the content in this volume. Neither the publisher nor the individual author(s) shall be liable for any physical, psychological, emotional, financial, or commercial damages, including, but not limited to, special, incidental, consequential or other damages. Our views and rights are the same: You are responsible for your own choices, actions, and results.

Table of Contents

Introduction

There are many who are married, but they don't know how to be married. Many have the door of divorce in view, but they are trying to find another possible door before considering what looks like the inevitable. There are many who are hesitant to take such a big step because they've seen so many failed marriages.

In marriage, you have to know how to be married. After finding the person we believe to be the one set apart just for us, we tend to pack our clothes, our attitudes, and our ungodly ways. After the ceremony, we begin to unpack these disastrous mindsets and hope that our new spouses can embrace them. We also bring our good qualities in, believing them to be enough to sustain our marriages. In truth, the mate does not have to conform to our ways; instead, our ways, and our spouse's ways, should conform to the WORD of GOD. The WORD is the meeting ground where there is no door for strife to enter. Nevertheless, the average man or woman enters marriage with a "meet me where I am" mindset.

This book is a roller coaster that is going to take on the ups and downs of yourself and help you to change the course of your marriage by changing the direction of your ways. You will learn more, you will understand more, and you will become a better spouse. GOD has already placed within you the weapons that you need to fight off the enemy; the lesson is learning how to locate those weapons, learning to hold them, and learning how to become an effective warrior.

You will learn why we make certain choices for our lives and how to destroy the root of those choices that have divided marriages for generations.

In this book, prepare to laugh as we journey on the highway to self-discovery and self-recovery.

Buffer

When one does not conform to the world's view of how to walk, talk, and think, they are usually diagnosed with a disorder. Merriam-Webster Dictionary defines disorder as: *to disturb the order of.* We must realize that the order of the world conflicts with and challenges the order of GOD. Therefore, obeying the WORD of GOD, to the world, is disorder. What the world sometimes perceives as a disorder is a simple reflection of its lack of understanding. That means that everything that looks abnormal may be super-normal. Super-normal means: *out of range with the man's limited perceptions; superior.*

Let's think of a cell phone. Each cell phone provider has towers in certain areas, and each tower sends out and receives signals from within a specific mile radius. When you go outside of that provider's range, you lose the signal. When you travel outside of the world's range of understanding, you have crossed over into a place where their signals of comprehension cannot be reached.

In dealings with our spouses, the majority of us witness what we believe to be disorderly behavior. Maybe hubby left the seat up on the toilet, or the wife seems to be a little too sensitive. Either way, we consider their behavior disorderly simply because we can't understand them. Does this make them horrible covenant partners? Not at all. The way to tear down Satan's strongman of strife is to build more towers. You have to be willing participants in the disabling of any live ammunition that the enemy may use against you, and you must work together at building more towers. In doing so, your understanding and tolerance will allow you to travel greater distances without losing your connection to one another.

One of the most common reasons for divorce today is recorded as irreconcilable differences. That means the couple was unable to resolve their problems mutually. When you stand in a court room, or in a lawyer's office proclaiming irreconcilable differences; you have just lied on the LORD. There are no differences that are impossible to resolve in CHRIST. The real problem is that one or both spouses have tried to resolve the issues on their own without involving the LORD. Their failure to do so glorifies GOD because it shows that we need HIM in our marriages. Nevertheless, this gives the once sacred union of marriage a bad name.

So many of us have fallen victim to our parents' warped views and opinions on marriage. We tend to follow in the footsteps and mindsets of our parents. This is why we have to get the WORD of GOD in us, so we can be changed by the renewing of our minds. Renew means "to make new again." As babies, our minds are innocent, and we aren't burdened by fear, past hurts, and generational mindsets. As we grow older, however, we begin to pick up on our parents' mindsets unknowingly, and we try to fuse them into our marriages. Children of divorced parents are more likely to go through a divorce than children of parents who remained married. This is why your mind has to be renewed or restored back to the point where faith kept you innocent.

When we become victims of these mindsets, it is usually because we have permitted lies to reside in our hearts. They become our ways of thinking, and our thinking patterns will always direct our decisions. Do not allow a lie to introduce itself to your mind and move into your heart. When lies start to court you, liars become attracted to you. You hear a lot of single women proclaiming, "I must have a magnet on me that attracts liars and losers!" When one is deaf to the things of the spirit, they often spoke the truth, yet they do not hear it. When a woman finds herself always attracting the wrong type of men, it is because she doesn't understand that there is no "type" that is right for her; instead, there is only "one" who is right for her. Nevertheless, because of her way of thinking, she attracts the wrong men because she hasn't learned to be the right woman. Something within her puts out a scent in the spirit realm that attracts demonically obsessed or possessed individuals. Until she gets delivered, she will always find herself attracting men to her but never attracting "the" right man to her.

Note to the Ladies

Are you sleeping with the enemy? The enemy is not your spouse; even though it may feel that way at times. The enemy is Satan, and the enemy is self. At times, we can be our own worst enemy.

Mrs. Wife: You wake up, and there he is. He's lying there sound asleep, and you've had trouble sleeping all night. How can he sleep in such a thick environment? Here you are, an emotional pile of rubble. All you want to do is fix the problem by talking about it again and again until you are satisfied with his response. Ladies, men have been on to this for years. We want to talk, talk, and talk some more until he is torn down; and we can build him up the way we think he should be built. The problem is you are trying to fix a problem using a problem. How does this work? You have to rid your marriage of the problem, rather than trying to repair it. Ladies, we are built to look Ford tough, but at the throw of something as little as a misunderstanding, our airbags deploy; our alarm starts going off, and we're ready to call a tow truck because we have trouble understanding that emotions and truth cannot mix. Think of it this way: Babies cry instinctively because GOD instilled this in them as a means of communication when they cannot talk. As they get older and learn to speak, they begin to cry less because they have found a better way to communicate. When we witness a child four-years-old or older crying uncontrollably, and the parent of the child tries to pacify that child, we shake our heads in dismay. That child has learned to use his or her vocal cords as a way of demanding what they want, but because they are old enough to communicate better, it is no longer a means of communication, but now a means of manipulation. Paul said in 1 Corinthians 13:11, *"When I was a child, I spake as a child, I understood as a child, I thought as a child: but when I became a man, I put away childish things."* It is imperative to stop pacifying childish behavior.

Having an emotional fit is the way of a child and is also one of the wiles of the enemy; it is witchcraft. How can you pray in one breath and use witchcraft with that same tongue? This may be your old way of doing things, but as you got older spiritually; you should have divorced this tactic. Until you are of the right age; spiritually speaking, you should not be married because any man who is more mature than you becomes a spiritual pedophile when he marries you. This is why GOD tells us, in Matthew 6:33, *"But seek ye first the kingdom of GOD and HIS righteousness; and all these things shall be added unto you."* If you seek a mate first, you are out of the will of GOD, and the enemy will subtract from you even the peace that you have now.

When you seek a husband, you will not find the one that GOD has appointed and anointed for you. Instead, you'll find a man. When a man is married, he doesn't become a husband; he becomes a married man. There is a difference between a married man and a husband. A married man is a flesh led creature who serves himself through sin. A husband is a super-man, dressed and anointed by GOD to take on the duties of leading a home. A husband can lead a wife because he has learned to follow the LORD, but a man will never make a good leader because he is still following the lustful and selfish desires of his own heart. When you marry a mere man, your lesson will begin and life will become an unmerciful professor. Some children learn in the biblical classroom; meaning they follow the instructions of GOD as spoken in the Bible. Other students have to go to boot camp. Being married to a mere man is like climbing a mountain barefoot. In addition, you are out of

GOD'S will when you seek a husband, because the bible tells us, *"Whoso findeth a wife findeth a good thing, and obtaineth favour of the LORD" (Proverbs 18:22).*

Secondly, when you have not followed the order of GOD, you are blind to the next level of your ministry. Since marriage is a ministry, you will walk into it with no vision. You may have ideas about the direction that you want your marriage to go in, but without GOD; you won't be led to the right place because you will have no visual ahead to see where you are going. In obedience, we are elevated level by level. It's like a set of steps that appear before us every time we step forward in CHRIST. With each level of ministry, GOD instills in us a certain amount of knowledge to sustain us in that level and help us to get to the next level. The ability to hold our mates and our marriages together is within us, but only obedience will draw it out of us. Yet, many of us have allowed romance novels and movies to cause us to want to fast-forward past GOD'S will for us, and go straight into the 'happily ever afters.' When we go through the honeymoon stage, we want to pause this part of the relationship; but when that relationship is tried by fire, you will know if GOD put it together or not. If HE didn't call it together, it will chaff away. If HE did call it together, it will withstand the tests of time. Nevertheless, GOD will explain HIS will for you through HIS WORD or through your suffering. It's not that GOD wants to break you down; HE is simply building your faith up in HIM. In HIS will, you will be molded; but outside of HIS will, you will be chiseled.

Maybe you lacked intimacy growing up on behalf of your parents. That's okay, but it's time out for victim status. If you live in the past, you'll die in the future. One of those parts of you has got to be buried.

As for me, I got married to my first husband at a young age, physically and spiritually. Spiritually speaking, I was probably barely a year-old; fresh out of the world, and a backsliding mess of a woman. At that time, I felt I needed the love of a man to complete me. I'd just given up partying, and was beginning to frequent church. Of course, I thought this was enough because I went to church every Sunday. My idea of "good" was in comparison to where I'd just traveled from spiritually. I can remember going to church, and watching men and women praise GOD with tears in their eyes. They had their hands extended, and they worshiped the LORD without shame. I marveled at this because I didn't understand what they were feeling. I excused their behavior, believing they were simply going through something, and church seemed like the right place to let the tears flow since there were people there to pray for them. Again, I was young. I jokingly love to tell people how, by the end of that marriage, I was one of those people. I finally understood. I had tried to assume a role that was not my own, and I watched GOD hold me together and strengthen me when I was falling apart. I learned to cry out to HIM; I learned to tell HIM my problems; I learned to thank HIM when HE brought me through; I learned to talk to HIM one on one. In short: I not only learned to say HIS NAME; I came to know HIM intimately.

When we are receiving the lashes associated with disobedience, so many of us begin to turn on GOD. I couldn't because knew I was wrong. At the time, I didn't fully understand everything that was happening around me, nor did I understand the art of warfare; but I understood that I'd came in through the window (sin) to get into that union, but consequence opened the door and kicked me out.

Note to the Gentlemen

For centuries, your eyes have been your enemy. Even some of the most renowned men of the Bible met their demise because of their choice to follow after curves and long lashes. GOD warned you over and over again about dealings with immoral women. Proverbs is full of pearls that basically tell you when the WORD of GOD is lacking within you, foolishness will thrive. But just like women, sometimes you get a little impatient, think that GOD is taking too long, and you run out and become someone's illegal husband.

Mr. Husband: There is a marriage ceremony that should have taken place with you before you ever put a ring on a woman's finger. That ceremony is the becoming of one between you and the WORD. To marry the WORD, you have to court the WORD, know the WORD, and study the WORD. When you travel the road that GOD has placed before you, you will find the wife that HE has called for you along the way. But when you go your own way, you will find a wounded woman. She's sitting there, still bearing the souls of the men of her past; and she is emotionally scarred, spiritually broken, and physically tampered with. Nevertheless,

you want to add your soul to the bunch because you think that you will bring her to a place of happiness and healing through your love. There's a problem with this, however. In order for this to be true, GOD would have to be a liar, and we know that it is impossible for GOD to tell a lie. So, since two words are coming at you (the WORD of GOD and her words), you have a choice to make: embrace reality or embrace truth. The two are different. Reality is what manifests itself to you, but this doesn't necessarily make it true. It's just a manifestation of what you believe. A good example would be the value of a diamond. In the world's system, a scale is in place that weighs and declares the value of that diamond, but the truth is; it has absolutely no value. If you don't believe me, go out and buy the biggest diamond you can find, and when a demon starts attacking you, throw the diamond at it.
A better example can be found in the WORD of GOD when JESUS spoke with the Jews that were questioning HIM. *"JESUS answered and said unto them, Destroy this temple, and in three days I will raise it up" (John 2:19).* In their reality, JESUS was talking about the church building; but in truth, HE was speaking about HIS death and resurrection. Our reality is limited to what we realize, but truth goes far beyond our comprehension because truth is divine. Reality is established on the foundation of what is real to us. Therefore, your reality was a lie because it was not established by GOD. It was established by your senses.

If GOD has called you to be married, you are already anointed to be a husband, but you must first answer the call of GOD to be HIS son. Coming into a marriage with no wisdom is like skydiving without a parachute. While the wind in your face may be pleasant, impact is inevitable. You must accept that your anointing goes far past just being someone's husband, but in marrying prematurely, you abort a lot of the plans that GOD has for you. Like Jonah, you are running from your calling, and when the whale of truth swallows you whole, you will cry out from within its belly.

Going out of the will of GOD for your life is the easiest road map to a treacherous and manipulative woman.

"It is better to dwell in the wilderness, than with a contentious and an angry woman" (Proverbs 21:19).
"It is better to dwell in the corner of the housetop, than with a brawling woman and in a wide house" (Proverbs 25:24).
"A continual dropping in a very rainy day and a contentious woman are alike" (Proverbs 27:15).

GOD is warning you of what is out there. When you go outside of HIS will, you go inside of Satan's will.
You're probably ready to be married, and the woman before you looks and sounds like a good woman. She goes to church, cries during a sad movie, and she seemingly needs you. Reflect back to these words: looks, sounds, seemingly. These are all words that let you know that you are basing your understanding on the flesh. You are using your carnal understanding to make a decision about your spiritual future. *"For the flesh lusteth against the Spirit, and the Spirit against the flesh: and these are contrary the one to the other: so that ye cannot do the things that ye would" (Galatians 5:17).* You can't go to the flesh for guidance because it only knows the way of death. You have to trust GOD and follow HIM wholeheartedly to find your way to HIS heart and the discovery of who you are. *"Trust in the LORD with all thine heart; and lean not unto thine own understanding. In all thy ways acknowledge him, and he shall direct thy paths" (Proverbs 3:5-6).*

Your wife is waiting for your arrival. She is out there, but GOD has to transition her from being a woman into being a wife. This transition takes place as she submits herself to GOD, and her flesh is killed. Without this transition, she will not be a wife, but she'll be a married woman. Again, there is a difference between a wife and a married woman. The difference is one is led by the flesh and one is led by the SPIRIT. GOD said in Proverbs 18:22, *"Whosoever finds a wife finds a good thing, and obtains favor of the LORD."* HE did not say that he who finds a woman finds a good thing, but he who finds a wife finds a good thing. A wife is hidden in GOD and only found in obedience, but a woman is common and always found in disobedience.

In addition, GOD has to tear down your flesh to build you up spiritually, so that you can be the husband HE has called you to be. It is then that HE can be that three-fold cord in your marriage, and the kingdom of darkness won't have any power over that union, but it will rest under your feet. Nevertheless, because of impatience and lying eyes, many find themselves on one knee, proposing to some woman and all of her demons. After marriage, they find themselves on both knees praying and asking the LORD for a way of escape.

Exercise the spirit man by gaining wisdom, knowledge, and understanding. These are your spirit's food and will help strengthen you for the journey ahead. Let GOD build you up so that you can be the leader whom HE'S anointed you to be.

Resolving Problems

Reflect back to the cell phone tower example. You have to stay within the tower's range to have service; otherwise, it will not work. Sometimes, we travel outside our spouse's range of understanding. This is not the time to fight, but to discuss how to build more towers.

One of the most common issues in marriage is unwillingness to bend. Each individual believes that compromise is a waving of the surrender flag, an acknowledgment of being inferior to the other mate, and a quick way to spoil the mate. So each one would prefer to be stubborn rather than give in to their spouse's demands. Being inflexible is the same as being a bundle of walking divorce papers. You have to broaden your range because GOD did not call you to stand still. You will travel outside of one another's understanding sometimes. The both of you will often be elevated, and sometimes demoted; but you need to be able to communicate with one another so that you won't "grow apart." Both parties should have more than just a desire for the marriage to work, but a declaration that it will work. They've also got to put in work. Your attitude must be: We will not divorce. Foremost, the WORD of GOD must be established as law in your home. The WORD draws the borders for you, so you do not have to be known as controlling by trying to establish rules yourself. By establishing the WORD of GOD as your life and law, you are also denouncing manipulation, control, backbiting, lack of forgiveness and all the devices of the devil that destroy marriages. You cannot run to both sides of the battlefield trying to see which side will win so that you can claim victory from that side. You have to choose who you want to serve: GOD or self. In serving the LORD, you have to accept that you will not win every argument, and you will not always get your way. This goes both ways. The both of you should declare the following: "I will not always get my way; you will not always get your way, but we will always choose GOD'S way." And don't bend on that. When you find yourself tempted to use manipulation, shock that devil by rebuking it, renouncing its ways, and submitting to the WORD of GOD. The Bible says in James 4:7: *"Submit yourselves therefore, to God. Resist the devil, and he will flee from you."* How does one resist the devil when they are angry? Think about this: If you're lifting dumbbells, you will find that the pain intensifies anytime you lift the dumbbell; but when you lower the dumbbells, the pain will subside. It takes more strength to lift the dumbbells than it does to lower them. When you're angry, it takes more strength to restrain yourself from saying what you want to say, and doing what you want to do; but it takes little to no strength to lower yourself. Let times of disagreement act as your marriage dumbbells. Instead of lowering yourself into any argument, resist the anger and the temptation, and lift up your spouse by saying the opposite of what your flesh wants to say and doing the opposite of what your flesh wants to do. For example, when you want to tell the spouse how awful of a spouse they are, try simply saying, "I love you, and I'm sorry." This requires a **lot** of strength because your flesh will be pulling you in one direction, and you will want to rest yourself in the flesh by not opposing it. Nevertheless, when you oppose the flesh, you come into the will of GOD, and this will ultimately drive the devil out of your presence.

She's checking your cell: I've come across quite a few

conversations between women wanting the right to check their husband's cellular phones. This topic has brought on a lot of fights and flights. Guys, I want to share a secret with you: If you find yourself at the other end of your wife's mouth about wanting the right to check your cell phone, give it to her! The quickest way to detonate a bomb is to pull its string. If you find her hiding and checking it; don't yell, just bring her the phone charger. Sure, it's a not-so-smart move on her part, but a lot of women do this out of insecurity. Just laugh and walk away. This will humiliate her and teach her not to give in to that desire to check it. Eventually, when she hasn't found anything to arouse or confirm her suspicions, she will lose interest in checking your phone. Resisting her won't make the problem go away. If she doesn't trust you, you need to find the root of this lack of trust and destroy it. You do this by answering questions truthfully and openly. *"But I say unto you, That ye resist not evil: but whosoever shall smite thee on thy right cheek, turn to him the other also" (Matthew 5:39).* If your wife wants to check the phone, go out and order detailed billing and hand it to her. You will only discourage her and make her feel humiliated. Satan knows this truth but many have been taught that life is a game that one has to play to win. This mindset is rooted in pride and pride is like a balloon full of hot air. It may lift itself up, but it takes a prick to bring it back down. The WORD tells you to resist the devil and submit yourself to GOD. By not giving in to the temptation to argue, you are resisting the devil. In doing so, you will cause your wife to face herself and her own faults. It is then that she will recognize that the problem is stemming from herself, and it is then that she may pray or seek guidance to be delivered from this mindset. Expose the devil, no matter where he is hiding. Stop trying to force your spouse to look in the mirror. The WORD of GOD will cast a true reflection of her heart to her. While HE works on her, your job is to pray for her and keep the peace in your home and marriage.

He's jealous: You're at work standing outside, waiting for your husband to pick you up. Your shift has ended, and he's running a little behind. Outside with you is a handsome new supervisor, who you have absolutely no romantic interest in. Trying to be polite, you engage in conversation with the newbie, and here comes your husband pulling up. He's gawking at the two of you in a threatening way. As you enter the car and close the door, the questions and comments begin.

1. Who is that?
2. Why are you standing out there talking to him like that?
3. I saw how you were laughing; you like him.
4. I can see it in his eyes; he likes you.
5. He's no good. He wants one thing from you.
6. So, that's why you dress up to go to work?!
7. Does the management team know that their leaders are flirting (or having affairs) with the staff?
8. I don't want you talking to him.
9. Come to think of it, our one-year-old kind of resembles him.
10. So, this is why you've been so distant lately. I get it now.

And this conversation goes on and off for weeks, months, and sometimes years. Now, this is simply a mental hijacking by the enemy. Yes, it's frustrating when you are innocent, but as a wife, your job is to go to the LORD on his behalf. First, you need to understand that there is a reason behind your husband's insecurities. It could be that he was hurt a lot in his life, or it could be that he's guilty of the same crime that he's trying to implicate you on. Either way, to stop this fruit from continuing to grow and flourish, you have to pull the tree up by the root. In other words, get to the bottom of it. How to approach the situation should be decided based on how he perceives women. A man who, for example, saw his mother engaging in promiscuous behavior will tend to view all women as promiscuous. It's similar to having a dog that you know will bite anyone that comes within a certain distance of you. When walking the dog, anytime someone is heading your way, you will shorten the dog's leash. In his mind, he has to shorten and tighten your leash to keep you from acting out on what he believes to be your instincts. Now, he shouldn't have been married anyhow until he was delivered from this mindset and the pain that drives it, but what's done is done. Now, you have to find a way to fight the demons that he brought into the marriage. His views won't change based on how you conduct yourself as a wife and a woman. Even in your innocence, he will judge some of your words and behaviors as admissions or displays of guilt. This man needs deliverance, and he has to be changed by the renewing of his mind. He needs the WORD to come in and purge that mentality out of him.

Stay in prayer and be sure to keep your husband's head in the WORD. He doesn't need oxygen as much as HE needs to drown in GOD'S WORD. The WORD of GOD is the Sword of the SPIRIT, and it is the Sword that will slay every demonic source that attempts to infect him with lies. In the meantime, don't feed that demon by arguing. Feed your husband's spirit with love. Reassure him, cook his favorite meals, and always reward his right way of thinking. Never feed the insecurity by trying to explain away your every move or decision. What you are doing is resisting that spirit of pride and strife. If you have to, go out and order a t-shirt with his face on the back and wear it proudly; or get a key chain with his photo on it. Sounds crazy and humiliating, right? It's not about being humiliated; it's about going into warfare against whatever spirit is attacking his mind. You have to understand that the kingdom of darkness feeds on strife and no matter how stupid your husband's words or actions may be; he is simply acting out because his mind is in captivity. Your first ministry is to go after that soul. Be slow to anger, slow to speak, but quick to listen.

Pride: The Marriage Slayer

What is pride and how does it affect my marriage? Merriam-Webster Dictionary defines pride as:
1. Inordinate self-esteem: Conceit.
2. Delight or elation rising from some act, possession, or relationship.

Reading from these definitions, it is of no wonder that GOD said that HE hates a proud look. (*See Proverbs 6:17*). GOD has raised us up, and it is HE that elevates or demotes us. Our obedience, knowledge of HIS WORD, love for HIM, and faith puts us in line for elevation. Therefore, we have no right to be puffed up because JEHOVAH is GOD alone. With a simple blow of HIS breath, GOD can knock us off our little idolatry pedestals. Pride is esteeming self, and basically trying to sit our hearts on the throne of GOD. It is a false sense of elevation, where one takes GOD'S glory and tries it on. The second definition is: delight or elation rising from some act, possession, or relationship. This definition doesn't have to be explained; it speaks volumes for itself. How can we stand before the face of GOD and allow ourselves to be puffed up because of something we did or have? GOD is GOD alone.

Every good thing that we have comes from HIM. Therefore, all glory belongs to HIM; not you nor me. But, when we begin to bask in HIS glory, we are putting ourselves in harm's way.

Pride affects a marriage the same way that it affects our relationship with GOD. Reflect back to Uzziah. Pride entered his heart, and he got bold enough to enter the temple of GOD, even though only the Levites were supposed to enter it.

"But when he was strong, his heart was lifted up to his destruction: for he transgressed against the LORD his God, and went into the temple of the LORD to burn incense upon the altar of incense.

And Azariah the priest went in after him, and with him, fourscore priests of the LORD, that were valiant men:

And they withstood Uzziah the king, and said unto him, It appertaineth not unto thee, Uzziah, to burn incense unto the LORD, but to the priests the sons of Aaron, that are consecrated to burn incense: go out of the sanctuary; for thou hast trespassed; neither shall it be for thine honour from the LORD God. Then Uzziah was wroth, and had a censer in his hand to burn incense: and while he was wroth with the priests, the leprosy even rose up in his forehead before the priests in the house of the LORD, from beside the incense altar.

And Azariah the chief priest, and all the priests, looked upon him, and, behold, he was leprous in his forehead, and they thrust him out from thence; yea, himself hasted also to go out, because the LORD had smitten him.

And Uzziah the king was a leper unto the day of his death, and dwelt in a several house, being a leper; for he was cut off from the house of the LORD: and Jotham his son was over the king's house, judging the people of the land" (2 Chronicles 26:16-21).

If a little fit of pride could cause a king to be lifted up so far in his heart that he felt that the hand of GOD was not strong enough to withstand him, just imagine what a hint of pride can do to a marriage.

It has been reported that infidelity is the number one cause of divorce in the United States; but while infidelity may have its well-deserved reputation, pride has taken more marriages and destroyed more lives than anything else that has risen up against GOD'S people. The reason pride is so successful is because it grows from within and, like a cancer, it often goes undetected by the person who has it. Someone can hold their head down low and still be full of pride. One can speak with fear and still have pride within. The problem today is many of us don't recognize the wiles of the devil simply because we have been taught to see through the devil's windshield. Our vision is blurred by what we have been taught. Our parents and our schools taught us which color to call red, which animal to call a cat, which animal to call a dog, which letter of the alphabet is called a Z, and so on. If you saw pride the way that GOD sees it, you would not embrace it nor participate in it.

How is pride the marriage slayer? *"He that is of a proud heart stirreth up strife: but he that putteth his trust in the LORD shall be made fat" (Proverbs 28:25).*

The Honeymoon Stage

In this chapter, you will learn about the honeymoon stage, how to maintain it and what and whom to avoid.

The honeymoon stage is the period immediately following the honeymoon, where the couple is in love with the idea of who they think their mates are. As we get to know our spouses, we begin to fight the character that they are, in hopes of resurrecting the character that our imaginations had erected. In the honeymoon stage, there is little to no arguing. At this time, we project what we want in a spouse onto our new husband or wife. For example, if you've always wanted a man to serenade you, protect you, and hold you when you're sad; you're probably imagining your new husband is going to do these things. And maybe he's serenaded you, protected you, and held you before; but you've made it up in your mind that he will spend the rest of his life sending you into the clouds. You might be right, but the part that doesn't show up in your imagination is the work you've got to put in to maintain this stage. Just as easy as it is to fall in love, one can fall out of it. Why so? Because the term "fall in love" is not truthfully real love.

It's a stage in which a person or both people are charmed. To be charmed is to be bewitched by an illusion. When we are charmed, a high-like feeling ensues that we refer to as cloud nine. It's not actually love because a couple can fall "in love" or basically be charmed by one another after a few hours of meeting. It is simply a stage where we float above reality.

When our reality doesn't match up with our imaginations, our fangs come out. This is when marriage gets real and the commandments of GOD have to come into play. A wife is commanded to respect her husband, and a husband is commanded to love his wife. There is a reason that this had to be a commandment. Women often lose respect for their husbands when their imaginations and their realities don't see eye to eye. Men, on the other hand, can be emotionally depriving and walk away from a relationship because it doesn't match up to his idea of what a marriage was supposed to be.

GOD allows trials and tribulations to draw us closer to HIM. These are the lessons of life that make us stronger and allow the name of the LORD to be glorified. Marriages have their fair share of trials, but the trials can draw you closer to your mate instead of pulling you apart. For this to happen, the two of you have to mutually agree to follow CHRIST'S direction, and to keep your pride at bay. Don't despise the trials that test the strength of your marriage; instead, welcome it as an opportunity to see the gaps that need to be filled in your marriage. You are slowly bleeding Satan out of the marriage by doing this. If you want to maintain the honeymoon stage in your marriage, you have to learn and accept the truth about your spouse and vice versa. The two of you are not perfect; you make mistakes, you will make mistakes, and you have made mistakes. You have to move beyond these errors to get to the secure holding center of love. For example, if your husband isn't the loving and doting man he once was, it's time for a family meeting. The truth is, he may not be this loving and doting character you fell for. This was just his cover letter to get into your heart. Now that he's comfortable with you, he's sitting on the couch, reading the newspaper, and he's not getting lost in your eyes like he used to. He's not declaring his love for you like he used to. It doesn't mean that he doesn't think it; it only means that he's conquered what he wanted to conquer, and now he's resting. Allow him this space, or you may push him further away. Explain to him how you feel, but do not shed tears or show any signs of negative emotion. Men are like reflectors; whatever you project onto them, they'll reflect it back to you. If you show any negative emotions, what you thought was going to be an emotionally charged reunion of two hearts will become an all-out sword fight. Then, you will surely have his attention because men are programmed warriors. While he may have chased and captured you like a treasure hidden in the enemy's camp, he won't recognize you as his little teddy bear when you lose your fluffiness. You'll only draw the warrior part of him out when you come in brandishing a bad attitude.

Instead, loving moments are great moments to talk; create them with a smile and no negativity. While in the honeymoon stage, you need to draft and mutually agree upon a way to handle disagreements. And ladies, we sometimes think that because Daddy was moved by our tears that our husbands will be too. Don't forget, your husbands had sisters, and they often found their sisters' tears annoying or funny. Men aren't highly emotional creatures. They often see tears as manipulation, and sometimes they are right. So, when you come before them in tears, you're not going to trigger a good response; you'll only trigger a flashback.

When you are able and willing to accept your spouse's imperfections and love them as they are, honeymoon won't be a stage for you; it'll be your reality. Welcome each trial as an opportunity to grow together as one. Needless to say, you shouldn't go and introduce problems to your marriage just to make up. That's an unhealthy relationship. No one wants to live on a roller coaster. There are people who like the idea of making up, so they create extremely painful chaotic situations in hopes of getting an extremely gratifying make up session. To them, there's something about telling your husband that he's a useless waste of skin and teeth that recharges the libido. Of course, such a marriage is built on the wrong foundation and is scheduled for an extreme end.

There are also people who live for the honeymoon stage, whether it's in a relationship or a marriage. Once this euphoric stage is over, they disappear and move on to the next man or woman who tosses them into the clouds. When they land again, they're out. In high school, it was normal for you to meet someone like this; someone who spent hours on the phone charming your heart. Sometimes, you'd fall asleep on the phone, and no matter what your parents said to you, you'd find a way to talk to this person who had you charmed. Most of the time, the man is the charmer, and the woman is the one being charmed. And many children find themselves in sexual relationships because they've been charmed out of their clothes. Then they find themselves hurt, ashamed and disappointed when this character is able to walk away from the relationship with such ease. Why did he or she do this? Because they are people of extremes. In their reality, if something is not all the way up, it's too far down. There is no middle for them; there is no cruise mode; they want exceeding the speed limit relationships. They'll take you on this emotionally charged ride to Never-Ever Land, where you'll experience things that you'll never ever get from them again. In many cases, people with this demonically charged drive have a goal, and once that goal is attained, you are not entertaining for them anymore. Where there is no wisdom, foolishness thrives. But you thought because she sounded wise, that she was wise. She may have spoken what she's heard or lived, but true wisdom is displayed not only in words, but in life choices. Or he may sound educated, but man's education is nothing close to being spiritually educated. And words are and can be deceptive.

Ladies and gentlemen, there are some men and women who will marry you just because you, at that moment, have them where they want to be. They're not happy people. They are people who look for love streams outside of GOD, and their definition of love isn't the same as GOD'S definition. In many cases, when you show up

as yourself and your plane reaches a safe altitude and begins to cruise, they'll bail out on you. Then you'll see them in the ice cream parlor with their new partner, charmed and repeating the cycle. Pray for their soul and move on. If they remain undelivered over the years, they're going to create soul ties with tens, hundreds, if not thousands of souls in their search for happiness.
In addition, there are those who love to intentionally float another person just to crash them. Again, these are not happy people, and this is why GOD has instructed you to seek first the Kingdom of GOD and all its righteousness. HE said that in doing so, everything else will be added unto you. What is everything else? Wisdom, knowledge, understanding, discernment, joy, peace, healing and so on. In gaining these blessed tools, you will avoid the paths of men and women who are obsessed with extreme personalities because discernment will ring your mind until you answer.

If you want to live in and maintain the honeymoon period with your spouse, here's how. First, realize this: There will be times when you will come down and times that you will soar. The key is to not crash. Look at it this way: Sometimes the plane has to change altitudes to maintain a safe and smooth flight. You shouldn't turn on the panic button every time you feel yourself or your marriage descending.

Here are some helpful tips to stay afloat:
1. Bite reality, but swallow the truth. The reality is, your mate isn't perfect; but the truth is, he or she can be a better spouse through time, and so can you. Never ever think that your spouse is the only one who needs to change. You shouldn't be trying to mold them into being what you want. Instead, the both of you should be allowing GOD to mold you into what HE wants.
2. Manipulation is witchcraft. Don't use that on your spouse, or you're inviting a host of demonic guests into your home and into your marriage. Find ways to communicate and always be willing to pray about everything.
3. No sex before marriage. In fornicating, you are cursing that

union; plus, there won't be any surprises for wedding night. Keep it blessed so you won't end up entering matrimony without the holiness.

4. Avoid placing the yoke of expectation on your spouse. Here are the basics: Your spouse should remain faithful to you, never hit you, never call you out of your name, provide for you and be there for your children. But, if the stability of your marriage stands on the foundation of what you expect, it will fall. For example, as a man you shouldn't expect your wife to be in the kitchen every day cooking for you. Get up and cook for her sometimes. As a woman, you should not expect your husband to carry your emotional baggage. That heaviness should be dropped and left.

5. Be spontaneous. Remember the law of driving. Do not follow a vehicle too long, or you may become relaxed and fall asleep behind the wheel. In other words, don't be boring or predictable.

6. Grow with your spouse. Keep this in mind: Everything that lives must be watered and fed to stay alive. In ministry, you should learn something new every day; in life, you should learn something new every day. Marriage is no different. Marriage is ministry, and it's now your life. Learn to do new things together that the both of you will enjoy. Don't become complacent with where you are; always reach higher.

7. Keep complaining to a minimum. If you can, block its access altogether. Complaining doesn't cause your spouse to hear you; it only teaches them to become immune to your voice when it reaches a certain pitch. If you want positive results, plant positivity as your seed. This is the only way that you're going to reap it. Sometimes, we default to temper tantrums when we don't get what we want, but this isn't cute. We're adults, so we have to put away childish behaviors.

8. Envision your marriage as a house. Lock wisdom, love, knowledge, long-suffering, and understanding in; but lock out jealousy, frustration, unforgiveness, confusion and fear. If you and your spouse are willing, you should establish a program to keep out these things so that you can always have a line of defense against the enemy. So when, for example, the husband sees that you are speaking negatively because of fear, he can be your

sharpener and say, "Baby, I see fear trying to get in here, but it's not welcome. Let's pray about it, talk about what took you there, cast it out, close that door and bind it shut."

9. Pray for your spouse even when they're wrong. Stop praying against them. You are one with them, so whatever happens to them, happens to you. You're too close to that earthquake to not feel at least an aftershock.

10. Plead the Blood of JESUS over your spouse often. It does not matter whether today is a good day or a bad one. There are many emotions that we refer to as love, but when the troubles of life shake its foundation; if it crumbles, it is not love. True love never fails. You can't wish your wife happy today and dead tomorrow, and think what you're feeling for her is love. That's obsession and fear that has been triggered, and its murderous cousin is opting to be the assassin.

Love is not an emotion; love is a spirit. The scriptures tell us that GOD is love. Hate is not an emotion; it is the absence of love, or better yet, the absence of GOD.

Always be willing to build more towers, and there is no greater time to do so than the honeymoon period. A wise king doesn't wait for war before he decides to fortify his country. He has to do this in times of peace and tranquility; otherwise, he'll find himself in someone's dungeon, or buried in an unmarked grave. Never think that your relationship is immune from the attacks of the enemy. The message here is: Learn how to fight together against a common enemy, rather than becoming enemies and fighting with the enemy against each other.

The honeymoon doesn't have to end; you just have to learn how to manage it. It's like having a business; some days you'll earn a lot, and sometimes you'll spend more than what you earn.

Growing Up In Your Marriage

Every situation you enter, you come into it as an infant. A good example would be a job. Because you were untrained in how the day-to-day operations were, you were not knowledgeable in regard to how to operate in that company initially. This is why you had to be orientated and trained. The goal wasn't just to teach you to be an associate, but to teach you how to become a knowledgeable and fruitful associate. As you went through training, you learned more, and you began to step up into the different levels of accomplishment.

Levels of Professional Accomplishment:
(Definitions provided by www.thefreedictionary.com)
Rookie or New Hire: An untrained or inexperienced recruit.
Intermediate or Basic: One that is in a middle position or state. (Most hires never go past this stage. This is when one simply learns enough to successfully do the job.)
Expert: A person with a high degree of skill in or knowledge of a certain subject.

When a relationship begins, most individuals put on a face that is not their own. As people, we tend to listen for what our new or potential partner wants, and then we try to morph into that person. It's our way of living a lie.

As the relationship grows, we begin to put our guard down and show more of who we really are. This is why the world's way suggests that you get to know a character at least one to two years before marrying them. Many believe that in this window of time, whatever is in your new mate should begin to come up for air. But this system doesn't really work because there are individuals who can be as patient as they are evil. There were many who got married after knowing their spouses for five or more years, only to have their marriages fizzle out faster than their courtship. This happens when we have more expectation than we have love. When our expectations are shattered beyond recognition, our true faces begin to show.

Again, you have to remember that when you walk into an unfamiliar situation, you are walking in as a baby, or rookie. It doesn't matter if you've been married six times, all marriages do not look or act the same because all people do not look or act the same. One of the keys to learning your mate is by first examining expectations and releasing one another from them.

Expectation is a heavy yoke and will weigh down even the strongest man.
Example: Imagine the joy you felt when you were a child, and you told this guy in a red suit what you wanted for Christmas. You walked away happy, planning what you were going to do with your new toy. Then, on Christmas Eve, you tore through the boxes looking for it, and it wasn't there. You were hurt and angry because you did not understand that the real culprit was Mom and Dad, their lies, and their limited income. How could he do this? Your expectation not only hurled harm at you, but at your parents who may have wanted to get it but couldn't afford to, and didn't want to tell you the truth about the infamous guy with the reindeer.

Now, today you're a grown man or woman, but you still allow yourself to stand on the heavy expectations that you've buried your spouse under. This load is too heavy for a man or woman to carry. The only expectation that should be in your marriage is: Your spouse to be everything to you that GOD has instructed them to be.

Being inflexible does not carve a new road for you and your new spouse to travel. New paths sometimes have to be created so that both parties can reach your united destination in peace. And this can be done. You simply need two willing participants with the attitude that their marriage will not fail.
Remember, where there are no signals of comprehension, you have to build new towers. The best way to break down the walls of expectation is, of course, through prayer. Stop allowing your thoughts to become your emotions. Cast down ALL evil imaginations, not just the ones that are blatantly evil. Rebuke those thoughts that the enemy throws into your head. Your thoughts are the window to your heart. The enemy comes in through that window to seduce you with lies. Arrest him with the WORD, and stop allowing him to establish lines of communication with your heart. You should get to know your spouse, learn their strengths, learn their weaknesses, and so on. The both of you should tackle those weaknesses until they become strengths, as well as further strengthen those areas where you are strong. Sometimes we can be strong, but not strong enough. The enemy knows where to hit you and how hard to hit you.

As you grow together, you will find that things that once bothered you in the beginning won't bother you anymore. You probably started off in the relationship with ways that you grew up with; however, as time passes, you should have found different, Godly ways of coping.

In my case, whenever I was angry I used to go for a walk or a drive no matter what time it was. Now, this wasn't the best way of doing things, but this was learned behavior. I grew up in a home where a fist or knife fight could break out in the click of a clock. To keep from fighting, I would leave so I could think, cry, and pray. As I grew into a woman; in the beginning, I was still a violent creature. It was what I knew. I felt this overwhelming need to hit the man who was hurting me and to prevent this, I would leave. Well, my career in hitting ended swiftly in my first marriage. I learned that some men hit back, and after less than a year of marriage, I was a recovering rage-aholic. I grew up watching my Mom and Dad fight it out, so I thought this was normal. Well, my Dad just ducked and moved, and my Mom would go full charge at him because she knew what he'd been doing.

And one of the ways that I have found that works for me and Jean is to have a family meeting. The act of becoming angry with the person who's done wrong only renders you guilty.

Oftentimes, we feel the need to make our spouses aware of how we feel, regardless of whether they already know it or not. As spouses, we are sometimes demonically reminded of previous conversations that we had with our spouses about the current unresolved issues in our marriages. Truthfully, some spouses do forget, while others make light of past agreements made between them and their spouse. This isn't a time to charge them or attack them, but it is a great opportunity to tackle the root of the issue. There are the times when a spouse will openly disregard past discussions and requests made by their significant other. This is an act of pride and rebellion. The proper way to deal with a hard-headed spouse is to lovingly communicate with them about their choice to rebel against any previously instated verbal agreements. If they still refuse to honor your request, take it to the LORD and leave it there, and it goes without saying; pray that stronghold off your husband or wife. Bind every demonic spirit that is attacking, attaching to, or seducing yourself or your spouse. You have the power in your tongue to send it to the pit and command that it stay there until the day of Judgment! Don't use your mouth to curse the one you love; use it to bind the real enemy.

Here are a few helpful pointers to help the both of you to grow:

1. Create an age chart and chart your progress. We use growth charts to show how much a child has grown over the months and years. Parents will often place these on their children's bedroom doors and have their children to stand against them to record their heights. Create a growth chart for your marriage and chart how it has grown over the years. Every month, measure your marriage's progress against the previous month. When you don't see growth or when you see that the marriage seems to be shrinking, actively do something to grow it up. Whatever you feed will grow and whatever you starve will die. Initiate new and fun programs for you and your spouse to involve yourself in. Please do not do this when you are angry or to intimidate the spouse; otherwise, they'll despise the idea.
2. Do a negativity fast with your spouse. If he or she agrees, the two of you should dedicate yourself to a whole day of not speaking anything negative about one another or anyone else. You can make this fun by offering rewards or penalties. For example, a reward can be a weekend getaway to the winner's favorite spot, and the punishment could be a week of washing dishes for the loser. After you've mastered doing this in a day, amp it up and start doing negativity fasts that last a few days to a week. Keep increasing the time frame until negativity is squeezed out of your marriage and your vocabulary.
3. Whenever you feel the need to say something negative to your spouse, switch it up and humbly say something positive. Please avoid sarcasm. This requires a lot of strength, but it will often breed the best results. Stay innocent and do nice things for the spouse. This will make them consciously aware of their own faults and it'll teach them to check themselves, rather than coming against you. This doesn't mean you're weak; it means you're strong enough to hold you back to let GOD go forward.

Whatever you do, use times of peace to try and maintain peace. We all know that the first year is the hardest, but it's just your first hurdle to get over. Leap high for love!

Habitual Strongholds

What is a habit? It is a recurring behavior that becomes a part of one's daily routine. Now, having a habit of harming people with your mouth is a habit that should have been extinguished long before you met your spouse. Nevertheless, there are many lost souls who wander into a marriage, and their deadly habits become their spouse's daily doomsday.

We are vessels, and whatever is in us will pour out of us. It is no wonder that deliverance should come before marriage; otherwise, you are likely to subject your spouse to emotional and verbal abuse. But, let's say that you didn't get delivered before marriage. What should you do when you feel the need to set your spouse straight? Jot the following statement down and place it somewhere you can see it daily: Don't open your mouth when your heart is in captivity. Your heart is in captivity when it wants to be a slave to your anger. This is when you want to say the wrong things to your spouse because they may have done or said something that you did not like. When your heart is in this place, you need to steal yourself away to go and pray. In this hour, your heart is diseased with evil and needs to be quarantined until you've been delivered. Your spouse will not and cannot deliver you; they can only help you to feel better, but they can't tackle the root of you not being able to control your anger.

Proverbs 18:21 reminds us, *"Death and life are in the power of the tongue: and they that love it shall eat the fruit thereof."*

Let's say that you are already married, and you tend to spit out venom whenever the spouse rubs you the wrong way. You want to stop; you just don't know how. First and foremost, give it to JESUS. That is a burden that you were not supposed to carry. Your venom (anger, hatred, unforgiveness) has a source, and you have to attack it from there. Your spouse is not the source of your anger. Unforgiveness is almost always the culprit behind venomous speech. You may have allowed indignation, hatred, doubt, and fear to be poured into you over time. Maybe it's because your spouse has hurt or betrayed you before. When you chose to stay in your marriage, you were supposed to divorce his or her past. Since you chose to stay, you have to stop having an affair with the past. It is hard to love and respect our spouses the way that we should love and respect them when our hearts are somewhere else. The core of unforgiveness is disobedience and rebellion, and this is not something that you want the LORD to find in you, no matter what your spouse did. You must attack and destroy the root of anything that comes between your relationship with GOD. You do this by repenting of that sin, renouncing that sin, and submitting to the WORD of GOD. Never be led by your feelings, but always honor GOD above your feelings. James 4:7 explains: *"Submit yourselves therefore to God. Resist the devil, and he will flee from you."*

Follow the lead of 2 Corinthians 10:5: *"Casting down imaginations, and every high thing that exalteth itself against the knowledge of God, and bringing into captivity every thought to the obedience of Christ."* Don't entertain those thoughts that rise up in your mind; cast them down. Sometimes a devil will tell you that your spouse is cheating when he or she is not. A devil will tell you that your spouse wants to fight, when they aren't even in that zip code. When you allow evil thoughts to repeatedly seduce your mind, your heart will eventually let them in, and they will become your fears. This is when your thoughts will begin to match up with your reality.

Always pay attention to what GOD speaks, *"For as he thinketh in his heart, so is he" (Proverbs 3:7).* Your thoughts are powerful, and your words are even more powerful. Whatever stands up in your mind; if it is not in line with the WORD of GOD, it has to be cast down, or it will sit down in your heart and become a stronghold. Your mind is a waiting room, and everything that comes in it is trying to get into your heart. The WORD of GOD is the police that comes into that waiting room and arrests any and everything that has the wrong intentions. When you don't allow the Police in, each criminal thought is subjected to your own understanding. Your understanding is limited and can't comprehend spiritual things, so it'll always tap into the natural for guidance. When something introduces itself to your mind; if it is not cast down, it will eventually get a pass into your heart. If it gets into the heart, it cannot be cast down anymore; now it has to be cast out, and this becomes an issue of deliverance.

Never think you're so smart that a devil can't fool you. Always be willing to humble yourself before GOD. Humility and obedience are both powerful weapons. When we stand in agreement with the WORD, there is a protective shield that surrounds us that no devil can penetrate. GOD sees what is happening in your home, and HE will expose the workers of darkness if you'll only walk in HIS light.

Habit: Are you accustomed to frowning at your spouse anytime he or she leans in for a kiss? At first, you thought this was cute because they'd laugh it off and kiss you anyway. Negative ways that have been accepted as the norm don't go unnoticed, and they definitely don't secure your partner in the union. Instead, as human beings we often learn to become immune to the venom of our partners. Eventually, these negative ways add up and become an elephant sitting on your marriage. You should be looking for ways to remove every issue that is lurking in your marriage; even the small ones. Our life's choices set in motion other strongholds to be released and established in our hearts. This is why it is necessary for you to make the right choices, so that the right sequences of events will set your blessings in motion. The wrong choices stir up consequences, and these consequences often destroy or critically wound marriages.

Do not allow your tongue to call negativity to you. Have you ever woke up on the wrong side of the bed? You're angry and everything that follows goes wrong. Your alarm doesn't go off; you spill your coffee on your shirt; your car won't crank; your children are lagging around; your spouse is acting a little too chipper, and when you arrive at work, you find that your boss wants to see you? We, as Americans, love to say, "When it rains, it pours." But the truth is you are a holy city, and you determine the weather. You had a choice when you woke up. To acknowledge the first bad thing that visited you, or to acknowledge the GOD who woke you. You chose to acknowledge the negative, which set off a negative sequence of events to come. With GOD, you don't walk into your environment, your environment is set by you, and comes to greet you where you stand. So, you have chosen to have a bad day. All you had to do was to submit yourself to GOD, and resist the devil and you would've had a shower of blessings; but you chose to predict a storm and a storm came.
When it comes to our lives, we are some of the best meteorologists around.

Make this a habit: Speak to your day. Speak blessings to it. When it starts off wrong, take a moment to pray and praise GOD. Do not give your day to Satan. What if you woke up to a thief in your bedroom and your gun on the nightstand sitting next to you? You'd probably blow him into the next room, or you'd hold him at gunpoint until the police arrived. Why don't you do the same with the enemy when you wake up to him invading your life? He comes in to steal your joy; so why are you handing it over to him when you could easily pick up the Sword (your Bible) on the nightstand and arm yourself? The WORD of GOD is your sword. Decapitate that devil, and continue on with your day. Bring your family together for morning prayer. There is power in prayer, and there is power in unity. CHRIST said, *"For where two or three are gathered together in my name, there am I in the midst of them" (Matthew 18:20).*

In prayer, you are resisting the devil and inviting in the HOLY ONE. Your habit of speaking death over yourself and gloom over your day has got to stop. Your mouth is a giver of life and whatever comes from it takes the form of life. Speak blessings and blessings will live in you and begin to overtake you.

The Spirit of Sexual Perversion

I pity the woman or man who is married to someone who is bound by the spirit of perversion. Sexual perversion is a filthy spirit. This spirit leaves its mark wherever it sleeps. This spirit is a flesh demon, and it thrives on numbers. As with any demonic spirit, the spirit of perversion enters through disobedience. It desires and seeks to become one with as many souls as it can bind. This is a gluttonous demon that is never satisfied for it has the belly of hell. One person is never enough to satisfy a person bound by this spirit. Anyone carrying this spirit will have an almost unquenchable sexual appetite, and a need to experiment in the bedroom. Anyone married to a person bound by this demon will find themselves going to lengths ends trying to satisfy this undying lust in their spouse. Many believe that by going above and beyond the realm of normality that they can keep their spouses happy at home so that they will never stray. The reality is that you can never appease the appetite of a demon; it has to be cast out.

Some people bound by the spirit of perversion are able to control themselves, thus rendering the demon dormant; but never absent.

Others try to feed their flesh with whatever it demands just to calm it down. Nevertheless, we have to be delivered from any and every demonic entity that attaches itself to us. A dormant spirit is still a wicked and dangerous one, and it will often become active again when a traumatic event occurs in its host's life.

A spouse with this spirit will usually be an unfaithful man or woman. Any demonic spirit roots itself in selfishness since selfishness is the foundation of sin. An unyielding and unquenchable sexual appetite or a desire to explore the body in ways that it was not built for is evidence that the man or woman is perverted. Perverted doesn't mean to be sexually twisted; perverted means to turn away from the original order or design of something. If someone is perverted; they aren't just perverted sexually, they are wholly perverted. This means that they have turned their heart away from the LORD. It doesn't matter if they frequent church or if they often speak of the LORD, when someone is perverted, their heart is turned away from HIM. When someone is sexually perverted, their body has followed their heart. Anytime the heart is perverted, the whole man becomes perverted.

A perverted person will always seek generic gratification from whatever source avails itself to them or whatever source is attractive to them. This type of gratification is generic because it is a perverted form of what GOD allows for HIS children. For example, a married man can enjoy the pleasure of having intercourse with his wife, but if his heart is perverted; what he has is not enough. Again, anything rooted in perversion is demonic and has the appetite of hell.

Being married to such a soul is challenging because, as a spouse, you may desire to enjoy sex as GOD has designed it with your spouse, but trying to appease the perversion in them can prove to be physically draining. Someone with this spirit may frequent pornographic websites and desire to do to their spouse what they are seeing on the videos. They have been tricked into believing that perverted sex can produce a greater orgasm than ordinary sex.

This isn't true, but because they believe it, they will experience greater releases of serotonin (the feel good hormone) when indulging in illegal bedroom acts. Nevertheless, couples can experience intercourse that is far more gratifying within the normal realm of coming together, but this first has to occur in the mind. Whatever we believe; we will receive. Therefore, if you believe that sex is better when you are probing the spouse, it will feel better to you that way; but if you believe that it is better when it is passionate, you will have a better experience during passionate intercourse. This means that sexual perversion is rooted in our beliefs. If a spouse views their partner in a negative way, they may not be aroused by that spouse, but if they are sexually perverted and the spouse offers to gratify their lusts, then they may become increasingly aroused. As you can see, this has nothing to do with love, but has everything to do with self pleasure.

But how do you know if you or your loved one is linked to this wicked spirit? Here are a few signs to look for:

- Unquenchable desire to bring more things into the bedroom, be they metal, plastic or cotton.
- Unquenchable desire to indulge in a sexual affair with another person other than the spouse. This can be a private affair or one that involves the spouse.
- Unquenchable desire to engage in acts that the human body was not built for.
- Desire to watch someone else engaged in intercourse. This includes pornography or eavesdropping.
- Becoming aroused by anything other than a human being or becoming aroused by odd things and circumstances. (Example: someone getting hurt, someone being raped, any form of violence, a dog howling, etc.)
- Unquenchable desire to pleasure one's self....before or during marriage.

- Pedophilia (Being aroused by children...the desire or fulfilling of that desire to have sex with a child.)
- Bestiality (Being aroused by animals....the desire or fulfilling of that desire to have sex with an animal.)
- Necrophilia (Being aroused by dead people....the desire or fulfilling of that desire to have sex with a corpse.)
- Strange fetishes (Example: being around by certain bodily features or desiring to have intercourse in strange places like a public restroom, church or store parking lot.)

Of course there are more that are not mentioned. Basically, a perverted person's mind is stimulated by illegal acts.

When you see these signs, it is time for fasting and prayer. Why fasting? Sexual perversion usually roots itself in the flesh, but it is the result of a perverted heart. You must repent and turn your heart back to GOD, and then submit the flesh. When the Disciples of CHRIST witnessed a child convulsing, they could not cast that demon out of the child because that demon was rooted in the flesh. JESUS told them how to deal with such a spirit *"Howbeit this kind goeth not out but by prayer and fasting" (Matthew 17:21).* Why couldn't we just pray to the LORD to have it removed? Because that spirit has attached itself to the physical man. Fornication, for example, is a sin against one's own body. (See 1 Corinthians 6:18). Because fornication is a sin against one's own body, the body has to be submitted to the LORD by the tearing down of the flesh. The flesh is torn down through fasting because it is not being fed with its desires, but is being starved and caused to submit to the spirit. For the spirit of a man wars with his flesh! During a fast, the body is not only starved of food, but it is also starved of sex. This is why a husband or a wife must get permission from their spouse before submitting to a fast. *"Defraud ye not one the other, except it be with consent for a time, that ye may give yourselves to fasting and prayer; and come together again, that Satan tempt you not for your incontinency" (1 Corinthians 7:5).* During a fast, the person is submitting their flesh as a living sacrifice. *"I beseech you therefore, brethren, by the mercies of God, that you present your bodies a living sacrifice, holy, acceptable unto God, which is your reasonable service" (Romans 12:1).* Anything that roots itself in the flesh must be torn down through bodily submission. In other words, you need to fast. In addition, pray and ask the LORD how long you need to fast. Many people will try to fast a flesh demon off in a 24 hour fast when they may need to submit to a 30 day fast. It's hard to comprehend going this long without the things you love, but this is because you have developed a wrongful relationship with these things, and it is hard to break it off with them to form a right relationship with them. During a fast, the layers of a man's soul are peeled away, and any spirit that is harboring itself in that man's flesh is exposed more and more. It is literally being stripped away from the man.

The first stab at it is admitting that it is there. You are taking control of your flesh. If your spouse has it; chances are, you have it too. Fast with them, or you'll be its source to re-enter the spouse. You do NOT want this spirit to come back once it has been vanquished. Why? Luke 11:24-26 warns us, *"When the unclean spirit is gone out of a man, he walketh through dry places, seeking rest; and finding none, he saith, I will return unto my house whence I came out.*
And when he cometh, he findeth it swept and garnished.
Then goeth he, and taketh to him seven other spirits more wicked than himself; and they enter in, and dwell there: and the last state of that man is worse than the first."
Therefore, before going through deliverance, the party being delivered has to want deliverance and be determined never to go back. In addition, once you and your spouse are delivered, you have to continually fight to remain delivered. The scriptures tell us that any and every demonic spirit will eventually attempt to come back. It may start off as a simple Internet search for a bakery called Rose's Cakes and Muffins. And some pornographic site comes up with someone named Rose. The minute that he or she clicks that link out of curiosity, they have just opened the door for

that demon and its new buddies to enter. If that spirit is allowed to come back, it will bring seven more evil spirits with it, which means that the person will be far more wicked and perverse than they were before. Not to mention, deliverance would take much more fasting, long-suffering, and prayer. *"When the unclean spirit is gone out of a man, he walks through dry places, seeking rest, and finds none. Then he said, I will return into my house from where I came out; and when he is come, he finds it empty, swept, and garnished. Then he goes, and takes with himself seven other spirits more wicked than himself, and they enter in and dwell there: and the last state of that man is worse than the first. Even so shall it be also unto this wicked generation" (Matthews 12:43-45).*

The spirit of perversion always destroys the marriage, or the married couple. It's not attracted to your wife, and it's not attracted to your husband; it is attracted to your disobedience. Demons link themselves directly to death and this is why a man or woman who is sexually perverted may often find themselves aroused by choking one another, spanking one another, or cutting one another.

Now, if you've been married for a while, you will know that every sexual encounter with your spouse is not the same. Some days are okay and others are great. A person who is under the power of that demon goes through those same feelings. A couple could reach a higher level of orgasmic heights by being monogamous and learning to love one another unconditionally. When the mind is submitted to love, it responds throughout the body. The more the two of you obey GOD, the better the sex will be. In truth, the level that the devil is telling them about can only be found in a GOD-fearing union, with no need for any objects or outsiders.

Sexual perversion is pure and unmasked evil that renders the man selfish and heartless. The proof is in the discarded and raped bodies of men, women, and children that are thrown on the side of the roads, placed in wooded areas, or buried in shallow graves. The person who committed this crime is spiritually sick. That spirit is broken. While others have committed their life to GOD, someone who has this spirit will often commit themselves to feeding it. That's why you will find that some parishioners have molested the very children they were trusted to protect. A title doesn't deliver someone, it makes them more of a target for a demonic attack, and if they are not fortified with the WORD of GOD on every side, they will be captured and sold into slavery.

But, what if you or someone you know has it? What can you do to be delivered from it? How can you stay delivered?

1. Admit to yourself and realize that it is there.
2. Repent and denounce it.
3. Ask GOD to cover you, or that person with the Blood of JESUS.
4. Ask GOD to give you power from on high, and to fill you with the HOLY SPIRIT.
5. Praise GOD. A little "thank you" praise is good, but a deep, shouting and reverential praise is much better! Even if you have to leave the house to be alone and praise HIM from your vehicle, do so. Your praise tells that devil that he is outnumbered and surrounded. It tells him to surrender or flee.
6. Go into a fast and ask GOD what type of fast that you should do. You may have to do the first 24 hours with no food or water, so you can be open to hear the voice of GOD. HE may tell you to continue on for four days without food or water, or HE may tell you to do a Daniel's fast.
7. Obey GOD.
8. Avoid all pornography and perverse people. (This has to be continued and maintained, so that perverted friend of yours just became your ex-best friend.) Remember: deliverance or death.
9. Bind that spirit and cast it into the pit. GOD says that whatever we bind on earth will be bound in heaven, and whatever we loose on earth will be loosed in heaven. Bind it and send it to the pit (abyss) and use your authority to bind it there until the day of judgment. (That way, it doesn't go out searching for seven more to bring back to you.)
10. Once you are delivered, stay delivered. Don't even entertain that spirit or another like it for even a half of a second. Bind it immediately and send it down, don't raise it up.

11. Stay in GOD'S presence.
12. If you feel yourself becoming aroused at something or someone that you shouldn't be aroused by, don't panic. It doesn't mean that this demon is attached to you, it could be one nearby trying to entice you. Bind it and send it down; don't raise it up. Sometimes, when in the presence of someone else who has that spirit, you may find yourself becoming aroused, only because you are sensitive to that spirit. Go into warfare immediately, and if you're not working with that person stay away from them. If GOD calls you to bring them towards the altar of deliverance, do so. But, ask GOD what HE wants you to do. Please note that devils come in different ranks and unless you can match that rank in the spirit, you are unfit to fight it. That's why you have to fast.
13. Believe. You can't cast something out if you don't believe in GOD. You say that you believe in GOD, but HE looks straightway at your heart. And in many cases, there are some questions there. You have allowed science and life to place dust on your heart. You can't cast anything out this way. *"Then certain of the vagabond Jews, exorcists, took upon them to call over them which had evil spirits the name of the LORD Jesus, saying, We adjure you by Jesus whom Paul preacheth.*
And there were seven sons of one Sceva, a Jew, and chief of the priests, which did so.
And the evil spirit answered and said, Jesus I know, and Paul I know; but who are ye?
And the man in whom the evil spirit was leaped on them, and overcame them, and prevailed against them, so that they fled out of that house naked and wounded" (Acts 19:13-16).

What went wrong? Why couldn't they cast that evil spirit out? The scriptures make it clear that they didn't truly believe. They said, "By <u>the</u> JESUS <u>whom Paul preacheth.</u>" Meaning, this was not their gospel. They were exorcists, using other techniques to try and rid people of demons. They saw how Paul had effectively cast out demons in the name of JESUS, so they thought that HIS name alone would be another tool in their duffel bag. Wrong answer. There is power in HIS name, but you must first believe to activate it.

14. Never again entertain perversity. There will be some days when you want to do something odd with your spouse. There is only one place on a woman's body that GOD has created for entrance (sexually), and there are no places on a man's body that was created for entrance (sexually). Everywhere else is out of line. Don't entertain that perversity. You're only picking up demonic residue and telling demons that you're desiring another brush with perversion.
15. Throw away every perverse thing in your house and in your wallet. Sex toys: throw them away. Pornography: destroy it and throw it away. Don't let what snared you, ensnare someone else. Never think something is harmless. Whips, chains and handcuffs represent bondage and control; get rid of them. Stop trying to reason with yourself and that demon. Stay away from pornographic sites and all forms of pornography. If you have to take extreme measures, try blocking them, so that you can't open them on your computer again.
16. Last, but not least, pray for and cover your children with the Blood of JESUS. If that spirit has been in your home, it has tried to molest your kids. That's its nature. Don't you ever think that a demon is as nice as you are. Because we, as people, tend to believe that even some of the most vile and evil people alive will murder adults but have pity on children. That's not the case. While your children may have resisted entertaining those thoughts, they may very well act on them one day. Cast it away from them, and down into the pit to be held there until the day of judgment in the name of JESUS!

Always remember, whatever or whomever you allow in your house, you are allowing access to your children. Because whatever spirit has access to that visitor does travel with them, and when it is welcomed into your home, judgment is declared upon that house. Even if they claim to be followers, leaders, and partakers of the Body of CHRIST; you are to look for their fruit. If they are evil, they will be dropping evil seeds in your home. Everyone who comes in contact with you is bearing some type of fruit, and everywhere they go, they are sowing the seeds of those fruits. If their fruit is good, they will serve a blessing wherever they may go; nevertheless, if their fruit is bad, they will serve as a curse wherever they go. Your assignment from GOD is to test the spirits by the SPIRIT to see if they be of GOD. How so? By knowing the WORD of GOD, you know the law of GOD. When you know the law of GOD, you get to act as a lawyer in HIS courtroom. As such, you can try the spirits according to the Living WORD. In other words, you'd better submerge yourself in the WORD of GOD. Drown yourself in it. Be captivated by it. Make it a dependency. Because when you do not, you become gullible and will receive any and every one who appeases the right-now version of you. But as you get delivered, you may find it hard to separate yourself from them or vice versa. When you invite such a soul into your home, whatever is attached to them comes with them and now has a key to your house and access to your family, because judgment has already been declared on such a man. 2 John 1:9-11 confirms this, *"Whosoever transgresseth, and abideth not in the doctrine of Christ, hath not God. He that abideth in the doctrine of Christ, he hath both the Father and the Son. If there come any unto you, and bring not this doctrine, receive him not into your house, neither bid him God speed: For he that biddeth him God speed is partaker of his evil deeds."*

But, when someone with the spirit of perversion, or any demon, for that matter, is allowed access to you, you become guilty of evil communication. Communication is the transmittal of information through spoken, written, and other exchanges. Communication is not just carnal, it is spiritual; meaning, since words have power, who we allow to communicate with us are given access to the most intimate parts of us. GOD has warned us in Proverbs 4:23 this way: *"Guard your heart above all else, for it determines the course of your life."* That is to understand that everyone who comes into your life pours into your life, and whatever is poured into you will eventually begin to overflow. Do you want to overflow with lustful thoughts? Burning desires that seem unquenchable? If not, be careful and pray about e-v-e-r-y-o-n-e who enters or attempts to enter your life. *"He that walketh with wise men shall be wise: but a companion of fools shall be destroyed" (Proverbs 13:20).*

In addition, stay submitted to GOD in every area of your life. GOD desires that we obey HIM because HE loves us and wants to protect us from the evil that follows sin. Talk to your spouse, and if the LORD leads; seek Christian counseling. Be sure that you go only where HE leads you to for this counseling. Never feed the perversion in a man or a woman. If your spouse requests lewd and lascivious acts, you are not helping them by submitting to these acts. Instead, you are helping that demon to grow. Remember, whatever you starve will die, and whatever you feed will grow. This is why a fast is necessary. That spirit needs to be starved out and prayed out. Obedience will keep it out, but giving in to the selfish and deadly desires of the flesh will always open the door to let it in.

Temptations and the Birth of Consequence

Temptations are tests designed to try the man or trip the man. We all pass through temptation from time to time, and it definitely doesn't go away once we get married. Temptation is the devil's seductive dance. Sometimes you can clearly see his presence on whatever or whoever he uses to test you, and sometimes his presence is well hidden because it is masked by something we desire. Whatever uniform he wears, his objective is clear: kill, steal, and destroy. You're just a pawn in his game.

Whatever tempts you attempts to have you, and when you are married, it attempts to have your entire family. A great example would be an adulterous affair. There are millions who have lost their families because they chose to engage in adultery, and they will openly tell you that it destroys more than one person.

But temptation is seduction. Once seduction has taken place, the act of becoming one ensues. This is when one has given in to seduction, and allowed themselves to fall prey to its devices. Shortly thereafter, a pregnancy follows. The baby who is being carried is called Consequence. Labor and contractions (tribulations) come before Consequence's birth. This is the time when the victimizer may become belligerent, untrusting, fearful, indifferent, generous, aggressive, and dangerous. People panic when they know that they are pregnant with Consequence or when they can see Consequence's head beginning to crown.

The birth of Consequence is a trying time for all parties involved. This is the time in which the seed that was planted has grown up and been reaped. Sometimes consequences include: the loss of a job, divorce, the loss of life, the loss of blessings, etc.

Ladies: Temptation doesn't like women much, because women are strong-willed creatures. When a woman makes up her mind to be faithful, she will wear it proudly. Temptation does have an angle over us, however, and it's called "emotions." Our thoughts provoke us, and we often allow those thoughts to sit down in our hearts and cause us to react negatively. Ordinarily, women react more because many of us have been shifted out of order by our experiences. If you were disobedient to GOD in the earlier years regarding relationships, chances are you were damaged by those relationships. Moreover, if you have not fully submitted yourself and your problems to JESUS, your husband will unwillingly become the representative for every man that has ever hurt you. If you are undelivered, you are still bound by soul ties, and because these ties are still present; it is impossible to tie up to the husband the way a wife should be linked to her spouse. This will undoubtedly destroy the marriage because the husband was not given a fair chance at winning your heart and making his own mistakes. Instead, he is made to pay for the choices of others.

Deliverance: First, you need to renounce the sin, repent of the sin, and ask GOD to remove the root of the sin from you. If that root is the presence of soul ties from past relationships, you will need to fast because the soul tie was established in the flesh during an act of disobedience.
Also, you have to begin by practicing and start living in your

deliverance. The most common thing for people to do nowadays is to wait for deliverance. This is error because deliverance has to be approached, embraced, and lived in. Anytime you feel a soul tie trying to reattach itself, tear it down with a fast.

Let's just say, for example, that every man that you know has cheated on their spouse. Your Dad cheated on your Mom, your Uncles cheated on your Aunts, your brother cheated on his wife and so on. You have met many women who proudly explain this away. They say that all men cheat. This makes sense, because all the men that you knew have been adulterers. Nevertheless, this is a lie. All men do not cheat; worldly men do. What if your husband is exhibiting behavior that warns you he may be involved in an adulterous affair? Why fight with him? You can't stop an adult that has made a decision from acting out their decision. All of your arguing, checking his cellphone, following him around, or timing him will avail you nothing. I speak this from experience, for experience is the teacher of the deaf. I was deaf, but experience spoke the truth loud and clearly. Anyhow, you have seen so many cheat, and now you are going to new depths, heights, and widths trying not to become a victim of this very act. When you use the flesh, you inflame the flesh. What this means is, when you're trying to stop your husband by acting up, you're only inviting more spirits into the marriage to entice him. The bible tells us in James 3:16, *"For where envying and strife is, there is confusion and every evil work."* The minute you open your mouth to argue, or your arms to fight you are inviting devils to a party of ignorance. Ignorance is their favorite food next to fear. Your arguing is music to them; your fighting is entertainment, and the grand finale is your divorce.

Resist temptation. Yes, this even includes the temptation to go shopping when you know there are bills that need to be paid. When you take that credit card to shop for shoes, when your closet is full of them, you are under a stronghold of poverty. The bible tells us, *"A good man leaveth an inheritance to his children's children: and the wealth of the sinner is laid up for the just"*

(Proverbs 13:22).

Sow a seed. Proverbs 31 talks about the righteous woman who sold to the merchant ships. Her hands were blessed because her mind and heart were blessed. Find fertile ground and plant seeds, as directed by the HOLY GHOST. Water it with your praise. By being the woman GOD has called you to be, you are fighting off any spirit that may attempt to enter your husband, your home, your children, or yourself. You have the power to plead the Blood of JESUS over hubby, rendering that adulterous spirit powerless. All this power comes from your willingness to obey the voice of the LORD. If your husband is committing adultery against you, all you have to do is go out and sow a seed. Rather than following him and arguing with him, go and be a blessing. We'll talk more on this subject later on in this book.

The gist of this is: Resist temptation! You are setting the motion for your life. If you want good fruit to grow and show up in your marriage, you have to plant good seed. Never listen to any devil who tells you that through manipulation, crying, arguing, and fighting that your husband will become a better man. Remember this: The devil is a liar.

Fellows: Temptation loves to knock on your door because of what you've been taught and what you've witnessed. Many of you grew up believing that to be a man, you have to be weak. You're tempted easily by money, power, and sex. All of these things offer up temporary highs, and this is as far as many of you can see. Devils love to get you on the ship of sin, wine you, dine you, and give you the impression that you're going to have the cruise of a lifetime. He keeps you so busy with deadly pleasures, that you don't question where you're heading. After he has had his fill of you and the journey is over, you will reach the shores of Hades, where you'll find that your sins were a one-way trip to nowhere.

Money: Since the beginning of time, man has dreamed of having enough money to retire and live out life without worries. To man, money seems to be the answer to everything. Money is not the answer to anything, but it does have the power to erect itself as a god in one's life. When you see secular ways to make money, you need to turn it down because once the love of money has you in its grip, death will more than likely be the only thing that will pry you out. Yes, GOD can deliver you, but you won't find a rich man who wants to be delivered. He may want the blessings, but when he has to give up the glory and the money for the blessings, he will walk out on the LORD. Proof of this is written in the story of the rich young ruler. Mark 10:17-27 reads:

"And when he was gone forth into the way, there came one running, and kneeled to him, and asked him, Good Master, what shall I do that I may inherit eternal life?

And Jesus said unto him, Why callest thou me good? There is none good but one, that is, God.

Thou knowest the commandments, Do not commit adultery, Do not kill, Do not steal, Do not bear false witness, Defraud not, Honour thy father and mother.

And he answered and said unto him, Master, all these have I observed from my youth.

Then Jesus beholding him loved him, and said unto him, One thing thou lackest: go thy way, sell whatsoever thou hast, and give to the poor, and thou shalt have treasure in heaven: and come, take up the cross, and follow me.

And he was sad at that saying, and went away grieved: for he had great possessions.

And Jesus looked round about, and saith unto his disciples, How hardly shall they that have riches enter into the kingdom of God!

And the disciples were astonished at his words. But Jesus answereth again, and saith unto them, Children, how hard is it for them that trust in riches to enter into the kingdom of God!

It is easier for a camel to go through the eye of a needle, than for a rich man to enter into the kingdom of God.

And they were astonished out of measure, saying among themselves, Who then can be saved?

And Jesus looking upon them saith, With men it is impossible, but not with God: for with God all things are possible."

From just looking at this story, you may come to believe that it is against GOD to be rich because JESUS said, *"It is easier for a camel to go through the eye of a needle, than for a rich man to enter into the kingdom of God."* Abraham was rich and righteous, and so was David, Isaiah, Job and many of the Prophets. Read it again. JESUS never said it was a sin to be wealthy, but the LORD made it clear that the man trusted in his riches. His wealth didn't come from GOD because GOD never gives the wealth without giving first the wisdom. That means that his wealth would not have served as a snare if it had come from the LORD.

Let's read it again: "It is easier for a camel to go through the eye of a needle, than for a rich man to enter into the kingdom of God. And they were astonished out of measure, saying among themselves, Who then can be saved? And Jesus looking upon them saith, With men it is impossible, but not with God: for with God all things are possible." What HE'S saying is a camel **can** go through the eye of a needle if GOD called it to go through. GOD has called you to be the lender and not the borrower, but before you get the wealth, you must get the wisdom. Man has twisted up the scriptures for centuries reporting that money is the root of all evil. But, that's not what GOD said. *"For the **love** of money is the root of all evil: which while some coveted after, they have erred from the faith, and pierced themselves through with many sorrows" (1 Timothy 6:10).*

Don't allow someone to contaminate you talking about getting rich. Get JESUS, for HE is all you need. With JESUS, you won't have a need that goes unmet. The world has to see the money to believe that they have it, but as a believer, all you have to do is pray about it, lower it down with your praise, and it's all yours! No car notes, no mortgages, and no monthly payments. This is to help you understand that the love of money is out of order and demonically driven.

"Be careful for nothing; but in every thing by prayer and supplication with thanksgiving let your requests be made known unto God" (Phillipians 4:6).

Power: Power usually comes with money. What is power? The ability to do things that others cannot do. What is power? Glory. But, have you learned that you cannot hold GOD'S glory? It's too heavy for you; it's too bright for you; it's too wonderful for you. Just like Satan, many desire to have the power and the glory of GOD. One of the most common reasons for wanting power is unforgiveness. The man who desires this believes that if he were to rise above all who hurt him, he could exact revenge on them without fear of consequence. But this is not of GOD. Another reason for wanting power is to be like GOD. Some people want to be over people, when they have no calling to do so. People who are worshipers of self want power because they have erected themselves up as their own god. Power, to them, means that man would have to serve them and their lusts. This way of reasoning is demonic. When a person wants to rule a nation or a group of people, and they have no WORD of GOD in them, they are demonically charged.

Our life is a chance to glorify GOD, live for GOD, and the opportunity to get our passport to return to HIM. When GOD charges a man up with power, that power is to live, heal the sick, raise the dead, and cast out demons. This is so HIS Name is glorified, and not your own. Don't despise power, but despise any power not given by GOD. Only desire to do the will of GOD. When GOD sees that your heart is not in captivity, HE will empower you because HE knows that HE can trust you with that power to help others and glorify HIS Name. When an ungodly man is given a dose of power, he becomes consumed by it and addicted to it. It dictates his life and he serves it. He is snared and reserved for the pit. GOD desires to have him, but he desires to have the glory of GOD. How can one be jealous of GOD and covet HIS glory?

Sex: Ever since you had your first sexual encounter, you have more than likely wanted more. And once you decided what was appealing and unappealing to you, you began to link that to your sexual encounters. For example, most men want a beautiful woman with a certain body frame. There are some men who desire skinny women, others desire medium sized women, some desire curvaceous women, while others desire obese women. In addition, some men want women who are unattractive to them. They feel that this intensifies the experience because they believe that unattractive women are better lovers. Whenever a man's desire is fulfilled, his mind reacts more, causing his experience to seem heightened. In truth, orgasm doesn't start or end in the pubic region; it occurs in the brain and the brain transmits neurons to that area of the body. With men and women alike, when our heart's desire is fulfilled, we have a better sexual experience. Now, it is what is in our hearts that is the culprit. Because if you are turned on by something perverse, you yourself are perverse, and your heart is contaminated or under siege. You need to take your sanity back to get back to where GOD has called you, because perversion is a form of insanity.

But, lo and behold: temptation. Sexually charged temptations are the attempt of a flesh demon to enter into and siege that person. Many souls have fallen for centuries because they tried to walk away when GOD never said to walk away; HE said to flee fornication. Take into account the story of Joseph with Potiphar's wife. If Joseph had not run, he may have found himself being overtaken by temptation, but he was a wise man. He knew that he had to get out of there and fast. The scriptures tell us that he left his cloak in the hands of Potiphar's wife, and fled.

When you become the husband of someone, you are her protector in the natural. You should never introduce the enemy to your wife; instead, you should always be on your face, praying for her, and her for you. There is power in love and power in your prayers.

There are millions of immoral women out there who will try to tempt your mind so they can attempt to have your heart. Beware! The souls of the dead are within her. *"Drink waters out of thine own cistern, and running waters out of thine own well.*
Let thy fountains be dispersed abroad, and rivers of waters in the

streets.
Let them be only thine own, and not strangers' with thee.
Let thy fountain be blessed: and rejoice with the wife of thy youth.
Let her be as the loving hind and pleasant roe; let her breasts satisfy thee at all times; and be thou ravished always with her love.
And why wilt thou, my son, be ravished with a strange woman, and embrace the bosom of a stranger?
For the ways of man are before the eyes of the LORD, and he pondereth all his goings" (Proverbs 5:15-21).

Temptation is the devil's way of spraying perfume on himself, so you won't smell the death on him while you follow him toward the slaughter. Look around today. You will find many immoral souls; men and women who desire to have your soul. Tight fitted jeans, midriff tops, lingerie in the open, derrieres on display, and so on. The devil is launching a campaign for you and your children. He desires to slaughter your sons and rape your daughters, but he needs your help. He has to have your permission to come into your home and do these things. He gets it by tempting you out of the covering of the LORD and bringing you into sin. After all, death is your payment for sin. In addition, as a parent, you are showing your children what choices to make through your decision making. This way, he not only binds you, but he knows that your children will likely follow in your footsteps, since this will be learned behavior for them.

Man of GOD, don't give in to temptation; defeat it. Cast it down, raise up the name of JESUS, and be thankful for the wife HE'S blessed you with. If you are not married, but desire to be married, you may have to fight even harder because there aren't many who are saved that will tempt you. So, in choosing a wife, you have to be wise and discerning. With everything, go before the Throne of Grace and be led only by GOD.

If you have those fornicating or adulterous friends who like to brag about their rendezvous, separate yourself from them; otherwise your evil communication with them will ruin your life. (See 1 Corinthians 15:33). If you are watching channels that are sexually charged, ask your cable provider to turn off that channel. If there are magazines that come to your house that are sexual in nature, return them to the sender with a note asking that they stop sending those magazines to your home.

You have to proactively work to get rid of whatever serves as a snare in your life. Temptation will never go away, but you can control your space and stop it from coming within the confines of that space. Whatever tempts you, get rid of it! Unless it's your wife.

Adulterous Insanity

You think no one can understand what you're going through. You are overcome by the desire to be with other people, even though you're married. You burn with passion from within, and you can't seem to shake it. You love your spouse, but you want variety. Funny thing, sex with others isn't better than it is with the spouse, in most cases. It just has an extra bite to it because mankind often deceives itself into believing that anything forbidden has an extra ting to it. *"Whosoever is simple, let him turn in here: and as for him that lacks understanding, she says to him, Stolen waters are sweet, and bread eaten in secret is pleasant. But he knows not that the dead are there; and that her guests are in the depths of the grave" (Proverbs 9:16-18).*

If this is how you feel, you are temporarily insane. Merriam-Webster defines insanity as:
1: a deranged state of the mind usually occurring as a specific disorder (as schizophrenia)
2: such unsoundness of mind or lack of understanding as prevents one from having the mental capacity required by law to enter into a

particular relationship, status, or transaction or as removes one from criminal or civil responsibility
3*a* : extreme folly or unreasonableness
b: something utterly foolish or unreasonable

We often associate insanity with extreme madness or psychological disorders as defined by a licensed doctor. Nevertheless, insanity is basically perversion. Let's break down each definition, so that we can get a more in depth look at insanity.

1: a deranged state of the mind usually occurring as a specific disorder (as schizophrenia)
Deranged means out of order mentally. It means to have an abnormal state of mind. GOD is a GOD of order, and HE has designed this world, and the things thereof, to operate a certain way. With mankind, HE has given us the tools to aid us in fulfilling our assignments in the earth realm. We were built a certain way, and programmed a certain way, but when we go outside of our design, we are considered insane. If you purchased a microwave and tried to microwave some popcorn, how would you feel if the microwave started playing music instead? It wasn't designed to play music; therefore, you would likely return the microwave because it is not operating as it was designed to operate. You are the same way. You were designed to operate a certain way, and when you go outside of your design; your mind needs to be returned to CHRIST for repairs. Schizophrenia is a state of derangement. It is characterized by illusions. An illusion is, according to Merriam-Webster, the state or fact of being intellectually deceived or misled; perception of something objectively existing in such a way as to cause misinterpretation of its actual nature. Adultery is also characterized by illusions because the person engaging in adultery has been deceived into believing that either sex outside of their spouse is better, or that the person they are engaging in adultery with is a better fit for them than their spouse. The truth is, how we fit with one another is in accordance with GOD'S design and plan for our lives. Therefore, when a husband and wife are in the will of GOD, they will fit

together as one; nevertheless, because they are individuals, they will often think individually. This means that they will sometimes disagree. What you do with those disagreements will determine how your marriage runs. By man's own definition, adultery is a form of schizophrenia.

2: such unsoundness of mind or lack of understanding as prevents one from having the mental capacity required by law to enter into a particular relationship, status, or transaction or as removes one from criminal or civil responsibility
Here, derangement is defined as a lack of understanding. This stands directly in line with the WORD of GOD. Proverbs 6:32 reads, *"But whoso committeth adultery with a woman lacketh understanding: he that doeth it destroyeth his own soul."* In addition, Merriam-Webster relates this to not being able to have the capacity required (by law) to enter a particular relationship, status, or transaction. How true, indeed! A person that has an adulterous heart should NOT be in a relationship because they lack the capacity to love someone outside of their selfish limitations. Therefore, their status should remain "single" until they've been delivered.

3a : extreme folly or unreasonableness
b: something utterly foolish or unreasonable
Folly means foolish. Merriam-Webster defines derangement as "extreme" foolishness and unreasonableness. How foolish is adultery? How unreasonable is adultery? They stem from a wicked heart, and they rest on a selfish foundation because sin is self worship! *"For from within, out of the heart of men, proceed evil thoughts, adulteries, **fornications**, murders, thefts, covetousness, wickedness, deceit, licentiousness, an evil eye, blasphemy, pride, **foolishness**: All these evil things come from within, and defile the man" (Mark 7:21-23).*

Therefore, adultery is temporary, or in some cases, long-term insanity. Adultery starts first in the mind as a wicked thought. *"Casting down imaginations, and every high thing that exalteth itself against the knowledge of God, and bringing into captivity every thought to the obedience of Christ" (2 Corinthians 10:5).* When that thought is not cast down, it makes its way into the heart where it is conceived. *"For out of the heart proceed evil thoughts, murders, adulteries, fornications, thefts, false witness, blasphemies" (Matthew 15:19).*

When the thought is not brought into captivity, it will always imprison the heart because what introduces itself to your mind is trying to make its way to your heart. Any man or woman who lusts after another person has already committed the act of adultery because once it gets in the heart, it has already manifested itself. It's only a matter of time before one submits their body to it. "But I say unto you, That whosoever looketh on a woman to lust after her hath committed adultery with her already in his heart" (Matthew 5:28).

What has happened is, a thought came into you, and when you didn't cast it down, it began to play like a movie in your head. You began to consider that thought, and after it danced in your mind for a while, it was recorded by your heart. Think about this: Once someone memorizes a phone number, it is common to say that they know the number "by heart." As you can see, any thought not brought into captivity will eventually burn itself into your memory or heart. You may have given in to the desire by watching pornography or flirting with someone other than your spouse. Now you're dirty, and your spirit man reeks of adultery; but you want more because forbidden fruit tastes sweet until the after-bite. It's not that it was better; it was different, and it was with someone new.

There is a demonic spirit directly linked to adultery. It is, of course, a flesh demon and it craves to become one with as many souls as possible. When a man has intercourse with a woman, he deposits a piece of himself into that woman. He develops a soul tie with her; meaning their souls are now knit together as one. They are now husband and wife. If the man's soul is contaminated, his deposit is contaminated as well. Women, on the other hand, are receptors because they don't make deposits. Instead, women harbor whatever is given to them. When a man and a woman have intercourse, she receives him into her body. When intercourse is complete, she receives his seed into her body. When a seed is conceived, she becomes pregnant and carries the seed of that man until the gestation is up and the baby is delivered.

GOD uses the natural to explain the spiritual. With a woman, even if she does not become pregnant in the natural, her soul conceives and she begins to bare that man's soul. Eventually, she will deliver to him a blessing or a curse. If the act occurred during an adulterous affair, she delivers to him a baby named Consequence.

Nevertheless, you know the WORD. You know that adultery is wrong, but it feels so right. First answer this: Do you love the LORD? If your answer is yes, make it evident in your life. GOD said, "If ye love me, keep my commandments" (John 14:15). If your desire to commit adultery is greater than your love for GOD, you have erected in yourself an idol, and that idol is you. GOD'S love for us goes beyond our sins and encompasses us on every side. Our love for GOD should be so great that no person, place, or thing could outweigh or overshadow it. But, adultery is a crime of self-worship, and the person you are committing this act with is your living sacrifice. Whatever you worship, you make sacrifices for. If you love the LORD, the sacrifice you will make is self. That's why you fast; that's why you pray and give up those dirty ways and evil friendships. Even though you want to keep them, you let them go because GOD says so. We are so quick to say to our spouses, "If you love me, you wouldn't do that." Even though you want to do a particular thing, you refrain from it because of your love for your spouse. GOD said the same thing. HE said, again, in John 14:15, "If you love me, keep my commandments." This means that it is not deliverance that will hold you from sin; deliverance just drives the demon away, but you still have to refrain from sin and your love for GOD has to be great enough to hold you. If you find that your love for GOD isn't strong enough to keep you from adultery, or any other sin against HIM, you don't really *know* HIM. You know *of* HIM, and you've even chatted with HIM a few times, but to know HIM is to love HIM. To love HIM is to obey HIM. To obey HIM is to reverence HIM. This goes on and on. Everything you do should link up to your love for HIM. Trying to love your spouse enough to refrain from adultery will avail you nothing because, as a human being, the spouse will step on your feet from time to time. In your state of selfishness, this would be enough to drive you to stray. Your love for GOD, however, will keep you because GOD is perfect and you can't find any sin in HIM.

GOD wants to have you wholly, not partially. When you try to give yourself to GOD in portions, you are unacceptable, no matter how you cut up in church. Romans 12:1 reads, *"I beseech you therefore, brethren, by the mercies of God, that ye present your bodies a living sacrifice, holy, acceptable unto God, which is your reasonable service."* Do you think your body is holy when it bears the scent of fornication or adultery? Cain was a tiller of the ground, or a gardener. He tried to offer GOD of the fruit of the ground, and GOD did not accept it. The Bible makes a distinction between Abel's offering and Cain's offering. Abel brought GOD of the first fruits of his increase, but the Bible did not say that Cain brought in the first fruits. It said he brought in some of the fruit. GOD desires your best. He doesn't need it, but this is so you will learn to trust HIM. Your best is your obedience. When you obey the LORD, you are worshiping the LORD with your life, and are counted as HIS. But when you obey your flesh or the demon therein, you are worshiping yourself and whatever is tempting you. So, all of your shouting, going to church, and tears avail you nothing if you are not willing to give yourself wholly to GOD.

And ladies, each and every time you give yourself to a man, you become his wife illegally. That's why in the scriptures, GOD gives your husband the option to divorce you if you commit adultery. You become defiled with the soul of the man that you have committed adultery with. In adultery, a woman loses her peace and becomes a danger to her family because she wasn't designed to hold the souls of multiple men. She was designed to be a wife to one man. Every time you lay down with a man, a soul tie is established, and because the man is the giver, and you are the receptor, you will begin to birth the seed of that man into your life. If that man's seed or life is contaminated, you will become contaminated. It's like a sexually transmitted disease because, again, GOD uses the natural to explain the spiritual. Whatever is transferred to you during your act of adultery, you will birth in your home, and it will grow up alongside your children. Again, this wicked baby is called Consequence.

When temptation comes, it dances with your thoughts and should be cast down. When it has not been cast down, it crouches in the heart and becomes lust. *"But I say unto you, That whosoever looketh on a woman to lust after her hath committed adultery with her already in his heart" (Matthew 5:28).* Once lust has been conceived, it starts a period of spiritual gestation, and something will be born to your sin. As a woman, because two souls are within you, you will find yourself confused. Again, confusion is a state of derangement because GOD is not in it. Where there is peace, there is GOD; but where there is confusion, you will always find the enemy campaigning. "For God is not the author of confusion, but of peace, as in all churches of the saints" (1 Corinthians 14:33).

Adultery destroys families and ministries. It breaks up homes and introduces a new way of thinking to everyone involved.

Fellows: Your daughters don't trust men, so they turn to homosexuality or promiscuity. In many cases, they endure tumultuous relationships because they think that the highs and the lows of fighting are normal. They tolerate relationships where they are made to suffer time and time again while their boyfriends or husbands go out and serve themselves as many women (or men) as they can handle. If you'd taught them better, they wouldn't marry or continue on with this type of man. Your sons think it's okay to be promiscuous. After all, you've taught them that to be a man, cheating is a part of their genetic code. You are teaching your children to be reckless, flesh-serving, devil-worshiping souls with no real understanding of what's right or wrong. That's called insanity.

Ask any saved and faithful man (yes, they do exist), and he will tell you that when you apply GOD to your marriage, and you honor GOD with your marriage, you won't have a need or a desire for anything or anyone else.

Ladies: There are many of you out there who believe in withholding your body from your husband. This is error, and it is against the WORD of GOD. It is common for a woman to give herself to a man that is not her husband repeatedly, but once she gets married, she begins to withhold herself from him. When someone tries to wisely tell you that in doing so, you are opening the door for adultery, many of you reply, "If he wants to cheat, he's going to cheat anyway. It doesn't matter if I have sex with him or not." Yes, if he has adultery in his heart, he will submit his body to it. Nevertheless, if he doesn't have adultery in his heart, then what? You cannot open the door for the enemy in your marriage, and then complain when he comes in. 1 Corinthians 7:3-5 reads:
"Let the husband render unto the wife due benevolence: and likewise also the wife unto the husband. The wife hath not power of her own body, but the husband: and likewise also the husband hath not power of his own body, but the wife.
Defraud ye not one the other, except it be with consent for a time, that ye may give yourselves to fasting and prayer; and come together again, ***<u>that Satan tempt you not for your incontinency.</u>****"*

As a spouse, we should never withhold ourselves from our spouses unless it is done in agreement for fasting. But, let's say, your spouse has a raging libido, and it's too much for you. Everything has a root, and the root of him or her being that way should be sought out. Sometimes, an out of control libido is the product of a void. Then again, his or her libido may be normal, whereas yours may be abnormally low. Again, there is a root to everything.

Remember, where there are no signals of comprehension, you must build new towers. Instead of saying no and ranting on repeatedly about what you see as a problem, the two of you should come together in fasting and prayer to seek out answers. Find out what the root source of the two of you not being in agreement physically is. Saying no won't make his or her urges go away, and if there is a void in them, they will seek out a yes outside of you to pacify that void.

When adultery enters a home, it becomes a generational curse over that home. Your children are scheduled to follow in your footsteps. Reschedule them by following the footsteps of CHRIST. In doing so, you are helping them to see HIM as their source and their deliverer, rather than just a name to throw in the batch with Santa Claus, the Easter Bunny, and so on. *(And prayerfully, you don't or won't be teaching those lies to your children as well. All lies have a destination. Never put your children on the road to death).*

Our marriage to our spouses is a reflection of our relationship with CHRIST. If you carry on an adulterous relationship against your spouse, all in the same, you are carrying on an idolatrous relationship against the LORD. Adultery is very similar to idolatry because something or someone is being reverenced in a position that was not given to them by GOD. In idolatry, you worship something or someone else; thus giving GOD'S spot to that thing or person in your heart. In adultery, you worship yourself; thus giving your spouse's spot to someone else in your life. You see, when we are faithful to GOD, it trickles on down into our marriages, but when we are unfaithful to our spouses, our deeds rise up before HIM for judgment.

A moral and good person will not and cannot engage in an adulterous relationship with you. You may say, "That's not true! I'm not bad at all. I just messed up." You messed up because of what was in you at that time. You were a tree bearing the fruit of the seed from within. Notice I use past tense terminology, praying that you have been delivered, even if it was just three seconds ago when you committed the act. You are whatever seed is within you. *"A good tree cannot bring forth evil fruit, neither can a corrupt tree bring forth good fruit" (Matthew 7:18).*

What if you are currently suffering in a relationship where your partner is involved in adultery? As the spouse, the power is within you to shut that insanity down, but you have to stay sanely in GOD'S will to do so. You have to learn to activate that power, and not allow your emotions to render you powerless. If you discover it (the affair) to be true, you may decide that you want out of that marriage. It's a normal way to think. Your spouse is hurting you with one of the greatest sins against you that he or she can commit besides murdering you or your family. Now, imagine how GOD feels when you do this against HIM. I know that you don't want to hear about that right now, if you're going through it, but you have to. Each trial is a test of your faith and the ability to learn a lesson. Right now, you're toiling and planting seeds, and it's rough. In addition, if a trial hits you, don't you walk away from it broke. There is wisdom and wealth in a trial; you just have to be sane enough to reach for it.

When I was married the first time, I was never really at peace because I was constantly having to deal with affairs behind affairs. I didn't know what to do because I was still a babe in CHRIST, so I did what I knew how to do. I fought, talked, yelled, begged, cried, threatened, and then I fought some more. I was literally insane at that time. Over the years, I endured so much until one day I decided that I would get revenge. I would go out and have an affair to teach him a lesson. I'd served five years of faithfulness as a wife, and suddenly, I was just tired and starving for affection. So I went out and started my own affair. At this time, I knew that my marriage was over because, for five years, I called my virtuousness my crown. I loved being a wife, and I loved being a faithful wife. I felt so empowered by the fact that I was a virtuous woman, but my affair wasn't the result of what he did to me. I found out later that this was an issue still rooted in me; only it was lying dormant within me. Hurt is like a fire alarm; it'll wake up everything in you that's sleeping. Even as a babe in CHRIST, conviction wore me down, and I couldn't continue the affair. It was too much for my soul, so I ended it after a month. To me, the day I sinned against him, I lost my rights to be a wife and a crown. Of course, it wasn't revenge against him, because he never knew about it; nevertheless, it turned out to be me hurting myself even more, and worst of all, me hurting GOD. In addition, our sins are against GOD and GOD alone.

Now, I am remarried and I will never relinquish my virtuous crown because of my love for GOD. Anytime you are willing to have an affair in response to your spouse's affair, you don't love GOD enough to be still. GOD explained to me that I had loved that man more than I loved HIM. My actions always responded to his actions, but my actions should have been responding to GOD. An affair will always show you what is lurking with you. Your goal should not be to become a better spouse; your goal should always be to become a better son or daughter to GOD. In this, you will automatically become a better spouse. Even when your spouse commits adultery against you, it is not a reflection of their love or lack of love for you; it is a reflection of their lack of love for GOD. You just happened to be standing in the way.

For the ladies: We try to find any and every way to get our spouses to be faithful to us when they are unfaithful. I tried changing my hair, changing my wardrobe....you name it. I tried cooking new foods, talking about the issue, praying, asking questions, and then I went back to looking at myself in search for the answers. Again, I'd change something else until I discovered that my changing me did not change him. The person committing adultery is the one who needs to be changed; therefore, in changing yourself, you won't convince them to become faithful mates, since adultery roots itself in rebellion. In changing the outer person, you haven't even touched the root of the issue. After seven years, I gave up and filed for divorce, and I can remember my Mom coming to church with me and telling my Pastor what was going on. I didn't want her to say a word because I was ashamed of how my life was spiraling out of control. My Pastor nodded his head and simply said, "Sow a seed. He'll be back. Sow a seed; this is your weapon." (*Paraphrased.*) I didn't understand it then, but now I understand what he was saying. I didn't sow a seed because I didn't want to continue in that union, so I didn't follow through with his request; I followed through with the divorce. Was that the answer? Yes and no. It stopped me from having to deal with any more adulterous affairs, and I was able to get my sanity back. I was able to finally focus on my life, my faith, and my dreams. But, at the same time, I sinned against GOD because of the state of mind I was in.

If you are dealing with an adulterous spouse; sow a seed. You don't know how much power is in that seed. Sow that seed even in your tears, and watch Psalms 126:5 come to life. *"They that sow in tears shall reap in joy."* Don't go charging at your spouse because that will NEVER solve the issue or uproot that demonic seed that is within him or her. Instead, this is your time to develop and test your strength. Ask the LORD where HE would have you sow your seed, and sow that seed without hesitation. Speak over that seed, and tell it what you want it to do. Even if you're considering a divorce, sow the seed and ask the LORD to show you what to do. In addition, commit yourself to a fast. Ask your spouse to fast with you, but if they refuse (which they will likely do if they are in sin), ask permission from them to fast. *"Defraud ye not one the other, except it be with consent for a time, that ye may give yourselves to fasting and prayer; and come together again, that Satan tempt you not for your incontinency" (1 Corinthians 7:5).* If they still say no to you fasting, talk to your Pastor to see if he or she will pray and fast for you. It's a great idea to initiate that three-fold cord, but don't try to strangle your spouse with it. The hardest part is remaining level headed.

When you respect your GOD, you will automatically respect your spouse.

And if your spouse decides to leave you to be with that other person, forgive them and move on in CHRIST. The worst thing you can do is to hold a grudge, but the best thing you can do is to allow the situation to push you closer to GOD to discover your own mistakes. I now tell people openly that no one has sinned against me greater than I have sinned against GOD. If GOD could forgive me for my affair; then who am I to judge anyone else? I played the other woman when I was unsaved, so how could I say that he (the ex) or any of the shes I dealt with were wrong and deserved eternal damnation? I couldn't because that would mean that I deserved the same fate. This is how you get over what someone did to you! You look at what you have done to others, and then dare yourself to think you deserve leniency for whatever reason. Ask the LORD to put forgiveness in you towards the people that have harmed you.

I found that GOD has placed an alarm in us that rings loudly when our spouses are having an affair. During this time, a spouse will try to silence that alarm by getting confirmation of an affair or refutation of an affair. Most of the time, the offending spouse will refute or deny that he or she is having an affair because they don't want to get a divorce. They are simply selfish creatures who want to serve themselves the pleasures of having two or more bedroom buddies. When I went through this, my alarm would not stop going off when the then spouse would deny the affairs. Instead, it was like pushing “snooze” on the alarm because the fear, anger, and hurt would be put to rest for a little while, but that alarm would go off again...sometimes louder. When that alarm would go off again, I would be insane because I had two messages going through me, and I didn't know which one to believe. There was the truth that GOD had placed in me, and there were the lies that the man had told me. I often chose to believe the lies because they felt better to me. This made me question my own sanity.

To the offending spouse: What I learned in this is that GOD has an alarm in all of us, and that alarm is to be trusted. When you are the offending spouse, it is never good to lie to your spouse so that you can continue sinning against them. When you do this, they will stop trusting that alarm. That alarm isn't there just to tell them when you are committing adultery; that alarm is there to tell them when they are in danger, when your children are in danger, when they need to invest, and when they need to pull away. That alarm is there to protect us. Lying to a spouse is the same as disabling that alarm. In doing so, your spouse may be preparing to go to the park with your kids one day, and that alarm starts to go off. They don't trust it anymore, so they go anyway. At the park is a crazed gunman set out on destroying every person there, but amazingly enough, the park is empty that day. Everyone who intended to go to the park didn't go because they were distracted by this alarm, but your spouse and children are there.

There are many people alive today who barely made it out of situations just like that, but they will openly tell you that their alarm went off. Somehow, along this journey in life, they stopped trusting that alarm. That alarm is the voice of GOD, and anytime a person does not believe GOD, they are literally insane. The heart of a person is set up to hold the truth and spread the truth, but when you fill it with lies; you begin to destroy the man from the inside out. The heart of a man is supposed to be inhabited by GOD, but a man that is inhabited by lies is spiritually broken. To have an affair and get your spouse to believe that you are not having one, you would have to convince them to evict GOD from their hearts so that you can continue serving your flesh. This is pure witchcraft and idolatry. What should you do if you are having an affair and you don't know how to stop? Pray about it, fast on it, and be honest about it. Talk to your Pastor and seek wise counsel. Be honest with your spouse so that the two of you can tackle that spirit together. If your spouse leaves you because of the affair, take that time away from them to get yourself right with GOD. Many times, people will return to the union if they know that you regret the decision, and that you won't do it anymore. People usually leave when they see no end to your selfishness. In addition, change your phone number and order detailed billing. Give that billing to the spouse and ask them to check it daily. What you are doing is coming against your own flesh and whatever spirit has been attached to it. This would keep you from entertaining those ideas about calling the mistress or philanderer. Instead, when that fire arises, call your spouse. You have to proactively fight off lust because it is like an unquenchable fire that burns without mercy.

Lastly, remember an adulterous affair is pure insanity unchecked, undiagnosed, unrecognized, and unmerciful. If you are committing adultery against your spouse, stop it now. Don't worry about the outside man or outside woman getting hurt. What helped me to stop was my love for GOD. It ate me up that I was wronging HIM trying to get back at someone else. In other words, HE'D gotten caught up in the cross fires. This means that HE wasn't in the right place in my heart. When you feel tapped out, that's when you need to tap into your love of GOD to keep you. Just imagine how tag team wrestling is. When one man is beaten and cannot overcome his adversary, he stretches out his hand to tag his partner. His adversary does everything in his power to keep him from reaching his partner, but eventually, when he does tag his hand, the partner comes into the fight and overcomes his adversary. When you are feeling tapped out, it's not time to throw in the towel; it is time to tag the LORD. The worst thing you can do is to try to take revenge or to try to handle the issue on your own. Divorce court is a sore reminder that we are failures when we try to do things on our own. Let GOD be GOD. You already have your role; stay in it. If you feel yourself going crazy, the answer is NOT in checking your spouse; this is an issue that you need to address between you and the LORD.

Being Submissive

One of the hardest things I had to learn to do was to be submissive. Let's face it. One of the most undetected spirits in America is the Vashti spirit, and I had it in my ear. I felt the need to challenge any and everything a man said to me because I didn't trust men, and I didn't see men as wise creatures. A lot of women don't admit this, but many see men this way. A woman will oftentimes trust her husband's physical strength, but not his mental strength.

I can remember during my first marriage hearing him say, "If I tell you to sit down, you'll stand up and if I tell you to stand up, you'll sit down." At this, my response was always, "Yeah, because I'm a grown woman! I don't need another Daddy!" (Eye roll) I was truly proud of my rebellious state. I felt like I wasn't one of those women who could be controlled and mishandled. If we had to fight all night, then that's what had to be done, but no man was going to run me. Of course, this state of mind was rooted in pure pride and rebellion.

Then I got married again, and in the beginning, that Vashti was still on me. And this time, I married an African man, and boy was I in for it. (Don't laugh). As a matter of fact, a few of my immediate family members and closest friends laughed because they wanted front row seats to see how this union would play out. African men are believed to be controlling, and I had a little extra bite to me. It turns out, he was not and is not the aggressive or controlling type, but he was and is a stubborn man. If his heart is set to something, it'll take the hands of the LORD to pry it out of HIM. In the beginning of our marriage, I was still a baby because I jumped from one union into the next. (It was a stronghold that I had, but that's another story.) Initially, we argued continuously and vigorously. I wouldn't back down (humble myself), and he wouldn't back down (humble himself). So, pride was driving our marriage. I would verbally remind him that I was American, and he would remind me that he's African, and we'd have it out to see who'd break. Again, he is African. He's a professional at being unrelenting, and I'm American; so I was a professional at being mouthy. So after about a week of not speaking, I would try to have the infamous "we're adults" talk with him, and he'd still be hard-pressed to prove a point. Then we'd argue again, and I was back at it. I felt like I wasn't going to let him win, but GOD kept dealing with my heart about pride and the arguing began to take its toll on me. I began to see the wrong in me and I asked the LORD to change me (repentance). I desired to be that wonderful wife that I'd read about in the Bible, but I didn't know how. I just thought that if the man followed my advice that our marriage would be good. This frame of thinking was rooted in hurt and rebellion; therefore, it could not bring us to where GOD had called us.

I asked the LORD to make me that Proverbs 31 wife that I'd read about. I asked HIM to make me into a submissive wife. HE taught me that submission to your husband is submission to CHRIST. Your husband may be one of those men who makes a lot of mistakes, but as long as you stay in CHRIST and remain chaste, CHRIST will lead him in all matters. As an American woman, I wanted to walk equally with my husband because I did not trust his lead. Again, this behavior was undoubtedly a Vashti spirit, and it is on a lot of American women. We know their imperfections because we not only live with them, but we have dealt with some of the repercussions of their decisions. Nevertheless, GOD designed a man to get back up again. Sure, he may trip and fall, but if you are in CHRIST, your husband will rise again. GOD said you would win him with your chaste behavior. Many of you don't try to win him; you try to challenge him, hoping to wear him down so he can do what you think he should do. He is not designed this way! And anything that is designed to operate one way has to operate in that fashion or fall apart. Your husband cannot and will not be headed by you, and if he does submit to you, your house will be out of order and in line with Satan's will. 1 Corinthians 11:3 confirms this: *"But I would have you know, that the head of every man is Christ; and the head of the woman is the man; and the head of Christ is God."* When you come from under this order, you expose your head to witchcraft, because a woman's head was not, and is not to be exposed. Instead, it has to be covered by authority. This is GOD'S order even if you don't like or understand it.

Many believe that submission is doing what their husbands command them to do, even when what he requests is wrong. I thought that way too, and I refused to submit at first. Submission is letting your husband take the lead, and trusting GOD with him. You don't have to follow him down the wrong path. Instead, you are designed to stay on the right path, and be that extra lighting he needs to get back on the road. GOD taught us how to deal with a husband that's off-road. *"Likewise, you wives, be in subjection to your own husbands; that, if any obey not the word, they also may without the word be won by the conduct of the wives; while they behold your chaste behavior coupled with fear" (1 Peter 3:1-2).*

What you are to do is to pray for him, and believe GOD that HE will change the direction of your husband's feet so that he may get back on the right path. You can tell him that he is off track, but what you cannot do is grab that steering wheel or you'll run that marriage off the road. Don't head into sin with him, but stay in the will of GOD. If your husband wanted to throw away the vacuum cleaner, but you liked the vacuum cleaner...talk to him about it, and if he is insistent, let him throw it away. That way, you can let him buy a new one. Sometimes, we fight hard about issues that shouldn't have even become big enough to be called issues. Now, if he told you to sin against GOD, you would not do this because you cannot come from under the CHRIST head.

What has to happen is, you have to trust CHRIST to head up your husband. It's not easy if your husband is a sinner. You weren't supposed to marry him anyway or at least you weren't supposed to marry him in that season of his life. But you did and now you're upset because he's acting like a sinner. A sinner sins just as a mower mows, an iron irons, and so on! Now, as his wife, you have an obligation to win that soul and to show him the benefits of CHRIST, including having a chaste wife and submissive wife.

After the LORD began to change me, I found that Jean and I didn't argue as much. Truthfully, arguments began to go down by more than 95%! Things that used to bother me didn't bother me anymore. When hubby wanted to make a bad decision, and I knew it was a wrong choice; I told him without the attitude. If he wanted to do it anyway, I let him. I watched (and tried not to laugh) as he would bump his head, and come back and say to me that I was right. I didn't gloat when he said those things, I just presented to him what I felt was the right way to go. Amazingly enough, he began to listen to me more! He didn't keep bumping his head into the same walls or even new obstacles because he learned to recognize just who and what I am. I am his help-mate, co-pilot, and co-captain. When I wasn't trying to force my way upon him, he began to take the lead as he was supposed to, and we began to love one another in a way that I'd never experienced. Wisdom taught him that he could not control me, just as wisdom taught me that I could not control him. But he learned that a wife is a crown to have, and he learned to keep that crown sparkling. I learned that I could trust the LORD with Jean and come out on top always. During this transition from Vashti to Esther, an event occurred that made me laugh and showed me that I could trust the GOD in Jean. We were driving along on the freeway listening to the GPS, and I was behind the wheel; he was in the passenger's seat. The GPS was telling me to go straight, but hubby was telling me to take the exit. Now, when we first moved here to Florida, and I had that Vashti spirit in my ear, I would tell him to stop trying to be the GPS, and I'd follow that machine. I would argue about the fact that he'd run to the passenger's seat, and now he suddenly wanted to drive from there. But this time, I had to make a split-second decision. Listen to hubby or listen to the GPS. I figured it out. If he was wrong, he'd see it, and we'd probably end up in Tampa having to drive 20-30 minutes out of the way. If he was right, our distance would be shortened. I could feel the frustration, but I had to reject it. I felt a sense of calm come over me, and I took the exit, and he was right. That GPS was taking us the long way. He drives more than I do, so he knows the city better. For those times that he was right, I didn't suffer the humiliation of having to say to him that he was right, and I was wrong. He would rub that in until it burned. And I actually like the submissive wife role a whole lot better. He doesn't abuse his role, like I thought he would. Like most women, I thought if you let a man take the lead, he'd have you walking behind him, polishing his shoes, and treating you like a third-generation idiot. What I found instead was that I could relax and get back to being a woman, a wife, and more importantly, GOD'S daughter. I was not designed to take the front line, but to stay at home, shielded, protected and loved.

The LORD keeps me humble by reminding me that any woman who steps from under the authority of the CHRIST head (CHRIST heads man; man heads wife) is subject to demonic oppression because CHRIST covers the husband and covers the wife when she submits to her husband. So, on those days when the husband makes a request that I don't like, I simply tell him what I think in a polite way, and I leave it at his will to deal with. Sometimes, he listens, and there are some times when he does not listen. But, through it all, I trust GOD, and every time we always come out on top. We have learned to laugh and be friends, and I now know and understand that GOD will not lead us into temptation. GOD hasn't failed me yet; I don't think HE'S planning to start now.

Burning Old Baggage

What is baggage? In relationship terms, it is all of the emotional and spiritual issues one brings from past relationships. A person carrying past burdens has not been released from their very own prison of hurt because they have refused to release the person who hurt them. Each failed relationship teaches them another wrong way of dealing with relationships. Souls bearing old baggage tend to go to great lengths to ensure that they don't find themselves in the position of being hurt or taken advantage of again. So, while the beginning of the relationship might be heavenly bliss because they haven't invested their feelings into it, the end of the relationship is always bitter. As their new partner wanders deeper into their hearts, they become more and more panicked as the new person reaches the place where the last person dropped out of the race. Someone with old baggage will often begin to expect to be betrayed or may walk away from a relationship when a person crosses a certain zone in their hearts.

The key to understanding breakups and betrayals is allowing GOD to grow wisdom from within you. But, until one understands why it happened, they are likely to repeat the process over and over again, and each time they will pick up a new layer of baggage.

Spiritually speaking, baggage is a soul tie that has not been severed. A soul tie is the binding of two souls united into one through association, sex, or through lineage. Sex creates the most powerful of these bonds because sex unites the individuals involved as one person. GOD never said that a marriage union was instituted through a marriage ceremony; a marriage begins the minute sexual penetration is accomplished. In the act, blood is shed and the covenant is fulfilled. *"Therefore shall a man leave his father and his mother, and shall cleave unto his wife: and they shall be one flesh" (Genesis 2:24).* An example of a Godly soul tie is a tie between a husband and a wife, if they are both believers. A bad soul tie would be an unevenly yoked relationship; one established through fornication and one established through adultery.

Bad association: GOD told us that bad association ruins useful habits. Whoever you spend your time with will eventually become one with you, and you will begin to pick up on their ways and whatever else is attached to them. That's why one who has been freed from the demon of addiction can't hang around others still bound by it. A great example of a soul tie established through association is demonstrated in 1 Samuel 18:1: *"And it came to pass, when he had made an end of speaking unto Saul, that the soul of Jonathan was knit with the soul of David, and Jonathan loved him as his own soul."* That's why GOD warned us about evil communication in 1 Corinthians 15:33. *"Be not deceived: evil communication corrupt good manners."*

I have heard a lot of people say that they won't engage in a behavior just because their friends engage in those behaviors. People really believe that they have an answer that will override the WORD of GOD; but the truth is, you are whomever you hang around. Whoever you link up to will not only come into your home, your life, and your marriage, but they will also become one with your soul. This is why it is referred to as a soul tie, and this is what happened between David and Jonathan. If the people around you are foolish, you will become foolish. If the people around you are violent, you will become violent. If the people around you are wise, you will become wise. *"He that walketh with wise men shall be wise: but a companion of fools shall be destroyed" (Proverbs 13:20).*

Your relationships with others are also baggage that you bring into your marriage. When you bring evil people in, they unpack their evil in your lives. You and your spouse are one, and you have the responsibility to rear up your children in the WORD of GOD. When you bring people around your children, your children are likely to look up to the worst of those characters. Not to mention, everyone that is friendly is not your friend. It doesn't matter how many decades they have tolerated you or been friendly to you, they can still be an enemy in disguise. In addition, some people can be your friends when you are on a certain level, but once you start to elevate, you become a new creature. Oftentimes, when a person begins to change for the better, it is only then that they will begin to see the venom of their so-called friends. Wrong associations have destroyed many marriages, and will continue to destroy marriages until the end of time, but it doesn't have to destroy your marriage.

When a spouse feels obligated to continue in a friendship with an ungodly character, they will slowly pick up the ways of that person. What can you do if your spouse is hanging around someone that you know is shady? I can tell you what I did. Jean and I went to visit one of his so-called friends one day. When I met the guy, I could immediately discern that he wasn't a good character, and that he had no real loyalty or love for Jean. Because of this, I didn't like him, but Jean had known him since they were young boys. We stayed at this man's house a week, and I tried to keep my peace, but I was so bothered by the way he handled my husband. This man would talk over him, wouldn't listen to his suggestions, and kept lying to him. I knew that he was trying to assert himself as the alpha male, and I knew that Jean had become immune to his behavior; therefore, he kept talking as if he didn't know he was being disrespected. I shared my views with Jean, and he politely brushed it off as the guy having a lack of home training. I wasn't at peace, however, because I thought about a worst case scenario. What if Jean needed help, and his life was on the line? I couldn't imagine this character helping him at all. As a matter of fact, I felt like he'd push him on over the cliff because I could see envy in him towards Jean. I didn't press the issue, however. Whenever Jean and I would talk about the places we'd visited, I would make a clear distinction between this friend and his other friend whom I knew loved him. I would always say to him that I knew his friend Roger loved him, but this other character tolerated him. Jean would laugh and always say to me that I've never liked his bad friend, and then he would go on about the guy having a lack of home education. I wasn't buying it though, but still....I kept quiet. I did this because it is not up to me to convince my husband of who is good and bad for his life. CHRIST is his head, so I took the issue to CHRIST. It took a couple of years, but one day, this guy showed Jean just how much he despised him by mishandling one of his relatives. My husband came to me and basically said those words that I love to hear. "You were right." I didn't have to do a thing. I made it clear that I didn't like the guy; I made it clear that I could see that the guy wasn't his friend, and I left it alone.

One of the worst things you can do is demand that your spouse stop hanging around a person. This will only make them want to continue doing so because pride triggers rebellion. For the women, leave the issues at the head of the matter. The head is CHRIST. In addition, clearly tell your husband that you do not want that character in your home anymore, especially if you have children and you are worried about this person's influence on your children. If he rebels; take it to CHRIST and leave it there. For the men; be honest with your wife about her friend or friends, and then make it clear that they are not welcome in your home. Don't be aggressive with her. Just tell her that this friend isn't welcome. In addition, the only way a wife will allow you to pull the welcome mat out from under her friends is if you give up the friends she said she doesn't want coming over. You can't tell her to stop hanging with a person if you won't stop hanging around or associating with a character that she doesn't like. If you believe that this wouldn't work on your spouse because of pride and rebellion in that spouse, take it to the LORD. HE will fix it; guaranteed! You have to leave it at HIS feet, however. If you don't, the situation will only get worse.

There are many ways that soul ties are established. The key to being released from a soul tie is repentance. If that soul tie was established through intercourse, it cannot be severed by man because the WORD has already established that whomever you have intercourse with is now your spouse. One of the biggest undetected marriage destroyers is outside soul ties. A woman cannot give her whole self to her husband when pieces of her are scattered around. A man cannot faithfully dedicate himself to one wife when he has other rogue wives out there. Outside relationships, whether established before or during the onset of your relationship, will always have power in your relationship. The only way to relieve those relationships of their power is to repent and ask the LORD to sever the tie. You have to be divorced by GOD in order to successfully marry someone else. *"The woman answered and said, I have no husband. Jesus said unto her, Thou hast well said, I have no husband:*
For thou hast had five husbands; and he whom thou now hast is not thy husband: in that saidst thou truly" (John 4:17-18).
Breaking up with someone in body is not the same as breaking up with them in soul. Today's breakups are basically just someone relocating their body to another place, and eventually submitting their body to another person. This isn't a breakup; it's a broken union. Only GOD can separate you from your past lovers. *"Wherefore they are no more twain, but one flesh. What therefore God hath joined together, let **not man** put asunder" (Matthew 19:6).*

For the men: Let's say for example's sake that you slept around in your youth. And now you're married, but every now and again, you want to check out your ex's Facebook profile to see what she's up to. Chances are, you still have a soul tie present with her, because when the LORD delivers you, she'll be but a testimony. For the women: You're married, but you like to go and shop at the store where your ex works. Before you go, you have to get extra cute to show him what he left behind. That's a soul tie.

Excess baggage is almost always a soul tie that has not been severed, whether it's with an ex-lover or someone who you just don't like.

There are also soul ties established in unforgiveness. Unforgiveness is your unwillingness to release another human being from their sin against you. Until you release that person (forgive) and repent, you won't be much of a spouse to anyone. Whether it was Heather who took your boyfriend away, or Paul who gave you a black eye before homecoming, you have to unleash yourself so that you can be the man or woman that GOD has called you to be. A person bound by unforgiveness will always be the misery of their spouse because they themselves are bound.

Your choices as a spouse are the direct result of your choices before you became a spouse. Your spouse should never be made to pay for someone else's mistakes. Trust issues are the direct result of unsevered soul ties. All forms of baggage have to be unloaded in CHRIST, and not on the spouse. *Psalm 55:22, "Cast thy burden upon the LORD, and HE shall sustain thee: HE shall never suffer the righteous to be moved."* Any choices that we make should be for the betterment of ourselves in CHRIST, and for the betterment of our familiar structures.

When you find yourself still burdened by the past, it's time to seek GOD in the present, so you can be a blessing to your spouse in the future.

First and foremost, you must have it made up in your mind that you want to be a better child to GOD, a better spouse, and a better parent. You must first make up your mind that this new journey is necessary, and that you are going to complete it. You need endurance, but most of all; you need JESUS. For every journey you take, you will find obstacles in the road. Don't turn back when those obstacles present themselves, but instead, floor your faith and mow those challenges down.

If you've decided that you are ready and willing, please be advised that breaking up with Satan is never an easy deed. He's a stalker, and he'll try several tactics to weigh you down, but step in your place; you are more than a conqueror through CHRIST.

Say this prayer aloud:
"FATHER, I repent of all of my sins, both known and unknown. I have carried around a burden that you commanded me to cast upon you, and I repent of that sin. FATHER, I ask that you forgive me for all of my sins in the Name of JESUS the CHRIST. I ask that you cover me with the Blood of JESUS. I ask that you cover my body, spirit and soul with the Blood of JESUS, and let THY hand be upon me from on high and fill me with your HOLY GHOST, in the name of JESUS CHRIST. (Now worship HIM. Go into praise, HE is worthy.) FATHER, I cast all of my burdens upon you, and I ask that you sever every ungodly soul tie from me. FATHER, I ask that you strengthen and keep me, and send your ministering angels to minister to me so that I may not attempt to pick up that burden again. As I step forward in you, I ask that you destroy the road back to that sin, so that I may never return to it. You are GOD alone, and I understand that I can do nothing of my own. I need you. I want you. Please give me all of you, and none of me. Create in me a new heart and fill it with wisdom. FATHER, please draw all of the evil out of me, and its evil roots; cast it away from me so that it may never reattach to me or anyone else. Remove all evil communications from me and create in me a righteous heart after your own. FATHER, open my eyes to see the lesson in my trials so that I may walk away with the treasure of wisdom, and not

the treachery of defeat. To you, I commit myself. In you, I trust. In you, I will remain all the days of my life and even forevermore. I ask that you continue to keep me. In JESUS Name, I pray. Amen."

Get Out of the Past

Getting out of the past is easier said than done; right? What we live with is not a reflection of what we are going through; it often a reflection of what we have been through. A season passes through and is but for a moment, but your life is in the now. GOD is the GREAT I AM. HE lives now, and HE was, and HE will be forever. HE is not a GOD of time because time has no rule over HIM.

HE sent HIS SON, because HE did not want man to continue to be punished for the sins of their fathers and their father's fathers. It is your now that delivers you, and it is your now that condemns you.

When I remarried, I thought I was a better woman, but there were many situations that came about that showed me that I was still living in the past. I had reasoned in myself to never allow another man to have too much of me, and I had decided to walk away from any relationship that showed any signs of being faulty. I would always try to define Jean's actions, and I looked for the motives behind his actions. After I'd made my assessment and predetermined what I thought he was going to do, I would shut down emotionally sometimes, and other times I would become too emotional. I was still living in the past, and I was still bound. This means that I wasn't ready to remarry, but I did it anyway because I didn't know how to be without someone in my life. This was a generational curse upon the women in my family, and I was carrying it to the tune. I had to pray for deliverance, and I had to pray for total healing so that I could learn to be a better daughter to GOD and a better wife to Jean. As GOD began to deliver me, HE started stripping away layers and layers of hurt, fear, and everything that my disobedience had attached to me. Jean had to watch me go through deliverance and be transformed into a healed and delivered woman, but not before witnessing the ugly transformation. During the transformation, whatever is in you will first be exposed by fire. I had a lot of situations that came upon me that made me want to default back to what I knew. I searched for divorce attorneys online, and I researched what it would entail to divorce a foreign man. What I didn't realize was that my past was assassinating my future.

When GOD changed me, I became a new creature. I wasn't just being delivered from the hurt of past relationships; I was being delivered from the traumas of molestation, rape, abuse, word curses, and so on. I was being delivered from being a victim, and I was being moved into my Godly inheritance of being more than a conqueror through CHRIST JESUS. There was so much in me that I had hid behind a smile. Nevertheless, I submitted myself to the change, and I went through the painful purging that took place to get that stuff out of me. I would have never made any man a great wife, because I had settled into being a good wife, and good is not good enough. I share this with you to say that there are many broken souls out there trying to hold onto a marriage while holding onto their past, and they are wondering why their marriage is slipping away. In order for my marriage to last, I had to die to myself and let go of my past. My past didn't go away, but I had to take the right things from it and not the wrongs in it. I had to reach out and take the wisdom, knowledge, and understanding that my past had locked in its hands.

Too many people go into new relationships not totally healed, and they don't realize that they are still bound because they've learned to function in their pain. A lot of people don't realize they are carrying around pain from their past until they have been tried by fire in their present. This fire is situations that come to reveal to us what is in us. It is a refining that will burn away the lying face that we put on and cause whatever is lurking behind that face to be exposed. Healing is only a prayer away. You have to want healing, and you have to will yourself into forgiveness. Love will take you there and make you forget about all the wrongs so you can focus on all the rights.

You have to become all new again. This means you need to become a virgin again. A virgin is innocent, trusting, loving and pure; but a defiled person is guilty, distrusting, lusting and unchaste. The past was the past, and it brought many lessons with it; take what you need from it and move forward.

There are certain things people say that will show you where they are. The mouth is a GPS system, and when it is open, it will tell anyone who meets you where to find you.

How can you live in today? First understand that the issue is not your spouse; your issue is the choices that you are making for today. When we accept accountability, we learn how to address the problems that are within ourselves, rather than constantly trying to address what we perceive as our spouses' issues. Our spouses may not be the best in dealing with matters of the heart, but let's be real here; there are some issues that they shouldn't even have to face in us. If your spouse has never had an affair, for example, they should never deal with an untrusting you.

The worst responsibility you can give to your spouse is the responsibility of massaging your hurts or attempting to deliver you from that hurt. They can't do GOD'S job, and this is why so many failed marriages are logged into the system. Too many wounded souls get married and expect their spouses to play GOD. No man or woman can handle this role. Expectation is a prison that confines a person to your demands, and their only way out is to escape you. Deliverance starts as a conversation between you and GOD. It starts off with you repenting and surrendering yourself to GOD. You have to renounce the sin and everything that came with the sin. But, as much as GOD'S arms are wide open to receive you, you have to open your arms of faith to receive HIM and be received by HIM. We have to cut off that TV so we can learn how to live in real time.

Forgiveness may seem impossible, especially when someone has grazed an already weeping sore, but it is possible. It does not start in your communication with your spouse; it starts in your communication with GOD.

Another way we live in the past is by constantly reminding our spouses of the hurt that they have placed upon us. What if GOD reminded you constantly of what you'd done to HIM; how would you feel? We like our minds to be left in peace, and when someone takes it from us; we often respond strongly. When you are in your spouse's face about the past, you are robbing them of their peace. It is no wonder that they respond negatively. Sure, if it's on your heart, it is obvious that the devil has robbed you of your peace, but this doesn't give you the right to rob your spouse of his or her peace. The past is always better when left in the past.

The next time your husband or wife does something that upsets or hurts you, go off into a room to pray and ask GOD to sever strife from you and fill you with HIS love. Try speaking to the spouse and make your rebuke short and loving. "Baby, remember, we talked about this. We agreed to not do this and yet, you did it anyway. Could you please honor our agreement from now on?" Regardless of his or her answer, do not leave the safety of GOD'S will. Your spouse can be won by your love and dedication to the things of GOD. Simply excuse yourself to another room if needed. After prayer, emerge as your loving self. Don't come out of that room with teary eyes and threats. Get out and FORCE yourself to do what your pride is telling you not to do. Cook his or her favorite meal. Prepare a romantic night. Give the spouse a massage. Talk about positive things. What you are doing is worshiping GOD through obedience, and your praise will confuse the enemy. If the enemy just so happens to be parked in your spouse, this will drive that devil out because he can't stand in the midst of GOD. Your obedience keeps you in the will of GOD, and HIS will is open to HIS presence. Pride is evil, and GOD hates a proud look. When you resist pride, you are resisting the devil. Submit yourself to the WORD of GOD. We do this by honoring what the LORD said regarding our situations. GOD said, *"Wives, submit yourselves unto your own husbands, as unto the Lord" (Ephesians 5:22).* GOD also said, *"Husbands, love your wives, even as Christ also loved the church, and gave himself for it" (Ephesians 5:25).*

Stop looking for the spouse to recover you every time you get lost in the past.

If you are married to a person that is living in their past: Cover your spouse with prayer, pray with your spouse, and try to do whatever GOD allows to help them to heal. You don't know if you have tomorrow, and FATHER said in Ephesians 4:26-27, *"Be ye angry, and sin not: let not the sun go down upon your wrath: Neither give place to the devil."* Therefore, when we are harboring anger, we are allowing devils to pitch tents in our homes. Evict him with your praise, and lock him out with your obedience.

Here are a few tips to help you to live in the present.

1. Forgive others and forgive yourself. Everything that happened has happened, and life has no rewind button to go back and redo it.
2. Intercede for others. Intercession is a powerful weapon that helps others, all the while helping you.
3. Never bring up past issues. Your spouse deserves a presently happy you, and not a shell of a person being

inhabited by yesterday.

4. Embrace today and all that it offers. When you look back, you can't see what's ahead of you. Concentrate on making today a better day, and tomorrow even better than that.

5. Your spouse is entitled to his or her mistakes, even if they have done things that you would have never done.

6. Jot down what you would love to have in your future, and draw up a time line to get these things. What you are doing is redirecting your mind's eyes.

7. Seek Christian counseling. (Pray about it first.) Sometimes outside intervention and intercession is needed when the issue seems too deeply rooted for you to address.

8. Take it day by day. Today, focus on being the best child that GOD has, and the best partner your spouse could ever have.

9. When something triggers a fear in you, rebuke the fear, not the situation.

10. Get rid of anything that negatively links you to your past. Sometimes, it's the little things that keep us bound.

You can be free of yesterday, but first you have to be willing to admit that you have been living in the past. There is so much joy to be had, and so many blessings to be enjoyed....don't pass them up for a chance to relive your pain.

Living In the Now and Not the Later

"Take therefore no thought for the morrow: for the morrow shall take thought for the things of itself. Sufficient unto the day is the evil thereof" (Matthew 6:34).

Much of the strife that enters our home comes because we are not living in today. It comes because we are either living in yesterday, or we have channeled our thoughts to the future. If your spouse isn't saved, it goes without saying that you want them to get saved. You want that big house on the lake. You plan to reach an income where your spouse and you can comfortably retire. And your drive shows this. There are many things that you want to accomplish, and this is what drives you.

GOD is the GREAT I AM. HE has already decreed and declared what you have, what you will have, and in what season you will have it. Your choices are like a vehicle that will drive you through the seasons, and into this wonderful place that you so desire; or your choices will cause your life's vehicle to break down in the middle of nowhere. Therefore, to get to where you want to be; you have to remain where GOD has called you to be. HE has called you to operate in HIS will. Outside of it, you won't go through the seasons because your life's vehicle won't start, since JESUS is the key to crank it up. But you keep trusting your hands and not HIS Hands. And in doing so, you have allowed wickedness to store itself up in your heart. Your journey has now become a journey by self for self, and GOD is not invited to tag along since HE can't sit next to sin, nor will HE sit in the passenger's seat of your choices.

To have a driven spouse can be good, but to have a spouse in overdrive is not. We plant gardens today, so we can eat the fruit thereof on another day. We cannot plant every day, because every day is not a season for planting. Some days are days for watering; others are for gathering. But if we spend all of our time planting, and we never water what we have sown into the ground, nothing will grow up for us. If the LORD causes the rain to water what we have sown, yet we do not gather because we are planting continually, we will have an abundant harvest set aside for someone else to gather. What we have to do is learn how to discern the seasons and act in accordance with those seasons. We do this by staying in GOD'S face so we can hear HIS voice, and by paying attention to the weather in our lives. Your personal weather is witnessed by what is going on in your life. For example, if you find yourself in a season where you aren't gathering much; it may be your season to sow. If you find yourself being blessed all around (or challenged all around), it may be your season to reap. If you don't see either, it may be your season to water the seeds that you have sown. You water them with your faith, and your obedience.

We are creatures of season, and each season of our lives sets us up for the next season. Because many don't understand this, they go out looking for Prophets and prophecies. This sets them up for sorcerers and diviners to speak into their lives, and to cause a shift to occur in their lives in favor of the devil. This is because those souls that are looking for Prophets and prophecies want to know what is to come, rather than deal with what has already manifested for them. They have seed in their hands, but they don't know what to do with them, so they sow these seeds into witches masquerading as Prophets of GOD. Their marriages begin to fall apart, their children begin to rebel, and their lives start spiraling downward. Confusion sets in, and demons join the party because they were invited to serve. Many want to know what tomorrow brings, but they have buried the seeds of today. They live in fast forward mode, and in doing so, they are not completing the assignments that were given to them by GOD.

A spouse that lives in the future will be a driven spouse, one that can never seem to enjoy the perks of today because their hearts have been bewitched. Their minds have become a crystal ball that reflects to them the future that they want, but they have to forsake the now to get to the later. At least, that's what they believe. Imagine this: It's winter time, and there is snow on the ground. You're a gardener and you are eager to see your garden blossom with the beautiful blooms and flowers that it yields every year. So, you decide to go outside and shovel the snow away from your garden. You go outside to plant the seeds wearing flip flops, shorts, and a tank top. You would undoubtedly catch pneumonia, and your seeds would die because you have chosen the wrong season to plant seeds. Because you were anxious, you thought you could bypass the seasons, make winter pack its bags, and your garden to yield fruit when you were ready. Instead, you stopped pruning and caring for the garden that you have today. When the dawn of a new day sets in, and you notice that your garden has been withering, you can't understand why. You've put in hours of work doing the wrong thing.

This behavior is found in some marriages, and instead of building a better tomorrow, the overly driven spouse usually neglects and destroys his or her own family. A spouse driven by the things of later is setting themselves up for a long fall down into the pits of reality. Each day is to be lived, not sacrificed for the next day. In trying to fast-forward through the seasons, you presently rob your family of the love, support, and attention they want and need. It's great to have a plan, and it's even better to work towards it, but there has to be a limitation; one that is set up on the foundation of understanding. If you don't know or understand the seasons, you won't plant the right things or do the right things to yield a harvest. Instead, you will destroy what you do have trying to get to what you want to have. GOD is a GOD of order, and it is HE that will bless you. You simply plant the seeds and stay in obedience. *"So then neither is he that plants anything, neither he that waters; but God that gives the increase" (1 Corinthians 3:7).*

It is not usual to see a man that is so driven that he ends up losing his family. Eventually, he does arrive at his wealthy place, only to have it stolen by someone more driven than he is. Everything in life is designed to birth its fruit in due season, and any fruit that is out of season isn't ready yet; it is bitter. You don't want to end up bitter and distrusting, surrounded by snakes and wolves. The greatest accomplishment that you can have is love. If you are truly loved, you are rich already and you have more than most millionaires. Trading love for things is not a fair trade off, even though it seems to be right now. Instead, take the time to plant the seeds as GOD calls you to plant them, and spend time with your family.

More than anything, take the time to prove yourself to be a man or woman worthy of the Christian title. Let GOD be the architect of all that you do so that HE can be glorified, and not yourself.

Retaliative Mentalities

Okay, so you're hurt, you're offended, and you're upset. Now, you want to show that you're not stupid (pride); you're crafty (witchcraft), and you can deliver a lick harder than what was dealt to you (vengeance).

Wanting to take revenge against a spouse, or anyone for that matter, is sin.

Take off the mask and really take a look at you. Most of what is in you has been deposited or picked up along the way of life. As we go along in life, we marry the wrong way of thinking, and we divorce reason, and as a result, many marriages are destroyed.

But you're hurt, and you're angry with the spouse. You have to be able to come outside of your selfish feelings to see the whole picture of what is happening in your life. Dividing a home will not make it come back together the way you think it should fit together. As a spouse, you have to learn how to live life as one person with your spouse and stop bringing "me" into the equation.

Everything done and said should be GOD approved. GOD has to always be in the midst of the two of you, and for this to happen, you must always gather together in HIS Name; even in decision making. (See Matthew 18:20).

I was so accustomed to coming out on top that when I took the big dip into the marriage scene, I brought in some of my street smarts. For me it was simple: Good husband equaled good night, but bad husband equaled no sleep. If I was hurt, I would disrupt the peace in my home and want to stay up all night arguing, crying, nagging, attempting to reason, and so on. I tried to punish my husband for hurting my feelings. If I was hurt, he had to be hurt. This was learned behavior for me. I had to be changed by the renewing of my mind in CHRIST. It took a while, but I learned that what I was doing was a form of witchcraft because I was trying to manipulate and force Jean into surrendering to what I wanted. I thought my way was better, and I thought that my way would protect our marriage. Again, I am married to an African man, so this didn't work. He refused to lose an hour of sleep dealing with that broken creature that I was, so if he had to, he would go in the extra bedroom, lock the door, and sleep peacefully. He would leave me to myself with my own issues, and I'm glad he did that now. This forced me to take a good look at myself and see just how I was behaving. My behavior didn't reflect me as a Christian; it reflected selfishness, pride, and ungodliness. I went before the Throne of GOD and asked to be changed, and GOD did it; HE changed me. HE changed me because I wanted to be changed. I needed to learn how to deal with what I didn't understand without panicking. This wasn't an issue of Jean not being a good husband; it was an issue with a wicked seed that had rooted itself in me. I didn't understand how that man could sleep when the atmosphere was so thick and chaotic. Honestly, he had no problem going to sleep, but I couldn't get any rest because I was robbed of my peace. What I discovered was that he was able to sleep because he wasn't burdened by the issues that I had. They were my own, and even though he is my husband; he wasn't going to tackle these issues. Instead, he left me in a room alone with those issues, and this was pure torture for me.

Then, the LORD left me in the room with my own issues, and this was even more torturous. There was no one to comfort me and tell me that everything was going to be okay. Instead, I had a choice; I could let the situation ruin my life or I could get over it. I chose to get over it and submit the problem to GOD. More than that, I decided to submit my whole self to GOD, and I watched HIM change me from an emotional woman driven by flesh to a woman after HIS own heart, driven by HIS WORD. What a difference this made in how I viewed things, how I handled disagreements, and what results came about.

Satan's tactics always backfire. If you are married, I am sure you can relate to this scenario: Spouse does something that hurts you (intentionally or unintentionally), and you get upset. You're hurt and you attempt to reconcile the situation by talking to the vigilante, but he or she resists the communication and begins to argue. Now, you're more upset because all you did was attempt to communicate in hopes that the problem would be resolved, but instead, it was made worse. So, what do you do? For women, when we are hurt, we'll usually kick peace out of the house and launch a verbal assault. Men usually withdraw themselves emotionally, and let the woman run herself crazy, or a man will leave the home for a few hours until he feels the coast is clear. These are both devices that should not be used because they are formed as weapons designed to hurt someone that we claim to love. Everything that happens to the spouse is going to affect you. Your prayer should not be that the spouse suffers the way they've made you suffer; instead, you should be asking the LORD to draw that sinful nature from their hearts and draw them closer to the FATHER.

Retaliative mentalities are always a problem, and retaliation never produces an everlasting solution to your problems. Retaliation will sometimes give you the results that you want...temporarily, but the problems always come back stronger and more evil than before. If you want GOD to direct your marriage, you have to be a forgiving spouse that understands that vengeance belongs to the LORD.

Even if your spouse has done something that was extremely hurtful to you, you have to know your place and act according to who you are. You are not GOD, and vengeance is HIS. You cannot teach your spouse a lesson worth learning; only GOD can do that. Anger is a form of derangement as well; that's why we refer to being angry as being mad. Mad means to be insane or mentally ill. Your spouse is not driving you towards the insane asylum; what makes a man crazy is how he deals what is dealt to him. Ask the LORD for the blessed gift of long-suffering. Don't be afraid, because in doing so you will learn how to cope with the issues of life. Many situations that once looked like rugged mountains will become mere dust piles to you. What you are learning is not how to cope with problems, but how to view them from the eyes of faith and not from the eyes of fear.

If you want to properly handle a spouse that is mishandling you, you should submit yourself to GOD and resist the devil. At first, it may seem that the spouse is getting worse, but it's not because he or she thinks you've finally weakened up; it is because that devil in them is being exposed. Once it is exposed, it will be vanquished if you will only stay in HIS will.

Bad Association (Friends, Foes & Family)

The two of you have been hanging out for years, even before you met your spouse. Your buddy has been by your side through thick and thin, and you can't imagine life without him or her. Let's say that this character is a man. Sure, he has some issues that he is dealing with, but you can understand him better than anyone. After all, you know how he grew up in a dysfunctional home. You know how he was bullied and kicked around in school, and underneath that rough pit bull exterior cowers the shadow of a man with much bark, but little to no bite. So you justify continuing in the friendship, but a new problem is before you: Your wife doesn't like him. She feels he is a bad influence, and she launches heated attacks against your desire to hang out with such a character. Is she wrong? No. Well, maybe how she delivers the message, yes; but in truth she is saying to you the same thing that GOD said, "Evil communication corrupts good manners." But I'm sure you have heard it said, "Just because he does this, doesn't mean I will do that. I have my own mind. I'm a grown man." This sounds good, but there is no truth to this since GOD has already spoken on the issue, and because HE said it, it's signed, sealed, and delivered.

Therefore, you will pick up on his ways. It may not be his philandering and adulterous ways, but it could be his discontent and hatred for women, or his foul language. Eventually, what is in him will make its way into you.

Let's say that your friend is a woman. She's that jealous and negative character that you have learned to overlook, and she's not too fond of your choice for a husband. It's hard to ditch her though, because she has been by your side since you were children. She has fought for you, helped you financially, and just been there for you when no one else stood by. The bad things that she has done to you seem to pale in comparison to the good things she has done for you. You think that she is harmless to your life and your marriage, but she is not. Instead, she is one of the most toxic characters around you because she has keyed access to your heart, and she has plenty of venom to unleash there. How could you walk away from her after all she has done for you? She's not **that** bad, right?

You have to understand that we are to first honor GOD, and secondly know that we are not abandoning a lifelong friend; we are abandoning a lifelong prayer-hindering yoke that has masqueraded itself under the disguise of a friend. We aren't mistreating a person, but we are mistreating GOD when we esteem a person over HIM. After all, HE has done more for you and been there for you a lot longer than those so called friends of yours. Sometimes, the LORD will deliver us from people that have placed demonic sieges on our hearts for years. Part of that yoke is feeling that you owe the person something. *"Owe no man anything, but to love one another: for he that loves another has fulfilled the law" (Romans 13:8).*

Holding onto friends that should have been let go of will prove to be poisonous to your life and the life of your family. Maybe the friendship was intended by GOD to be seasonal, or maybe they will change their life when you get out of it. Sometimes we are the very ones who keep our friends and loved ones from seeking GOD.

Sometimes we unknowingly become idols to our friends, and they begin to depend on us for the friendship. This is absolutely dangerous because all idols have to be destroyed. You can never allow yourself to become a part of a man's habit or religious behavior. If they were called by GOD, they have to arrive at a place where they are acceptable to HIM, not to you. Chances are, being your friend was not their ultimate destination. GOD has a place that HE has called them to, but they don't feel like they have to change, and they don't hear HIS voice because sin has damaged their spiritual eardrums. Your loyalty to them can prove to be their undoing.

How does bad association affect your marriage? First off, whatever is attached to whomever is in your life is going to attach itself to you and everyone else it has access to. That's how demons work. They are like contagious viruses. When you know someone is sick in the natural, you avoid them out of fear that you will catch what they have. You wait for them to get well, and then you come around again. Well, the spiritual side of things isn't much different. When someone is spiritually sick, what is in them is contagious, and unless you are there on assignment as the doctor (deliverer), chances are you're going to be infected. It may seem harmless, but its mission is to do the work of its father, the devil. Its mission is to kill, steal and destroy.

Don't get caught up in the lies Satan tells you, which include, but are not limited to:

1. You are a leader. You haven't picked up on his or her ways in all this time, and you never will. Those scriptures were just for the weak.
2. Your spouse is just insecure. If you give in, you are feeding that insecurity.
3. You're the man. She's trying to step into a man's position, and tell you what to do? Before you know it, you'll be standing in the kitchen, wearing an apron and crying because she didn't kiss you good morning. Stand up and be the man.
4. You're a strong woman, and he's intimidated. You'd better stand

your ground and show him that he doesn't pick your friends. Besides, she's been your girl since 3rd grade and you're in her life to help her change into a better person. She's full of venom now, but she's making progress.
5. Look at all your friend has done for you, and here you are… you're ungratefully selfish. This friend would have never done this to you.

Remember, Satan is a liar, and his plan is to keep you in bondage. He never wants you to be free, and one of the tools that he uses to bind you is evil association. Being free is a choice, and if your friend chooses to stay bound; why are you visiting them in their own self erected prisons?

This mindset especially occurs within the family circuit. So many people deal with evil family members simply because they are family, and they feel a sense of obligation to keep in contact with them. JESUS associated family ties; not with the carnal side of things, but through our relationship or lack of a relationship with GOD. Matthew 12:47-50 reads, *"Then one said unto him, Behold, thy mother and thy brethren stand without, desiring to speak with thee. But he answered and said unto him that told him, Who is my mother? And who are my brethren? And he stretched forth his hand toward his disciples, and said, Behold my mother and my brethren! For whosoever shall do the will of my Father which is in heaven, the same is my brother, and sister, and mother."*

If JESUS saw it this way, so should you. If you have to get out of order to associate yourself with someone, you have chosen to forsake the CREATOR for a creation. Minister to the lost, but don't go into the wilderness trying to pull them out by your religious leash. GOD never arrests the will of a man to cause him to drunkenly come to HIM; instead, HE has charged that your love for HIM be what ushers you to HIM.

How bad is a wicked friendship? When I was a young girl, I was molested by relatives and friends of the family. My parents let any and everyone into their home, and their children paid the price for their choices. One of my Dad's best friends is one of the most memorable of those culprits. He started fondling me when I was twelve years old, and this behavior continued until I was fourteen. He called the house one day and told me to meet him at the corner store. He said that he was going to move me into this secret house that my parents knew nothing about, and he was going to take care of me. He would buy me clothes, a car, and he would let me drop out of school to be his woman. This panicked me because I wasn't romantically interested in him; after all, he was in his forties, and I was only fourteen. I had managed to avoid being alone with him so far by staying around my siblings when he would come over, but when he would catch me alone in a room for a few seconds, the touching would start. Now, here he was on the phone telling me to run away with him. I paced back and forward until my parents came home, and I finally told them everything that had been happening. I can remember my Mom picking up the phone to call him, and my Dad asking me a lot of questions. Then, my Dad got the phone and started crying and yelling at the guy. He'd told my Mom that he was just playing with me, and of course this angered an already scared me. I went to my room and paced back and forward some more because I was sorely afraid. The next day when I came home from school; this character was sitting in our living room, and I was horrified. I hurriedly went to my room, and my Dad came in and apologized. He said that they'd talked, and that this guy was threatening to commit suicide if he ended the friendship. After all, they'd been friends since before I was born. Sadly enough, my Dad continued the friendship, and I had to deal with seeing this man come over like nothing had ever happened.

Why do I tell this story? I didn't name the character because people can and do change, and I have since forgiven him. He may be saved now, and he may have repented, but the story has a familiar ring to it for a lot of people. Some people choose longevity over their responsibilities as a spouse, parent, and more importantly, a child of GOD. Longevity is nothing because Satan can torment you for decades, but this doesn't mean that he should be allowed to continue. Some people can hang around you for decades and still not have your best interest in mind. They can and do harm your spouses, your children, and your relationship with GOD. This is why you should never count months and years; you should always look at the fruit of the man, and if the tree is bearing evil fruit, the tree itself is evil. Chop it down out of your life.

Being in the company of wise men and women, you too will become wiser. In associating yourself with the workers of evil, not only are you picking up on their ways and demons, but you are sharing in the punishment that they will receive as a result of their choices. And of course, whatever touches you will touch your spouse and your children as well.

So, be sure to avoid all evil communication, no matter how long you've known the communicator. Remember, if what is coming out of a person cannot and will not be accepted by GOD, but is being transmitted to you, you are allowing yourself to become an evil receptor. Whatever is poured into you will eventually become a continuous river in you that will flow from you and drown you.

Bad Advice Versus Good Counsel

There are times in a marriage when we feel so overwhelmed that we may consider seeking outside counsel for help. This isn't always a bad thing, considering the scriptures tell us to consult the elders of the church. But of course, this doesn't always happen. Many times, we or our spouses go to the first one with a working set of ears to voice our problems.

You're hurt; really hurt. You're upset, and the spouse is just being cruel. You decide to reach out to a friend or family member, and they listen intently, encourage you, and then give you some good advice. Scenario: You're a married woman, and you and your husband just had a huge fight. You call a friend, and she advises you: "Honey, go home and talk to your husband. Stop being so emotional; that man loves you. You know men just don't deal with emotions too well, so go home and apologize to him for your role. Then after all is calm, go and talk to him calmly about the incident." You take the advice and it works. Sounds like good advice; right? Now, you want to call her every time you have a problem. The problem is her heart is not right before the LORD.

So, the next time a problem arises, you run out the door with your cell phone in hand. You call her, and she can hear your quivering voice coming out of the receiver. You begin to pour out everything your awful husband has done to you today. Again, she listens intently, and encourages you; but this time her advice is a deadly combination of truth and flesh. This time she says, "GOD has got you covered. You have got to stop being so emotional and going off every time your husband rubs you the wrong way. He's just a man! All men are the same. Yes he loves you, but he can't override his manhood! That's why you have to be smarter than him. Instead of crying, go to Wal-Mart and buy a new comforter set, a pillow, and a headphone set. Then make up your couch, and make him sleep there until he comes and apologizes. Don't kiss him; don't touch him, and don't let him touch you. By nature, men are like children who have to be trained. No sex for him until he apologizes, and you need to stick with this. Don't cook; don't clean. Just get up and go to work; and after work, take yourself to the spa, and treat you to some me-time. After a while, he will realize how much he needs you, and he will come to you and apologize. GOD didn't create you to be an emotional punching bag, and HE said, 'To whom much is given; much is required.' That means you have given the husband all the time and lectures he needs to do the right thing; now you have to require him to show that he's been paying attention. And if he can't meet up with your expectations, go into your prayer closet and stay there."

To some people, this sounds like good advice, but in truth, it is a cocktail of lies mingled with a hint of truth to intoxicate your judgment. GOD has already given us commands; not tips. HE told us what we ARE to do in our marriages; not what we CAN or SHOULD do, but what we are COMMANDED to do. The problem nowadays is, when turmoil arises, many of us want a quick fix, and GOD wants us to let the storm water our understanding. Even though the enemy may be attacking the union, GOD allowed this attack so that you could fortify that area of your marriage where the enemy is attacking. This is clearly an open area that needs to be sealed off with the blood of CHRIST

JESUS. GOD'S intention is for you to come together, pray, and fortify that area; but Satan's intent is to destroy the marriage. It is your decision which direction you take.

Either the two of you will come together and go against the enemy as a united front, or you will divide and be attacked by the enemy individually. This is the way the enemy works; he divides and then he conquers. When we begin to point fingers at one another, we are in the same working with the enemy to overcome our spouses. Once he's done tearing them to pieces, he will use them to tear you to pieces. The whole time, he goes undetected or unchallenged. As spouses, we want to attack the obvious issue; in other words, we want to attack what we can see. Nevertheless, we are not fighting a natural fight; this fight is spiritual. *"For we wrestle not against flesh and blood, but against principalities, against powers, against the rulers of the darkness of this world, against spiritual wickedness in heavenly places" (Ephesians 6:12).* This means that many are working hand-in-hand with the enemy to destroy their spouses unknowing and unwittingly. This is done because of lack of knowledge.

When you turn to someone for advice, you are welcoming their life's results into your life. Even if a person appears to have a happy marriage; it doesn't mean they are happy. Some people can give you a hint of good advice, followed by a flood of bad advice.

After mixing the truth with a lie, you will find that the advice begins to get worse and worse, and truth is rarely found in it. There's no need to mix in the truth now because you have opened up your heart and your home to this individual. Make no mistake about it; whomever you take advice from is now a third-party in your marriage, and as such, they will affect your marriage directly. At one point, they were serving you with a lot of truth, and maybe a piece of flesh would get into the mix. Now, their advice is a dose of truth followed by an overdose of fleshly lies. Before you know it, you're yoked up with an evil individual who is not going to take it well when you decide to stop taking her advice because now her name is on the line. She has now invested so much of herself into your union, and now she wants to follow through with what she has started. Suddenly, it's not about you anymore; this is a personal vendetta. You have handed your husband to her to be the face of all the men that has hurt her. In addition to unresolved marriage problems, you have created another problem. Now, you have to worry about your marriage problems being aired publicly by her, and making its way back to your husband.

Flesh is easy to recognize and once you recognize it, do not continue the conversation. If you see or hear things like emotional reactions, you have triggered the flesh. You can't trust your own flesh, so why would you trust the flesh of someone else? Better than that, you should always seek GOD for counsel. HE will either speak to you directly, or HE may provide a counselor that is after HIS own heart.

How do you handle this uncontrollable urge to lay out everything in your heart? Pray about everyone you associate yourself with; it's that simple. Ask the LORD to remove everyone from your life who HE does not want in it. In addition, ask HIM to place wisdom in your heart to govern your marriage (men), or ask GOD to place wisdom in your husband's heart to govern the marriage, as well as wisdom in your heart to trust the Head of your husband (women). Remember, Solomon asked for wisdom to govern GOD'S people. Do the same in regards to your marriage, and GOD will show you who to speak to. Don't be fooled by titles and cloaks. Everyone is not mature enough to handle your problems.

If you are in a position of leadership, you need to be extra careful about sharing your marriage problems. Some leaders aren't mature enough to handle your issues, and they may try to advise you out of conceit. After this, you will find that many will disassociate themselves from you because they aren't too happy with the choice you made in your marriage. For example, if you chose to stay when they thought you should have left; you will see a change in your relationship with them. Then again, many leaders will lose respect for you altogether and begin to view you as their son or daughter in ministry rather than their sister or brother. This is very common when leaders go to leaders who aren't anointed to advise them.

Scenario: A man of the cloth (Pastor) is having an issue in his marriage. Maybe his wife was getting too frisky with her boss, and he goes to another man of the cloth who happens to have a warped view of women. His obligation is to uplift you, sharpen you, and pray for you; however, he happens to know a single woman in his congregation who he believes is a better match for you than your wife. He indirectly tells you that she is much better than your flirtatious wife. He says, "Brother, I understand how you feel; the LORD can fix this for you. You know, women can be something else. I divorced my first two wives because they were like boats without an anchor; they were floating all over the place. Be encouraged, man of GOD, and know that if this isn't the wife GOD chose for you; HE is setting you up as we speak. As a matter of fact, there's a young beautiful and available woman who goes to my church and sits on the front pew every Sunday. I always thought she'd make someone a good wife one day, and I can actually see the two of you maybe hitting it off well." (Then he goes into a prophe-lie to tell you how he sees this woman as your wife).

Do you see how he has begun to put a wedge between you and your wife? This man knows nothing about long-suffering, being patient, praying, and glorifying GOD in his marriage, and now you've just given him the keys to crash your marriage into his opinion.

Be prayerful about everyone you pour into, because in pouring into them, you open yourself for them to pour into you.

My struggle was a filthy combination of being overly emotional and prideful. Anyhow, Jean and I went through a pretty rough storm in the first couple of years of our marriage. At one point, I was very sure we would not come out of it together. I was actually confident that this marriage was over because I was dealing with something I had never dealt with before, and I just didn't know how to handle it. It wasn't an extra-marital affair; for me, it was far worse. It was an in-law who wanted to bring her own warped views into my marriage. This wasn't considered a VERY bad thing in Jean's culture, so he didn't see anything wrong with it at the time. We were arguing every day, and I was crying every day. In the midst of this, a leader approached me and tried to order a website from me. In his initial contact, he began to do what I believed to be prophesying. HE began to tell me that the LORD had said I'd outgrown my church. I listened intently as he tried to get me to join his church. I told him that I would pray about it, and we continued talking about the website that he needed.

A week or so later, hubby and I were at it again. This in-law was advising him again about how to handle me, and I was livid. He called right behind an argument, and I happened to be in my room crying. I was actually throwing a temper-tantrum because I wanted out of the marriage. Anyhow, I answered the phone and told him that I'd call him back. Sensing stress in my voice, he asked if all was well. I thought to myself that I could confide in him. I could tell him what was going on, and trust him with this information; after all, he says he is an Apostle. I thought he would intercede for me, so I began pouring out my problems. I was beginning to feel better as I unloaded all of the hurt. That was until he told me how he'd had problems in his marriage as well. I really wasn't expecting a gripe session; I was looking for prayer. Not long after this conversation, he began asking me questions like, "If you and your husband were to ever divorce, would you consider remarrying?" I didn't know how to answer this, and I didn't want to accuse him of flirting. I tried to convince myself that he was just asking harmless questions, but I couldn't shake it; this was out of order. I thought Satan was trying to taint my view of this man, so I answered, "Yeah. All men aren't the same." Suddenly, he began referring to me as first-lady. At this time in my life, I was rather naïve, so I called a friend of mine and told her how I believed this man was flirting with me. She wisely counseled me to be firm with him, keep the conversation on business; and if that didn't work, to tell him to stop calling me. But, I wanted to be **sure** I wasn't reading too much into this. After all, he was an Apostle....or so he said. At that time, I respected titles and didn't know to look at the fruit. I didn't want to leave any room for me to question myself, so I simply began avoiding his calls, and that's when the text messages started. He asked me about my marriage; if all was well, and I replied that it was. He then went on to ask me if I wanted to be a first-lady one day, and I replied back saying that I am already a first-lady. Then the text I felt I needed came in, and it read, "Are you attracted to me? Because I am attracted to you." At that, I angrily sent a response, "I am a woman of GOD. I don't go to the left or the right. I go hard for GOD! With that, do not contact me anymore."

What's the moral of this story? Everyone who cries LORD, LORD won't enter Heaven. You can't even trust everything that presents itself as a prophesy, or everyone that presents himself or herself as a Prophet. Keep in mind that Pharaoh's magicians were able to mimic many of the miracles that Moses performed before Pharaoh. There are many magicians who disguise themselves as Prophets, Apostles, and other Christian leaders. Titles don't tell you what the man is; his fruit does.

Around this same time, I had another incident because, again, I was looking for help or a way out of the marriage. I was on the phone with a friend, when her friend began groaning and saying that the LORD had a word for me. I was in distress and wanted permission from the LORD to leave Jean, so I was hoping that this was the answer to my prayers. I had been begging to leave Jean because the in-law was dividing our home, and I was tired of him not doing anything about it.

Anyhow, this man began to speak and say just what I'd been praying for. "Woman of GOD; GOD says you're released!" What? I can leave him? Finally! (The only reason I had been staying was because I wanted to make sure GOD was in my decision. Even though I was still growing in CHRIST, I knew that a wrong decision would backfire.) I began crying uncontrollably; happy that I was free. I was just beside myself with joy as I listened to him go on and on about what he claimed the LORD was saying. He finally told me that GOD was going to give me a word in seven days as to where to go, and what to do. I was so happy that I began packing my bags and celebrating. During this wait, a brother in CHRIST who I consider a very dear friend contacted me. He seemed to always contact me when I needed someone to talk to, and I knew that he always told me the raw truth whether I wanted to hear it or not. I joyfully told him that I'd been given permission by GOD to leave Jean in a few days. I was friends with him and his wife, so I knew I could trust him. They'd prayed for me before, and counseled me before about my marriage. We were communicating via email, so he asked me, “Sister, what's your new number so I can speak with you?” I knew he'd be very pessimistic about the prophecy, but I thought I'd be able to convince him that it was genuine. After all, I felt better. That counts, right?

When he called me a day later, I told him what had been happening, and what had been spoken over me. I listened as he told me how he did not believe the prophecy was from the LORD because the LORD hates a divorce. I was countering with my thoughts when he asked me, “Sister, when you prayed to ask the LORD if you could be released from your marriage, did you pray aloud?” At this, I told him yes. He then replied, “Don't you know the devil can hear your prayers when you pray aloud? That's why you have to pray in the SPIRIT. Don't you know that our prayers go past the devil's bedroom?” I was so confused that my head started hurting. He then replied, “Just pray on it, sis; that's all I'm asking. Me and my wife will be praying for you as well, and if in seven days you hear from the LORD, listen and do what HE tells you, but we are going to bind up any spirit that is not of HIM, so no demons can speak to you on this day.” I agreed and left the conversation feeling depleted. I was back to square one, and I just hoped that GOD would give me permission to leave on the seventh day. When the seventh day came, I listened intently for the LORD. I stayed up all night listening for HIM, looking out the window, and hoping to see an Angel of the LORD coming with news. Nothing happened but silence. I didn't know how to feel. On one hand, I was happy because I didn't want to dishonor GOD. On the other hand, I was hurt because I just kept thinking, "You mean to tell me I gotta stay with him?"

As you can see, during this time, I sought out counsel from anyone that said they were of the LORD. I was open to anyone's counseling, and the enemy saw this. I just wanted out, and I wanted someone to tell me that GOD said that I could leave. Proverbs 4:23 warns us, *"Above all else, guard your heart, for it is the wellspring of life."* I didn't guard my heart; it was wide open for anyone with a title or anyone who at least went to church. I was going on prayer lines hoping that I would get a prophecy. My fight wasn't with Jean; I was wrestling with GOD. I had already made up my mind as to what I wanted to do, and I was looking for confirmation that I could do it. To hear that I had to stay was not a message that I welcomed because I felt like I'd made a mistake, and I wanted to do it over. I had been seeing women with their husbands at church, and that's what I wanted. I wanted my husband to be laid out and slain in the SPIRIT, and since this one did not match up to what I wanted, I was ready to repent of him and start over. Like many women, I did not realize that the man before me could have possibly been my GOD-sent husband that I'd married out of season when we were both still bitter. I saw a problem that I didn't know what to do with, so I reasoned within myself that the solution was divorce. This was a generational curse that was still on me at that time, and I was slowly being delivered from it.

When did peace come into my marriage? When did Jean's heart begin to turn to the LORD? When I stopped warring with the LORD on HIGH, and I learned to appreciate and support who Jean would become in the LORD, not who he currently was. When I humbled myself and stopped with the arguing, packing, and slandering of my husband's name, the LORD came into me and removed those wicked ways. The problem wasn't all him, after all. Sure, he had his faults, but I soon discovered that I was trying to be GOD in my husband's life. I was trying to change him, and I wasn't letting him make his own mistakes. That in-law had been successful with sowing discord because I was not fully covered with GOD'S armor. I wanted to wear the helmet of salvation, but every other part of the armor was packed away under my desires. When I stopped seeking counsel, my marriage took on a whole new life. I learned to get on my face before the LORD, humble myself before the LORD, and to stop trying to argue with Jean. I learned to talk to him, pray for him, pray with him, and stand in the gap for him. That is what made the devil flee. I had to get over myself to get under GOD. When I felt the need to battle it out with Jean, I went into another room, and I began to pray. The LORD would tell me sometimes to do something nice for my husband. It was hard to do at first because I was wrestling with pride, but I listened to HIM, and I watched the atmosphere shift in my home and in my marriage.

Wicked counsel is only successful when you are in rebellion. As I began to submit myself to GOD, many of the people whom I'd been associating with got away from me. Why is that? *"Submit yourselves therefore to God. Resist the devil, and he will flee from you" (James 4:7).* And hubby finally heard from his Head and stopped taking advice from that problematic in-law. It was amazing because I watched GOD easily work something out that I had been trying to fix for years. I held up the progress because I refused to submit to my husband, and as such, I was refusing to submit to the CHRIST head. GOD only needs one of you in the marriage to submit to HIM, and HE will do the rest. It doesn't take two people to make it work out; it only takes one believer who is wise enough to submit to the LORD. To submit is to stay in line with the WORD of GOD. If you are a wife, your duty isn't to come against your husband because CHRIST is his head. When the husband won't do what he is supposed to be doing as your spouse, you can talk to him about it. If he refuses to listen, you should go to his Head, CHRIST JESUS. Your words won't always be respected by your husband; it is the counsel or the chastening from the LORD that will get his attention, and cause him to submit to GOD'S will; not yours. *"Likewise, ye wives, be in subjection to your own husbands; that, if any obey not the word, they also may without the word be won by the conversation of the wives; While they behold your chaste conversation coupled with fear. Whose adorning let it not be that outward adorning of plaiting the hair, and of wearing of gold, or of putting on of apparel; but let it be the hidden man of the heart, in that which is not corruptible, even the ornament of a meek and quiet spirit, which is in the sight of God of great price" (1 Peter 3:1-4).*

Bad counsel took me through some of the roughest patches that I have ever had to go through. It's funny because all I had to do was submit to GOD and resist the devil. Then and only then, GOD would have worked it out. I took the long and hard road first, and found that there was no short-cut that would have taken my problems directly to the finish line and declared me a winner. You can't fix your marriage with your hands, your attitude, your money, or threats of divorce. Only GOD'S hands are big and strong enough to fix you, your husband, and your marriage. You can't mix your tries with a prayer or two. You have to fully surrender and let GOD be GOD. HE won't share HIS glory with you.

Forgive and Forget

The world has coined this phrase, "I can forgive you, but I will never forget." This has been echoed tremendously within the walls of the church, and sadly enough, many people saved and unsaved live by this. With this mentality, you will need to have a divorce attorney on standby because marriage does not work this way. GOD has to be in your marriage; HE has to head it off. This means you have to follow HIS lead with your marriage. How can one develop their own strategy in marriage? The LORD has already told us what to do in our homes, how to treat our spouses, and how to cope with marital strife.

We should mimic the lead of our FATHER. We have all sinned and fallen short of being worthy to be called HIS. Nevertheless, HE has forgiven us and continued calling us sons and daughters. *"And their sins and iniquities will I remember no more" (Hebrews 10:17).* Why is it that GOD said HE would remember our sins no more? Does this mean HE literally forgets what we did? And how can we literally forget what someone has done?

The word 'forgive' comes from the Greek word 'charizomai', which means to pardon. Pardoning means to excuse and wipe one's record clean, or to declare one innocent. That is, GOD does not hold you accountable, nor does HE punish you for whatever deeds HE has forgiven you for.

When the Blood of JESUS washes us from our iniquities; we are no longer guilty of those iniquities because JESUS bore our guilt. Therefore, old things are passed away and all things are made new. When one wants to repaint a car, they don't leave the old paint on the vehicle, or it will begin to show up as the new paint wears down. Plus, it would be hard for the new paint to stick to an already painted vehicle. They have to strip the car of its paint, buff it, and prime it before painting it. When GOD extends grace to us, the old ways are not covered by the new ways, but they are washed away. After our sins are washed away, we have to be buffed and primed to take on our new roles in CHRIST. This means that we can be delivered, but our old mindsets still have to be stripped away from us. Deliverance isn't just the casting out of a demon, but whole deliverance consists of the mind being renewed as well.

"Repent" comes from the Greek word 'metanoia.' Metanoia means to change one's mind. The average Christian thinks repentance is to simply apologize to the LORD for one's wrong doing, but their mind isn't changed. There is no change inwardly; just an apology to the LORD. Is this true repentance? Of course not. One's mind has to be changed, meaning they no longer see the need or desire to participate in the sin that they claim to be sorry for. Their minds and their hearts have to be returned to CHRIST JESUS. *"And be not conformed to this world: but be ye transformed by the renewing of your mind, that ye may prove what is that good, and acceptable, and perfect, will of God" (Romans 12:2).*

No one is worthy of GOD'S grace or HIS love, but HE loves us anyway. How is it that we want to hold our spouses accountable for whatever they have done, but we do not want to be held accountable for what we have done? This brings the parable of the evil servant to mind.

"Therefore is the kingdom of heaven likened unto a certain king, which would take account of his servants. And when he had begun to reckon, one was brought unto him, which owed him ten thousand talents. But forasmuch as he had not to pay, his lord commanded him to be sold, and his wife, and children, and all that he had, and payment to be made. The servant therefore fell down, and worshipped him, saying, Lord, have patience with me, and I will pay thee all. Then the lord of that servant was moved with compassion, and loosed him, and forgave him the debt. But the same servant went out, and found one of his fellowservants, which owed him an hundred pence: and he laid hands on him, and took him by the throat, saying, Pay me that thou owest. And his fellowservant fell down at his feet, and besought him, saying, Have patience with me, and I will pay thee all. And he would not: but went and cast him into prison, till he should pay the debt. So when his fellowservants saw what was done, they were very sorry, and came and told unto their lord all that was done. Then his lord, after that he had called him, said unto him, O thou wicked servant, I forgave thee all that debt, because thou desiredst me: Shouldest not thou also have had compassion on thy fellowservant, even as I had pity on thee? And his lord was wroth, and delivered him to the tormentors, till he should pay all that was due unto him. So likewise shall my heavenly Father do also unto you, if ye from your hearts forgive not every one his brother their trespasses" (Matthew 18:23-35).

In this story, FATHER is demonstrating the corrupt nature of man. We want to be forgiven, yet we are slow to forgive others.

You will be tested in your marriage; that's a given. Your spouse has access to parts of your heart that others don't have, and because of this, your spouse has the power to do more damage to you than anyone else. That's not scary because you have just as much power to do damage to your spouse because you have his or her heart; but in marriage, two people are coming together and vowing not to break that bond of trust. Nevertheless, when our spouses do or say things that hurt or anger us; it is normal to react, especially when we think our marriage to them is being threatened. The key is knowing the right reaction to have and avoiding emotional reactions. Anytime wrong is done to you, submitting to GOD should be your weapon.

How does one forgive or forget? It's not as complicated as it seems. In truth, it is easier to forgive than it is to hold a grudge. Forgiveness is simply pardoning one from their trespasses against you or someone else and going past your pride to love and treat them as if they have never done anything wrong. The hardest part of accessing forgiveness is reaching past our own pride. I found that in almost every marital problem that had attempted to tackle my marriage, the spirit of pride was the one that kept hubby and I from giving the issue to GOD.

Every spirit has some ranking, and many spirits never enter or attach themselves to a man alone.
For example, a lying spirit always brings pride, and pride always brings offense. What if you are trying to get to the truth, but you can't seem to find it in your spouse? It's hidden in the spouse somewhere, so you continue your journey to try to extract it out of him or her. You attempt to talk to your spouse, and the first spirit that meets you is pride. Pride is telling your spouse that this problem you seem to be having needs to be viewed as a game that he or she must win. If they lose, you'll think you're the boss, and you'll only get more controlling. Pride and that lying spirit tells your spouse that you want to put him or her in a prison, and this is your attempt to lock them up. As a result, these spirits convince your spouse to send forward offense. Offense is like a rabid pit bull warning you that if you continue, you will be eaten by regrets. Nevertheless, you think you're almost getting to the truth, so you continue on and take that harsh attack that offense launches. You say a prayer and continue on because you believe that GOD will get you through these harsh deserts and rough terrains to get you to the truth. After all that suffering you go through trying to get to the truth, you find out that the truth wasn't in your spouse. JESUS

CHRIST is the truth, so you've been searching in the wrong place. *"Jesus said unto him, I am the way, the truth, and the life: no man comes unto the Father, but by me" (John 14:6).*

GOD told you to submit yourself to HIM and resist the devil, and this would make the devil flee from you. You've been deceived into believing that your detailed investigations, intense interrogations, and your unrelenting search for the truth would prove to be successful. Instead, you helped the devil to tear your marriage into shreds.

When you have chosen to forgive your spouse and others, the hardest part of the ordeal is not what they are doing and saying; it is how you respond to it. Love does not hurt, but some things that visit us in love do. You cannot be a willing victim and expect to live in peace. Victims are victimized and peacemakers make peace. Which one are you?

GOD is Love and HE said if you repent, HE would forgive you and remember your sins no more. That is the evidence of true love. Love stands taller than any issue that presents itself to us; we just have to stay in love to be guarded by love. You and your spouse should stand up and declare, like Joshua did, "As for me and my house, we will serve the LORD."

Unforgiveness always seems to live within us when we are not patient with the LORD. We want justice now; we want the truth now; we want what we want when we want it, and when we don't get it, we throw temper tantrums.

When you chose to get married, you were choosing to live in a continual state of forgiveness. Marriage is two people united as one, but the definition does not override the fact that we make individual choices that will sometimes conflict with one another.

Not only do you have to forgive the spouse, but you have to forget about what was done to you in the past. That doesn't mean that it will leave your memory; that means that you should never let those thoughts enter your head again, and you should never let words about those incidents exit your mouth. Every day, your spouse's slate should be wiped clean and so should yours, because the sun should not set upon your anger. That means that all issues should be resolved before you lie down to sleep at night. The next day is a new day, and GOD'S mercies for you and your spouse are renewed. You have to extend mercy as well because you are an imperfect being, and it is hypocritical for you to try to measure yourself and your choices against your spouse and his or her choices. It's not easy to do, but it's not impossible either. GOD has to be the reason for every decision that you make in order for it to be the right decision. Meaning, GOD has to be the driving factor behind every choice that you make. For example, let's say that the wife has disregarded your request that she stop spending money on shoes. You want to save up to buy a home, but she obviously has a spending problem, and now, to make matters worse, she is on the offensive. She rants on about your costly habit of wanting to eat out once a week, even though she knows that this was your attempt to date her. You can either respond to her offense, her choices, or you can respond to GOD'S will. GOD'S will is that you forgive her and lead your home by making a Godly decision. Of course, you'd need to pray and ask HIM what the right move is because the flesh has plenty of ways that it would like to handle her, but GOD has an answer that will be more effective than anything you could have conjured up.

It's a new day; forgive your spouse for whatever they did yesterday, last month, last year, and years ago. This is how you stay in the will of GOD, and how you continue to elevate to a better place in HIM. You will find that in forgiveness, a lot of things that used to anger you won't anger you anymore because you will learn to live in the peace of GOD. At the same time, you will provide a more peaceful marriage to your spouse, and they will do the same for you in return. Don't worry about the creation's choices, when you can go to the CREATOR about their choices.

When you forgive, you can live in peace and remain in a loving marriage. Sure, you could choose to be hostile and intimidate your spouse into doing what you want; but to do so you'll be inviting Satan and his host into your marriage. If the devil comes in, peace will escape you, and problems will pursue you.

Excessive Arguing– Uprooting the Root

All too often, we all get into an argument or disagreement with our spouse, and most people believe that the disagreement stemmed from their spouse's choices, misconceptions, or words. On that same not, their spouses believe that they are the root of the problem. This breeds a contentious environment where the lines of communication are closed, and the signals of comprehension are not being reached. For everything that springs up in life and in your marriage, there is a root. Everything on this earth starts off as a seed; whether it is an idea or an action, it is first a seed, and then it begins to develop its roots and grow. A baby started off as an egg, and that egg had to be fertilized before it began to take on life. Marriage is the same way. Everything that presents itself in your marriage first starts off as a seed that has to be fertilized. When it is an evil thought, it needs to be cast down before it is fertilized and takes on a life of its own.

Have you ever seen the dog referred to as the Saint Bernard? Saint Bernards are huge dogs. What if the dog's body kept growing, but its legs stayed the same? Undoubtedly, that dog would not be able to walk because his legs could not sustain the weight of his body. Therefore, GOD has caused all living things to grow up as a whole and not individually. You want to mature in your marriage, but many times there are areas that are often ignored for the sake of keeping the peace or keeping the power. Some spouses will tolerate behaviors from their partners just to keep the peace. Over time, the tolerant spouse becomes silently venomous, while the offending spouse is not aware of the cancer growing in his or her marriage. Then, there are the spouses who have gained a sense of power over the other spouse because of an incident that occurred which rendered the powerless spouse guilty. For example, maybe the husband was discovered by his wife to be staying in touch with an ex-girlfriend. As a result, he becomes unrecognizably humble, while the wife abuses her source of newfound power. The marriage cannot grow because one or both spouses has decided to take on an excess burden or to place a burden upon the other spouse. This makes the marriage top-heavy, meaning that one or both spouses begins to be smothered by the choices of the other spouse.

To come into your marriage, Satan must first have an entrance. When you are both believers, the enemy will try to create an entrance if he cannot find one. Unlike many believers, he knows that everything on earth starts off as a seed; therefore, he begins to sow seeds in the minds of one or both parties in that union. Out of nowhere, for example, one spouse may suddenly become insecure and distrusting. Or one spouse may suddenly begin to demand more freedom. Each issue has a root, and that root is starting to sprout. All too often, we look at what is growing up, and we try to mow that down, but the root is often ignored. Because of this, the situation is pruned but never uprooted. To uproot the issue, one has to get to the bottom of the issue. Why is one spouse suddenly distrusting? Could it be that the spouse has a best friend who is sowing confusion into his or her head? That's a possibility, of course; but it has to be explored. Why is one spouse suddenly interested in having a life independent of his or her partner? Could it be that some of his or her co-workers has been bragging about spending time away from their spouse and going on mini-me vacations? This is a possibility, but the issue has to be explored. As you can see, it is not always what we think it is. Sometimes, we become paranoid and believe that our spouses' intentions are to betray us. Many would assume that the spouse who was suddenly super jealous is having an affair, but this isn't always the case. Many would assume that the independent spouse is attempting to have an affair, but this isn't always the case. Sometimes, the seed was sown by a simple conversation with someone else.

You have to fortify your marriage to keep the enemy out. Your marriage is a country, and you have to protect that country from invasion. Every access door has to be closed, and every wall must be fortified. Satan is persistent; therefore, the both of you have to be consistent in arming yourself and challenging anything that dares to approach your marriage. Even if you close one thousand demonic access doors, if there is one still cracked upon, the enemy will come in through it. All doors have to be shut.

Pride is the root of all continual issues in a marriage. *"Only by pride cometh contention: but with the well advised is wisdom" (Proverbs 3:10).* When you see an issue repeatedly rising up in your marriage, rather than fighting the issue, sometimes you need to come against pride as a unit. The real issue in these cases isn't always what the spouse did or did not do, but the issue is pride that's causing the spouse to offend their partner. When we try to fight the issues that we can see, we fight the winds. When we pray about issues that we can see, we pray amiss. Oftentimes, the issue is obvious, but it goes undetected because of our own blindness. The best thing to do is to go to the spouse and ask if the two of you can both come together against pride. Start binding it, cursing it, and renouncing it.

Trust Issues

Now, I have to admit, I have had some major trust issues in the past. Coming from a home where my parents divorced after discovering my Dad's adulterous relationships and outside children didn't exactly help me in my love life. On top of that, I was raised to believe that oh-so-common lie that all men cheat. Because of this, I began early on trying to be the heart-breaker so I wouldn't get my heart broken. Then I got married, believing that all men do not cheat, but they have to be watched to keep them from thinking about it. When I discovered my spouse was no better than my Dad, I tried fighting him, but that didn't work. My pride was fully intact and hadn't suffered any blows from my childhood. I didn't want to be that woman who was cheated on, laughed at, and always fighting just because my husband could not control himself. So, I did what I saw my Mom do; I divorced him. I was determined not to stay 16 years in like my Mom, so I cut it down by a decade and ran towards the first divorce attorney I could find. Trust and I weren't friends; we weren't even on speaking terms. We were foreigners to one another, speaking two different languages. Therefore, that tower could not be built at that time. Lack of trust was my couch and I sat on it often.

Overcoming Trust Issues

Overcoming this was no picnic, and it wasn't as easy as I'd hoped it would be. I tried on so many different personalities and thinking patterns...but none of them worked. The issues were still there when I remarried. I looked for complicated solutions such as trying to be silent when my mind was screaming, but the solution came in the form of a mental diet.

If you were overweight, how would you lose some of that weight? Dieting and exercising, of course. You have to watch what you eat, avoid certain foods, and exercise often. Trust works in that manner. Your spouse may not be the problem. The problem could be that you have not forgiven someone who has hurt you, or your way of thinking is wrong. You need to intake new information and shed the old information. You do this by praying for wisdom, knowledge, and understanding. You also do this by proactively taking on the root of your insecurities. When you feel yourself become suspicious or insecure, don't challenge the spouse; challenge your feelings. This is when you need to quarantine yourself so that your negativity does not spread to your spouse.

Head into another room and begin to pray about the issue. If your spouse is curious as to what you are doing, be honest with him or her. Humbly and lovingly tell them that you love them, but you are battling trust issues, so when an issue starts to rear its head, you are scalping it until you get the chance to decapitate it. You will find that when you are lovingly admitting that you have a problem, your spouse just may join you in coming against that problem. You can even ask them to come and pray with you about the issue. If they don't want to involve themselves, don't pressure them. Be polite and loving. Remember, the issue isn't always the spouse; sometimes the issue is rooted in you.

If your spouse has trust issues, your job is to be proactive in helping your spouse to overcome this. Sure, you may or may not be the reason behind their trust issues; nevertheless, any problem that your spouse has will directly affect you and your children. It is better to come at the issue together as a unit than it is to send the spouse away to deal with it on their own.
Where are you going?
Who is that on the phone?
What took you so long?
Why do you need to shower all of a sudden?
Why do you suddenly need new clothes?
Who keeps calling you from _ _ _-_ _ _ _?

Those questions are irritating, especially if you're faithful and you have done nothing to cause the distrusting spouse to become distrusting. To battle the issue is not the same as battling the spouse, because the issue is not with your spouse. Don't attack the projected issue; go straight to the root. When this happens, you should call a meeting with you and the spouse, but always remember to remain calm and loving. If the spouse doesn't like face-to-face discussions, try passing notes to one another or emailing one another. Sure, this sounds childish, but there are people out there (men especially) that don't like eye-to-eye engagement when their hearts are being searched out. A lot of men don't like to hear that their wives want to have a talk with them about an issue in their marriage because men tend to default to their warrior side when they feel challenged. Women, on the other hand, love those discussions because it gives them a chance to unburden themselves of whatever has been weighing down on them. Most women feel that such talks will make the marriage better, whereas most men tend to think that such talks will make the marriage worse.

To get the spouse to go into such a conversation without being guarded, you have to show him or her that you are willing to accept whatever answer they give without getting emotional. The first few conversations may seem tense for the spouse, but after they have tested you to see how you will handle what they say, they will decide how much further they want to go. For example, if you believe your wife has a secret bank account, and this has been bothering you, it is normal that you would want to talk with her about it. Your fear may be that you think she is planning to leave you eventually, but this just may be her doomsday preparation kit that she was taught to keep out of your reach. To go into such a conversation, it is not wise to bring in negative energy or negative emotions. The better way to get her to confess is to start by sharing your secrets with her. Tell her how much you love her, and reassure her that you don't intend to ever leave her. After the two of you have discussed life in general, then you can bring up the issue, but don't press it. Let her know that it bothers you, and look for the root of the issue. Again, her intentions may not be wicked in nature; they can be rooted in trust issues, or this can be something she was taught. Look for the positive side of this; if something was to happen to you, or if the two of you separated, she would have something to fall back on to take care of the kids. If she does have a secret account, don't try to get access to it or know how much is in it because this means that you are trying to disarm her. If her weapon is not to harm you, but to protect herself, you shouldn't be offended.

During times of peace, you and your spouse should agree that when contention threatens to come into your home, you will both sit down, set pride aside, and talk about the issue. Agree that the two of you won't leave the table of negotiations until you have reached a peaceful settlement. Try going for a nice brisk walk together to talk and relieve the tension. Exercising the body does relieve the mind, and a nice romantic walk should put those fears to bed. Sometimes it is better to take your problems to your spouse outside of your home, because some people feel that these discussions let in a negative energy that tends to stick around for a while. Going to the beach or to a nice quiet park is a great idea because you can hold hands, kiss your spouse, and be more relaxed about sharing the issue. If it's too dark outside to go anywhere, try taking a chair outside and sitting there with your spouse. Again, the goal is to change the environment and relax the spouse. Be sure not to show aggression or negative emotions, as these will put the spouse on guard. In addition, ask a question and then invite the spouse to ask you a question. If the spouse feels like he or she is being interrogated, they may start being defensive or even lying to get out of the conversation. If they feel like you're having a discussion, however, they are more likely to speak with you.

If you are the one being questioned, answer the questions without sarcasm or venom. Try smiling, laughing, and lovingly touching your spouse to reassure them as you answer the question. Sometimes, the spouse may feel stressed about questioning you, and this may make them go on the offensive. Treat all discussions like a big sale in a store; everything said is being discounted and sold out. This means that you should not make a big deal out of the issue or out of their answers. This HAS to be a limited time offer; meaning an agreement has to be put into place that you will answer questions for a total of one week or one day, for example. After the agreed upon time, those questions must not be brought to the table unless otherwise agreed upon for the next discussion.

So, what you should do is:

1. In a time of peace, address the issue of distrust, and what should be done when one spouse is feeling the need to monitor the other one.

2. Exercise what you have agreed upon even in intense situations.
3. Agree on a time period as to when the questioning has to stop.
4. The spouse with the trust issues needs to talk about what it is that has caused them to be that way. Listen and love them, but do not baby that victim spirit. They have to overcome it, not nurture it. Come together with your spouse against whatever is attacking their mind.
5. After the agreed upon timing, do not answer previously answered questions, but begin to address the root of such questions. Attack whatever is attacking your spouse.
6. If you are the spouse that is having trust issues, or any type of mental battle, try not to make your war your spouse's war. Ask them to pray with and for you, but don't burden them with the issue, because the war is fought by choices. You can choose to entertain those thoughts or to cast them down and pray them away. If you choose to think negatively, it is not your spouse's responsibility to bring you back into a positive state of mind. Again, these are choices that you are making, and this is a great time for you to start potty training your mind. Anytime waste wants to go out of it, don't take it to the spouse, flush it out with the WORD. When you are feeling mentally under attack, go into your quiet place (prayer closet) and pray. Take authority over any and every unclean spirit.
7. Agree upon a solution to the problem and how to prevent it from reoccurring.

Family/ Friends

"Therefore shall a man leave his father and his mother, and shall cleave unto his wife: and they shall be one flesh" (Genesis 2:24).

Again, this was a major problem in my marriage because Jean was taught differently than I was taught. He believed that family was first and foremost over everyone, including the spouse. The spouse was just an external person who made vows to get into the family. Trying to get him to see things GOD'S way was a major issue because his way of thinking was grafted in traditionally.

Over time, I have met many men and women who have told me stories about monstrous meddling in-laws. At first, I thought my issue was unique because I'd married an African man, but I found that it is a relatively common issue in American society. The difference with us, however, is we often don't tolerate a family member of ours trying to demean our spouses. Sure, you will have that friend or family member that will try to test and see how far they can go, but Americans often nip the issue before it becomes a bud. Nevertheless, I did come across a few that had blindly let their parents (namely mothers) demean their spouses initially. They would excuse the issue or just try to avoid that parent's bad side, but their spouses often fell upon the harsh brutalities of their parents' words or actions. After a while, and a lot of prayer, they would finally realize that they were out of order for letting their family member have so many rights in their marriage, and they would put them in their respective places.

Position: Everyone in your life has a position in your life. Sometimes, people have to be repositioned in your life in order to continue having a relationship with them, and other times, people have to be repositioned out of your life to discontinue having problems with them. This includes friends and family members.

Oftentimes, you will find that some family and friends will try to reposition themselves in your life. This especially happens when you have made a change to your life. When you got married or when you get married, you will find that many of the people around you will try to reposition themselves to either a lower place to get out of your spouses' way, or they will try to take the place of the spouse and reposition the spouse under them. Anytime your family member or your friend tries to place their feet in your spouse's place, it is NOT the job of the spouse to set them straight.

Because this is someone related to you, you have the responsibility to ensure that everyone knows their roles. This minimizes arguments and misconceptions. Let's say that you were having problems with your husband's mother. She keeps coming to your house at all hours of the day unannounced. To make matters worse, she brings food from her kitchen as if you weren't a good cook. You talk to your husband, and he doesn't see the big deal. The problem is you are being challenged for your position as a wife because the mother has failed to stay in her place as a mother. She instead chooses to audition for a role as a co-wife. You have talked to your husband about this, but he does nothing but try to convince you that you are being unreasonable. In such a case, you should always speak to the spouse first and let him know that this is an issue for you, and that you won't tolerate it. Be loving but firm when you tell him that this is not up for negotiations; she has to know her role in his life and stop trying to borrow a seat on your throne. Warn the spouse that you are giving him the opportunity to address the matter, but if he does not, then you will have to address her directly. Don't expect an understanding response or a positive response because the two of you do not agree about her role. His job was to inform her of her position and to refuse to deal with her in any other place but as his mother.

You have a new and more important role to fill, and that is being your spouse's spouse, which by all means is more important than your relationship with your parents. Our marriages are reminiscent of our relationships with GOD. As we grow up in HIM, we learn that no one is more important than HIM, so we learn the correct placement and role for each individual. There is an order in the Kingdom, and it has to be commanded here in the earth realm. When that order is not honored, disorder takes its place and begins to destroy our marriages.

Our friends often challenge our spouses for their position; especially when the spouse is a newbie trying to get to know you. A friend, however, has to be invited into the union per-SE to give their advice. Relatives usually do this without invitation. We unwittingly give our friends permission to become equal partners in our marriages when we open our mouths to share with them what is going on in our home. As a result, you will find many marital relationships that are slowly being ripped to shreds by the advice or presence of one of the spouses' friends.

First off, telling your friends what happens in your home isn't wise. I used to do this, and I had to learn to stop it. I would call my friends when I was raging about something my husband did or said, and they would give me good advice sometimes, and other times, they'd give me bad advice. I knew when the advice wasn't right, but I didn't have the right to contend with how they felt because I brought the issue to them, thus giving them permission to insert their own opinions. After Jean and I would reconcile, I'd be over the issue, but my friends weren't. They would ask me about the issue, how Jean was now acting, and what I was doing. There were times when I was ashamed to admit that all was well because I could hear that all was not well with them. Then, there were the times when I would openly admit that we'd talked about the issue and reconciled, and I could hear judgment and disdain for my choices on the phone line. Were they bad for not wanting me to reconcile? No. They had not invested any money, love, years, or plans into my marriage; therefore, they could not value it. I was the one being naïve in sharing my problems with them. Again, when I stopped this behavior, my marriage approval rate went up more than 75% from Jean's point of view.

People will always measure your situation from where they stand. No one can tell you how much to sell a car for if they don't know its worth. No one on the outside has invested what you have invested into your marriage; therefore, they stand to lose nothing if you lose your marriage. This is how you have to see things. If you have a friend or a family member who without reason does not like your spouse, disassociate yourself from them. People like to keep these characters around for collateral, so that if the relationship doesn't work out, they could still call on this family member or that friend. Why not just call on the LORD?

Venomous Views

Over the course of time, things happen that can't be undone, and words are spoken that can't be unsaid. We not only see our spouse's good side, but we have a front row seat to their hearts. And if it isn't clean, we get the unpleasant view and stench of what is inside. But, GOD also sees this and HE is no more pleased than you are.

When a secret service agent is hired to protect the president, he is thoroughly researched to ensure that he can be trusted. Not only must he be trusted enough to be in the president's presence, but he has to be trustworthy with any confidential information that he may come in contact with. When a secret service agent is told secrets, they take a voluntary oath to refrain from speaking what was spoken or demonstrated to them. Most secret service agents take their jobs very seriously; more seriously than most folks take their marriage vows.

When you become a husband or a wife, you are taking a vow that is not only more important than that of a secret service agent, but your vow is sacred. What you view in your own home isn't to be used against your spouse, but it has to be prayed over, prayed out (if necessary), and covered. This means that whatever you know about your spouse, you should not share with anyone else.

When Jean was in Germany and I was in the States, we were both so very deeply in love. Everything between us was perfect, and I knew no flaw in him. As human beings, we substitute what we do not know with what we desire. We like mysterious men and women so much because we get to fill in the blanks with what we want them to be. That is, until we get the unrevised formation of truth.

I would fly to Germany to be with him, and we would only get to be together for a couple of weeks to a month at a time. This made it easier for us to fall in love and stay in love because we were able to keep on our good faces. I did see things that I did not like with him, but I had bigger fish to fry. I had to go back home, so I wanted to enjoy every waking moment in peace with him, and I'm sure the feeling was mutual. Then that great and ominous day came...we moved in together. It was still really good for the first couple of weeks, but as the time passed, he took off his mask and relaxed and I did the same. The same man who had wiped my tears away when we were dating was now suddenly irritated if I looked like I was ready to cry. That man who wanted to talk about it when we were dating did not want to hear about it now that we were married. I'm sure he could point out some of my coming-out parties too. I began to see the real him and he saw the real me, and this became a problem. We had to learn to merge who we really were together, and that merger wasn't exactly without its share of issues because we were both immature. This was my second marriage and his first, so he lacked the basic survival skills of marriage, and I expected him to know better.

During this time where reality was confronted by truth, we both had ideas of what we wanted from the marriage, and we were unyielding. I wouldn't humble myself, and he wouldn't humble himself. He came from a country where women didn't argue too much with their husbands, and I came from a country where a husband knew better than to argue with his wife. So, that was an interesting mixture of personalities that came together looking for something the other did not possess. He wanted a quiet and meek woman, and I was far from that. I would often tell him that he should have done his research before he approached an American girl. I wanted a man to take the lead but to listen to my guidance as well. Of course, my way of thinking and his way of thinking was misguided because we wanted each other to be to us who we could not be for one another. The wedding bells in our heads began to sound like the bells that ring before boxers enter the ring. I wanted to win, and he had to win; so we kept losing. During this time, couples begin to develop a venomous view of one another. How you perceive your spouse isn't always the truth; it is a warped view of them based on your experience before them coupled with your experience with them. For us, our views of one another didn't change until we submitted to GOD.

Venomous views can and do come from external influences such as family, friends, co-workers, and our church leaders. In addition, we develop bad views of our spouses when we have unresolved issues, overwhelming debt, undisciplined children, and so on.

How we treat our spouses externally is a reflection of how we feel about them internally. This is why it is necessary for us to guard our own minds during the course of the marriage. I had begun to despise Jean at one point because of what I allowed to get into my heart. Sometimes, these views don't come from the spouse, but it comes from within yourself. You have the responsibility of casting your burden to the LORD; you can't cast it on the spouse because it is too heavy for them.

Venomous views can also be introduced to us by people hoping to take our spouse's place in our lives or in our bedrooms. I have met many men and women who have gone on and on about how horrible their spouses are. They talked more about divorce than restoration. When I speak to someone like this, I often wonder who is on the other end of their love. What I have found is that in 97-99% of the cases where a spouse wanted to withdraw themselves from the marriage, it was because they wanted to insert themselves into another relationship. Either they had already begun the affair, or the affair was taking place mentally, but they were hoping to transition it into the physical realm.

I remember meeting a woman who'd been fighting with her husband. She told me how she could not stand her husband, how bad of a man he was and at the end of it, and she talked about the possibility of divorce. When she was done, I asked her if there was another man in her life, and she said that there was, but they were just friends. After that, she went on to tell me how wonderful her new friend was and of all of the great things he'd done for her. Suddenly, her husband had no value to her, but the new man was invaluable. Of course, I had to tell her the truth; she was bewitched with lies. She'd fallen for the other man because the only record he had with her was spotless since she really didn't know him, but her husband's record was full of flaws. She became the problem in her marriage and she magnified every issue in the marriage because she now had an alternative to her husband. The husband felt the need to defend himself against the verbal attacks that became frequent in his home and she felt the need to remind him of how unworthy of her that he was.

Her view of her husband had been warped by her own lusts and desire to try on another relationship for size. She believed that her husband was an awful man, and her new friend was sure to point that out to her when she told him the stories of her husband's flaws. This is error.

You have to see your spouse as your soul mate. You have to see your spouse as one of the best gifts that GOD has given you. You have to see your spouse as the best decision that you have made since baptism. And this sight begins in your imagination and finds its way to your heart. Imagine what you want with them, and do not let your imagination be steered by what you have with them. GOD is able to do exceedingly and abundantly above all that we can ask or think. What if you had a diamond that you'd saved up your money to purchase? That diamond was valued at six million dollars, and you worked hard to earn the money to get that diamond, but now that you have it, it doesn't sparkle like you thought it would. One day, while walking, you drop the diamond into the grass and because it's not sparkling, it's hard to find. Would you walk away and leave that diamond for someone else to find? Of course not; you would search that grass for that diamond until you have found it. Even though it did not sparkle, it did not lose its value, nor did it take away the fact that you'd paid a great price to have it. That's how marriage works. Your spouse does not lose his or her value when they fall short. Even when they are dull and boring, they are still valuable. The key is in determining the value and finding a way to make it worth your while. You need to always recognize that you have a great spouse, and that you are blessed to have them. When you see otherwise, you begin to discount their value and you will eventually walk away and let someone discover the treasure that you once had. A mother will not stop loving her children just because they didn't take the career move that she wanted them to take. She will continue to love them no matter what decisions they make. You have to be the same way in your marriage. Marriage is not conditional, it is unconditional. Lust, however, is conditional.

To learn to love your spouse again, you need to stop taking in negativity. Oftentimes, we fill ourselves up with negativity from the music we listen to, the television we watch, our associations, and so on. Everything and everyone that communicates with us is going to affect our lives. For example, you will find that we are all either a pessimist or an optimist. A pessimist will always find the negative in a situation, but an optimist will only see the positive side of that same situation. What you allow into you will determine whether you are an optimist or a pessimist. If you have a pessimistic friend, their energy will be channeled into you every time you talk with them. It doesn't matter whether you are a leader or a follower, negativity does not discriminate. I used to have negative as well as positive friends around me, and I noticed that every time I talked to a positive person, I hung up the phone happy. My day was either made better or it remained the same in dealing with them, but anytime I talked with a negative person, I felt drained. I would become pessimistic and this changed the atmosphere in my house. It's the same with Jean. Anytime he talks to positive people, he's happy and he wants to continue in that energy, but if he's talked to a negative soul, he's drained and he will continue in that energy. As human beings, we are effectors and receptors. We are like oscillating fans wherein we take in air from the atmosphere around us, and we push it back out at a greater speed. Pay attention to yourself when you are talking with someone that is negative. You will often feel the need to show them that you can relate to their hardships. You have to reach into the negative side of your brain to make them feel comfortable with you. Negative people don't like to be around super happy people.

Your goal should be to affect the atmosphere positively, and to do this, you have to take in positivity. What I learned to do with negative people was to speak opposite of what they were speaking. If they were ranting, I would start talking about how good GOD is. What I'm doing is attacking that spirit in them or that spirit that is attached to them. I have found that people like this usually find an excuse to get off the phone when I do this, and their phone calls slowly became less and less until they were no more.

Listen to music that uplifts you, encourages you, and promotes what GOD promotes. Stay away from negative people, media, and situations. You need to change your view of life so that your life can produce better fruit for you as an individual and as a spouse. In doing so, you will cause a systematic change to occur in your marriage where you will begin to see blessings line up for you and bad things fall away from you. How you view life and how you view your spouse is a mirror reflection of what is in your heart.

Lack of Knowledge

Isn't it funny how we expect people who do not do right by GOD to do right by us? One of the reasons that they do not do right by HIM is lack of knowledge. And one of the reasons that they do not do right by you is lack of knowledge. Meaning, they simply don't know any better. Sure, the information is available to them; however, they have not accessed it. Remember, every situation that we come into, we come into as a baby, and we have to grow up in it to mature in it.
The world gets this concept. Why doesn't the church?

You go to school and you are leveled up each year. You have to learn the lessons from the grade level that you are in order to pass to the next level. Marriage is the same. We all start off as children in our marriages, and we grow up into a mature and functioning union. The difference is that with marriage, two people have to learn to grow together in order not to break apart.

Would you spank a three year old for not knowing calculus? The same measure goes behind what your spouse knows. Why are you challenging them for not doing something you know is right or for doing something you know to be wrong? No matter how many times you tell them, they have to get it. I can tell that three year old a calculus problem twenty times, and each time he'll probably laugh at me and maybe even mock me. Maybe your spouse just does not understand why you don't like something or someone. Get to the root of the issue. Sometimes, our issues are our own and do not reflect on our spouses. Some things are just pet peeves, and this isn't something the spouse needs to submit under, it is something you have to learn to get over.

Example:
Rachel hates it when Mark chews with his mouth open. Plus, Mark forgets to put the toilet seat down after he's been to the restroom. If this is not enough, Mark has a huge flatulence problem because his diet consists of too much starch and not enough proteins. After years of tolerating Mark, Rachel is now considering a divorce. Marriages have ended for far less trivial issues. What should Rachel do? First, Rachel needs to find out what is wrong with Rachel. Why does she magnify Mark's faults? Why is her love for Mark so limited, and how can she break down those limitations? In addition, she could easily initiate a home program to help Mark break those annoying habits. Rachel could create a program where Mark has to give her a dollar every time he chews with his mouth open, and she has to go along by paying Mark a dollar for every time she fails to break whatever habits she has. Because this is hitting Joe in the pockets where it hurts, it will make him more conscious about the issue. Or Rachel could get over it. In addition, Rachel can have Mark to give her $5 ever time he leaves the toilet seat up. This would make change fun for the both of them and remove the negativity surrounding it. As for the flatulence, Rachel could introduce Mark to a healthier diet by learning to cook new and healthier dishes. The plan here is to offer a sound reason or find an alternative. Make it fun and funny, and you'll both enjoy it. But, if Rachel makes it a teeth- grinding episode of anger, Mark won't participate long, and their marriage

will eventually fall apart over nothing. The objective is to build more towers of reception and stop tearing down the old ones.

Pride

Pride is always at the stem of the issue. We have learned to be competitive, recognize craftiness and resist all efforts to be made a fool of. So, when we get married, many times we use these duck-and-punch techniques with our mates, and this is the wrong thing to do. Those are worldly ways picked up in our places of pain. Instead, Romans 12:2 has the answer. *"And be not conformed to this world: but be ye transformed by the renewing of your mind, that ye may prove what is that good, and acceptable, and perfect, will of God."* You have to think differently. Your mind has to be changed before your reality agrees with it.

One of the ways to combat pride is reacting positively to a fuming spouse. Hubby and I went on a cruise in 2010, and there was a man there that would come and sit with us anytime he saw us. Anyhow, he started talking about how he battled his wife when she was raging. He said that he would just nod his head and say, "You're right, baby. I'm sorry. It won't happen again." He said that in his younger years, he would argue with her, but he learned that this was taking him nowhere, so he learned to avoid the battlegrounds by just nodding along...even though he admitted to not knowing what he was agreeing to most of the time. Anyhow, we laughed and hubby tried that on me a few times, and it really bothered me because I wanted to get to the root of the problem, fix it, and kick it out of our marriage.

Another day, we went out to a Red Lobster here, and they had a thirty minute wait, so we sat down next to another couple. They told us that they'd been married, I believe thirty years, and Jean asked them the secret to their longevity. The man looked him in the eye and said, I just agree with whatever she says. I don't argue with her; I just agree. We all laughed, and I shared my experiences about Jean doing that to me. The lady and I connected on the issue because we were both bothered by it, but both men (her husband

and my husband) agreed that the fighting was minimized by their decision to pick their battles wisely. Am I saying that you should become a doormat? No, but what I am saying is that you need to learn to review what you are about to fight about and see if it's worth it. If not, excuse yourself from the ring. I have since started doing that with Jean. If I see an argument trying to brew, I humble myself and just smile at him because the fight isn't worth entering. For example, if your husband wants to argue about you spending too much time on the Internet, it is better to talk with him and spend more time with him. I remember talking on the phone with a client one day, and her husband interrupted her to ask where his shoes were. She politely asked me to hold on, and then she began to verbally assault him. After that, she came back on the line, apologized to me, and proceeded to give me the details of her order. Was this attack necessary? No, it was rooted in something evil. Spouses can be bothersome at times, but they don't need to find ways to live inside of the four walls of our limitations; instead, we have to find ways to break down those walls.

Bitterness

People tend to try to create a healthy balance of the WORD and the world, and this just does not work because the two cannot mix. You have to overwhelm the flesh with the WORD. The root of bitterness is insanity. Again, to be insane does not mean that you are crazy in the world's sense of the word, but it means that your normal thinking patterns have been altered. A bitter spouse is a perfumed cesspool. Even their good deeds reek of attitude.

Bitterness begins to root itself in us when we are disobedient to GOD. When we enter marriage through the window, and not through the door, we come in unprepared. The window represents thievery or premature gain. The door is opened by GOD. It is very common for a believer to marry the wrong person or to marry the right person out of season. This means that they entered the marriage through the window, and if they can't endure the trials that come, they will be thrown out of that very same window.

When you see that you or your spouse are angry all the time, get to the root of the issue; don't snip the surface. You can prune the leaves off a plant, but if it isn't uprooted, it'll grow back. You need to get to the root of the issue, and the two of you should team up against Satan and all of his workers instead of teaming up with Satan against one another.

Irritable Spouse Syndrome

Is your spouse always irritable? Just plain cranky. If the wind is blowing too hard, they open their mouth to complain. If there is nothing on the television, they want to throw the remote. If they can't get their hair to act right, they are ready to break the bathroom mirror. If you forget to greet them when you wake up, it's time to suit up for war. Or, are you that spouse?

As discussed in the previous chapter, everything that grows up has a root. Sometimes that root isn't as deep as you believe it to be, and then sometimes the roots are deeper than what you believe them to be. But, whatever and wherever it is, it needs to be destroyed.

Ladies, we are particularly bad about being irritable. With fluctuating hormones, and a never-ending sense of responsibility; we don't get a lot of time to just unwind and detox from all that has gotten underneath our skin or our soul, and sometimes, we growl. But is it fair to take it out on the people we love? I do understand that the hubby has access to the most intimate details about you, including the location of that panic button on your heart. Nevertheless, your panic button shouldn't have a hair trigger. Could you imagine if the button for the atomic bomb could be pushed just by breathing on it? This world would be in dire trouble.

Many of you are extremely sensitive and emotional. If your husband is laughing too loud, you're screaming at the top of your lungs. If the children are whining, you're ready to blow their eardrums out with complaining. I have been around women who seem to get irritated just by the laughter and movement of their children, and they are usually like that towards other people. It bothers them to see someone happy. A lot of times they can tolerate a smile, but laughter is too noisy; too much playing crosses their eyes, and joy seems to send them overboard. They don't like happy people because they are not happy themselves.

Rage is a spirit. A spirit cannot enter a man or camp around that man's heart unless that spirit has something to stand on. It has to have unforgiveness as its platform, fear as its foundation, or jealousy as its walls. An irritable spouse is under demonic siege. A demon cannot possess a Christian, but a demon can build up a siege ramp of sorts around a Christian's heart if that Christian is out of the will of GOD. Therefore, that spirit did not place them in bondage; they surrendered to that spirit. GOD set us free with the blood of JESUS; nevertheless, you have to be in HIS will to enjoy this freedom. Satan's will is that you are in captivity, serving his own lusts and devils. All too often, people say that they love the LORD, but they still practice ways that are against HIM. Many are professing to be GOD'S children, but they are taking direction from Satan. Because of this many of them inherit the lifestyles, fears, and consequences that are set aside for Satan and his demons. *"So then because thou art lukewarm, and neither cold nor hot, I will spew thee out of my mouth" (Revelation 3:16).*

Marriage can be beautiful. It is a serene place, but it can have its ups and downs like everything else in life. If you have not mastered the art of forgiveness, don't put yourself or anyone else through a marriage with you because in marriage, you better know how to forgive at the drop of a hat. We absolutely-unequivocally-without hesitation have to forgive any and everyone who has hurt us. Our salvation depends on it. Why give someone continued power over your life?

GOD is love, and HE must live inside you before you can enjoy the benefits of being HIS child. Your continued irritation is demonically driven. The spirit of offense is a guarding demon, and a lying spirit stands in as the adviser to anyone who has it. The spirit of offense guards whatever platform that spirit of rage is standing on, and that lying spirit lies to its host about the motives of others. It uses these lies to convince the host to let rage come forward to handle the situation. That way, truth doesn't come in easily because when someone tries to share the truth with the person, they are offended and guarded. To be delivered, your heart has to connect with the Truth. You have to walk in the healing that GOD has given you through JESUS CHRIST. You may not believe that you have been shattered by some of the things that have happened to you, but if you are easily agitated, you have been and you're still holding on to them. *"The spirit of a man will sustain his infirmity; but a wounded spirit who can bear?" (Proverbs 18:14)*

How do you know if your spirit is broken? You will know that your spirit is broken if you keep trying to break the spirit of someone else. Hurt people hurt people. Hurt people don't like happy people.

Unforgiveness is holding on to what you should have let go of. Unforgiveness is refusing to bury the past; even though it is dead. The stench of the decay of yesterday is something you've grown accustomed to and learned to live with. Maybe you buried the past before, and another issue arose that caused you to exhume it. Whatever it is, you need to understand that when your hands are full, there is no room in them to hold anything else. That is, when you are holding onto your past, your hands are not free to grab hold of your future.

Today is the day that you can be set free by simply confessing your sins and repenting of them.
Here are a few tips:

1. Get some alone time with GOD and talk with HIM. Tell HIM what is wrong so HE can make it right. HE loves you that much. Tell HIM what you want HIM to do for you. Call out every name of every person who has hurt you, and release them to HIM in love. Don't ask HIM to harm them; ask HIM to deliver you from them, and to deliver them from their sinful ways. Ask HIM to forgive them because JESUS asked HIM to forgive you while HE was yet on the cross. HE didn't give one second to unforgiveness. Even though you may feel that you want them to be punished; forsake the flesh and put on the will of GOD. Their sins will reap their consequence, but this isn't something to celebrate or gloat about. Instead, pray that the soul comes to CHRIST.
2. Get together with your spouse and first apologize to him or her for your actions. Tell them that you have already talked to the FATHER, and now you want them to stand in agreement with you for your healing. And the two of you, pray together. *"And if one prevail against him,* ***two shall withstand him****; and a threefold cord is not quickly broken" (Ecclesiastes 4:12).*
3. Get together with your children and apologize to them. Never be the type of parent who does not admit his or her own mistakes. Your children need to understand that you are not perfect, but you are humble enough to admit your faults and seek to become a better person. Tell them that the two of you (you and your spouse) have talked with the FATHER, and now you want them to stand in agreement with you for your healing. Now come together in prayer. *"And if one prevail against him, two shall withstand him;*

and ***<u>a threefold cord is not quickly broken</u>****" (Ecclesiastes 4:12).*

4. Put together a commitment journal to chart your progress, and document any relapses or withdrawal symptoms. It is similar to being delivered from drug abuse or alcoholism because you are learning a new way to cope with life. In this book, develop a diet plan to help you get through each moment where you may begin to feel irritable.

5. Make a fun game out of it.
Every time you act cranky, you have to give the person that you are directing it at $5. What you are doing is being made consciously aware of every time you default back to this behavior. You either obey GOD and do what's right, or sacrifice a $5 bill. *"Behold, to obey is better than sacrifice..." (1 Samuel 15:22).* It doesn't matter you have to give the last of your money, and you were planning to buy a box of washing powder with it; stick with this program. It is your in house rehab. This will make you more conscious of what you are doing, and it'll serve as a reminder to you to continually come against that spirit when it's trying to find its way back into you. *"When the unclean spirit is gone out of a man, he walketh through dry places, seeking rest, and findeth none. Then he saith, I will return into my house from whence I came out; and when he is come, he findeth it empty, swept, and garnished. Then goeth he, and taketh with himself seven other spirits more wicked than himself, and they enter in and dwell there: and the last state of that man is worse than the first" (Matthew 12:43-45).*

6. Last but not least, when you want to say bad things, force yourself to say good things. Do NOT be sarcastic with your words, or you'll draw out offense in the person you are speaking to.
Example:
•Husband is at it again. He is chewing with his mouth open, and something escapes his mouth and lands on your

eyeglasses. Calm down; think rationally, and be loving. Start talking about loving things. He will correct himself, or you can give him a loving reminder.

•Wife is doing that thing with her teeth that drives you into the arms of insanity. Get up and kiss her. Tell her how beautiful she is.

What you are doing is honoring James 4:7, *"Submit yourselves therefore to God. Resist the devil, and he will flee from you."*

Memorize Romans 12:21, *"Be not overcome of evil, but overcome evil with good."* You are more than a conqueror through CHRIST JESUS. You have to win against whatever is trying to overcome you and your marriage. Do not allow the enemy to convince you that through the failure of your marriage, you will have won. You won't win doing Satan's will.

Let's learn to stand on the WORD, live in the WORD, and we will enjoy the perks of being GOD'S children.

Paranoid Activity– The Plot Thickens

One of the hardest people to live with is someone who is suspicious and argumentative. When we come home from the merciless outside world, we expect peace, love and understanding. Worse than an argumentative soul is an argumentative soul who borders on paranoia. You know the type. They have a theory about what you're doing and why you're doing it. Sometimes that foolishness they conjure up makes really good sense, even though it's not true. An example is:

Peter goes to the grocery store to buy some seasoned salt, but Trish, Peter's wife, isn't at all happy about Peter's decision to go to the store. As a matter of fact, she's been noticing that he can't seem to sit still lately. To make matters worse, she has also noticed that Peter has been a little self-conscious lately. He's been talking about going to a dentist to fix his chipped tooth, and all of a sudden he wants to lose 30 pounds.

So, Trish waits patiently for Peter to come home, all the while those thoughts of another woman are haunting her. She can see it in her mind's eye: Peter is standing in front of a woman being attentive to her lustful needs. He is giving her the same look he used to give to Trish and complimenting her with the same soul-melting words he used to say to Trish. By the time Peter comes home, he is in danger because Trish has opened up her mind for demons to insert lies into. The lies that danced in her head are just that...lies. The truth is, Peter wants to look better for Trish. He's noticed that she's been a little grumpy lately, and he's worried that she may be falling out of love with him. He looked in the mirror and decided that he did not like what he saw. Can you see how Trish is about to damage, if not destroy her marriage due to allowing paranoid activity to take place in her heart?

Many souls are like this. The stories are always all over the headlines. There was a man who thought his wife was having an affair with the Pastor. Thankfully, GOD intervened in the nick of time before he could take that Pastor's life. There were women who believed their children were demon children, so they killed them to save the world. The stories go on and on, but the root word to these stories is "believe." They believed the wrong thing, and as a result, they did the wrong thing.

Some will say that their paranoia isn't that extreme. Yes, it is because it's the same spirit. Most people who have shown extreme signs of paranoid schizophrenia were considered at one time to be minor cases. The longer that spirit is allowed to dwell in a person, the more severe their thoughts become until they become almost unbearable. The only difference between an undiagnosed case and a diagnosed case is one person is seeking treatment, while the other person is not. In addition, treatment doesn't avail much because it's all rooted in a demonic spirit. The person needs to be delivered. Some people have believed too much of that demon's lies, and these are the obvious cases. Then again, there are people who have managed to keep some normality to their thinking patterns because they don't believe everything their minds have played for them. Their paranoia is often triggered by anger, trauma, or curiosity.

Having an unsound mind isn't an issue that you should take lightly. This is one that you have to and should want to be delivered from for yourself, your spouse and your children. It is too agonizing to live in a state of mind where your thoughts seem to do more damage to your heart than your life does. To a person with this spirit, everything is a plot, a scheme, or a divisive plan to set in motion to harm them.

How does one overcome this spirit? The answer is in the scriptures. *"Submit yourselves therefore to God. Resist the devil, and he will flee from you" (James 4:7).*
You submit to GOD by obeying HIM. When those thoughts come up, you have a small window of time to make a decision. Do you cast down all evil imagination and bring your thoughts into captivity, or are you sitting there allowing them to play like a movie in your head? Your decision will decide if this day is the day that you begin to walk in your free place or if you continue to be bound. And it just doesn't stop on its own, because thoughts are the devil's way of trying to introduce a situation to us. We then have the ability to believe or not to believe what is being thrown our way. GOD has instructed us to not even allow that mental conversation to take place. *"Casting down imaginations, and every high thing that exalteth itself against the knowledge of God, and bringing into captivity every thought to the obedience of Christ" (2 Corinthians 10:5).*

The point is, everything that makes sense to you is not true. Our senses are wired to our understanding, and our understanding is wired to our hearts. This is why GOD warned us in Proverbs 3:5-7 this way: *"Trust in the LORD with all thine heart; and lean not unto thine own understanding. In all thy ways acknowledge him, and he shall direct thy paths. Be not wise in thine own eyes: fear the LORD, and depart from evil."*
GOD warns us to be not wise in our own eyes. Don't think you have the answers; don't believe yourself to be wise, but understand that you know nothing, and every wise thing that departs from you comes from the LORD. Never let evil thoughts plant seeds in your heart. Don't let one thought give birth to another one. Submit yourself to GOD and resist the devil. You have to stop giving

Satan a bed to sleep on in your heart because he is a liar, a thief and a destroyer. Whatever you allow to sit in your heart is now a third-party in your marriage.

One thing you have to understand is that, even if your spouse is in error, you are not his or her GOD. You are the spouse and there is an order of things that has to be in place before GOD will move on your behalf. Whatever problem arises in your marriage belongs to GOD. HE doesn't want you to deal with it; HE wants to deal with it.

The challenge is for you to monitor your thoughts. Think of yourself as a security guard, guarding the President. You need to check that spirit's credentials to see if it is of GOD or against HIM. What you will find is that more than half of what you were allowing to visit your understanding was not of GOD.

Builder or Demolition Worker

We all have an assigned role, but each of our assignments is supposed to come together for the building of the Kingdom. As marriage partners, we are building together. What happens when we begin to tear down our spouses? What happens when we begin to, block by block, destroy our marriages? We become demolition workers, or better yet, demon-mission workers.

I had a dog and I loved him so much, but I was worried about his state of mind when I went to work. He would be at home alone, and he would cry as I left for work. I could see his head shuffling with the curtains as he attempted to get one last glimpse of me. And he would howl and cry as I pulled off. I couldn't let him roam the whole house while I was gone because he would entertain himself by destroying my home. So I put him in an empty bedroom that I had, and I called it his room. Leaving him alone began to bother me because I couldn't stand to see him crying. I couldn't imagine what it must be like to be at home, shut up in a room for eight hours alone. That sounded too much like prison, so I went and got another dog. Both dogs were Siberian huskies, and I figured that the duo would keep one another company and the crying would stop.

With the new dog in place, I smiled as I left the house the first day, but over time, I began to notice the curtains would shuffle on both sides. Then I saw two heads and heard two howls as I left for work, and now I had two dogs that were tag teaming my home when I was away. They were working together to destroy whatever they could get their mouths on. My plan had worked somewhat. While he did seem happier and less anxious when I came home, the impact of a lunging 70 pound husky was doubled because she would join him in welcoming me home.

They were builders and they worked as a team together. Even though they would break things from time to time, I still loved them, and I couldn't punish them for being what they were. They were Siberian Huskies, and it is their nature to destroy things when they are bored. This is one of their personality traits. I'd worried about him being alone, so I went and got another dog to join our family. GOD did the same thing for you. HE was worried about you being alone, so HE blessed you with a spouse. What exactly have you been doing with the soul that HE has given you to love? Sometimes, our spouses do things that we don't like, but they are human. A person cannot be a perfect creature for you when they can't be perfect for GOD. People will make mistakes, and we have to be willing to allow them to make and learn from these mistakes. This is what builds them up, but sometimes, we tear them down in hopes of rebuilding them the way we want them to be. This is error because we are not GOD.

Ladies

"Every wise woman buildeth her house: but the foolish plucketh it down with her hands" (Proverbs 14:1). Did the scripture say **some** wise women build their house and **some** foolish women pull theirs down? No, it is written that **every** wise woman builds her house, and **every** foolish woman pulls hers down with her own hands. Notice before and after the word 'foolish' there are no words indicating that GOD is referring to a limited amount or

certain group of women. HE made it plain; foolish women tear down their own homes.

A builder builds. If the weather isn't too harsh, the builder continues to build. If the weather is extreme, a builder will take the day off.

A demolition worker tears down buildings. If the weather isn't too harsh, the worker will continue to tear down what he is hired to tear down. Demolition workers will often work in more extreme weather conditions than builders because their job isn't to make the building secure; their job is to tear it down.

What's the weather like in your marriage? Do you continue to build on rainy days? Do you know when it's time to take off and rest? When stormy weather comes, do you change your builder's hat for a demolition worker's hat? You have to choose; either you are building that marriage, or you are tearing it down. You can't be a builder and a demolition worker in your marriage. Why work hard to build it, and tear it down when the storms seem too extreme for you?

There is a season for everything. As individuals we have seasons, and as married couples, we have seasons. Every season has a purpose, and that purpose is to prepare you for the next season of your life. When the rain comes, it comes to water every living thing so that it can continue to live and continue to grow. If there were no rain, every living thing on earth would die. But, we have learned to hate bad weather and welcome good weather. Wouldn't the sun be a nightmare if there were no water to quench our thirst or wash us off when the sun was beaming down on us? The weather has purpose, and when you understand the purpose for the weather, you'll learn to dance in it no matter what the forecast is.

•Every drop of rain that pours down on your marriage is meant by the devil to rain you in, but GOD has purposed it to fill you up and sustain the life of that marriage.

•Every rumble of thunder and every flash of lightning that strikes through your marriage is intended by the devil to scare the two of you and to kill your marriage, but GOD has purposed it to power you up. And even when you feel that your power is out, let JESUS be your generator.
•Every earthquake that quakes through your marriage is assigned by the devil to rip the foundation from between you and your spouse, but GOD has assigned it to cause you to hold on to one another a little tighter.
•Every hurricane that tries to suck the life out of your marriage can be the very hurricane that GOD uses to suck the enemy out of your union, and cause you and your husband to trust in the safety of HIS arms.

GOD'S plan is to build you up; Satan's plan is to tear you down. Which plan are you participating in when you need some work done?

But, you are a builder for the kingdom of GOD. Are you building what you were called to build? Even when times are rough, the workers shouldn't be cursing one another out; they have to continue to work together or they may halt the work. If the work is halted for too long, the city may place a judgment against that structure. If this happens, the demolition workers are sent to tear down the structure since it has been exposed, and has begun to succumb to the elements.

What are you exposing your marriage to? How do you and your spouse handle times of conflict? Are you putting off working on your marriage because you don't feel like doing the work? Did you know that the enemy is drawing up a petition against you and your marriage because you have left it exposed, and it is beginning to succumb to the elements of life?

Your purpose isn't just to head up a ministry, be a mother, or even a good woman. These are all parts of who you are, but you can't cut out the part where you were anointed to be a wife. Your role as a wife is the second most important role that you have been assigned to. Your role as the servant of the MOST HIGH GOD is the first. Women often take their roles as mothers as the most important assignment, and many lose their marriages and their ministries trying to do so. When you put everything in order, GOD will cause you to be an even better mother than the women who proactively sacrifice everything for the sake of rearing up their children. Obedience is better than sacrifice. When your number one role is mommy, you leave yourself and your children exposed to the elements because you cannot protect your children like GOD can. Will you go to school with them every day? Will you dress them in bullet-proof vests and sample their food to make sure it's not poisoned? Will you bathe them for the rest of their lives to make sure they don't drown in the bathtub? This is to get you to see that you need GOD to protect them. You can only protect them from obvious danger, but you can't protect them from everything. This is why it is essential for you to trust GOD and serve your role as HIS daughter first. Purpose is your vehicle. Stay inside of it and you'll go somewhere, but if you get out of it; Satan will be waiting for you on the side of the road.

Fellows

Proverbs 12:4 says, *"A virtuous woman is a crown to her husband: but she that maketh ashamed is as rottenness in his bones."*
A crown is worn on the head; therefore, if your wife is on your back, something is wrong. But, that doesn't mean that she isn't a virtuous woman. That means that your home is not in the proper order as set up by GOD.

When a structure is being built, everything must be positioned in order for the building to be sturdy. You cannot use the roof as the floor, the foundation as the walls, and the bricks as curtains. Such is your marriage. Everything has to be in order, and GOD has given you the role to head up the project. Every issue that springs forth in your marriage, you are accountable for. You have to be aware of what comes into your marriage and what is missing from your marriage. The people that come into your life all have a part in your marriage. Everything that you bring into your home has a part in your marriage.

Think of it this way: If you had a company and you hired a CEO to head up that company, you are going to expect him to run it and prosper it, right? He should have ideas to implement, knowledge to throw around, and understanding to crown him. You wouldn't give a four-year-old the position as CEO unless you were wearing a straightjacket. You were given the role as CEO of your marriage, and now you need to run and prosper that marriage. When you took on the role of husband, you were in the same way saying that you were old enough to head up a marriage union. Now, you have to prove yourself worthy.

JESUS is your head and you are to be the head of your wife. That is, you are led by JESUS. When this order is carried out, Satan couldn't break into your home if he tried. He has to ask for permission to come in, and he does this by introducing contention to you and your wife.

JESUS is the Architect, you are the builder, and your wife is your assistant. In order for that building to come together in beauty and strength, you have to follow the plan of the Architect, or you may end up with a structure that looks nothing like what's in GOD'S plan.

At HIS own expense, GOD sent HIS SON and the plan was given into your hands to carry out. HE gave you the tools, HE made the knowledge available to you, and HE sent you a helpmate. Are you building what HE has asked you to build, or have you developed your own plans?

Every woman wants a man to lead her, but he must be able to fulfill the role of a leader in CHRIST. I don't care how independent-minded she is now; she wasn't created that way, she became that way. As her husband, you should lead her by following CHRIST. However, when you begin to follow yourself, your friends, or any human being for that matter, you become a demolition worker in your marriage. On sunny days, you're building your marriage, but on rainy days, you're tearing down that marriage. When the sunny days come back around, you're starting over again and wondering why your structure isn't completed yet. To be a leader, you have to follow an even bigger leader. Whenever you follow a person, you are following whatsoever that person is following. So, if they are following a demon straight to the pits of hell, you are walking hand-in-hand with them. When you set your sights on man, you limit your potential, but when you set your sights on CHRIST, your potential is limitless.

Your wife should never disrespect you. She should love and honor you, but you have to love and honor the LORD. You have purpose and she has purpose. Let's go back to the story of the fig tree. Matthew 21:19 reads, *"And when HE saw a fig tree in the way, HE came to it, and found nothing thereon, but leaves only, and said unto it, Let no fruit grow on thee henceforward for ever. And presently the fig tree withered away."* What just happened here? Why did JESUS curse the fig tree? The season of harvest was upon it, but that fig tree was not operating as it should. It was not yielding any fruit. What about you and your house? You are a fruit bearing tree, but what kind of fruit are you bearing? What grows up for you is evidence of what is growing up inside of you. That's why you should learn to spread your leaves out and praise GOD in the rain. Could you imagine what would happen if a flower used an umbrella during the rain? The ground around it would dry up and that flower would die.

You better build.

•When you are building something, sometimes you'll hit your fingers with the hammer. As much as it hurts, the building must go on.

•Your wife needs you to head up the home. Your children need you to head up the home. But when the head starts acting like a butt, most of what comes out of your mouth is worthy of flushing. Learn when to speak and when to listen. A great leader doesn't always ask for service, but a great leader serves. *"After that he poureth water into a bason, and began to wash the disciples' feet, and to wipe them with the towel wherewith he was girded" (John 13:5).*

•Every marriage gets its share of seasons. If you fail to plant seed in the season of sowing, the only thing you'll find during the season of harvest is weeds.

•Love covers a multitude of sins. If you love her, you will forgive her. If you forgive her, GOD will forgive you. Even if today seems bad, you're still alive to make it better.

•If the building is not coming together properly, you are responsible. *"For unto whomsoever much is given, of him shall be much required" (Luke 12:48).* You were given a greater role in that marriage. It doesn't matter if you married her when you were a sinner, and now that you're saved she keeps tearing down what you are trying to build up. That is the consequence of disobedience. Now, your job is to win that soul for the LORD and to continue to build for HIM. HE will deal with her as HE sees fit.

A great leader isn't brought in to dictate. He comes to lead. So, don't confuse your role and think that your wife is supposed to serve your flesh. She is called to serve the LORD, so if you are being headed up by the LORD, she has to follow your every step because in doing so, she is following CHRIST. But, if you are being led by the devil, no woman wants to or has to follow you to hell. Remember, follow the plan and the building will come together properly. You don't have to develop strategies when being led by the HOLY SPIRIT. You only need to listen to HIM and obey HIM and all else will have to take its place.

Husband and Wife

You don't have to agree that you will never argue, but you should agree to always build no matter what. Divorce is so popular in the United States because it provides an alternative to doing the work. We like to abandon our assignments, void our contracts, and start building elsewhere. Then, when we get into other marriages, we discover that there is work to be done; sometimes more than what was in the first marriage.

Most of us know at least one person that is always at the altar, or at divorce court. They are married one minute, divorced the next, and then remarried again. They keep looking back at their previous marriages and then defaulting to the behaviors that destroyed those previous unions. Suddenly, you find them at the store without their spouse and learn that they are going through yet another divorce. But there's always someone with them waiting on the ink to dry on the divorce papers so they can take their shot at taming that lion. These souls have no building knowledge, no love, no long-suffering, and no loyalty. They don't want to build because they don't like doing the work. They look for already established structures that they can move into, but anytime they are presented with work, they want to void the contract and start a new one somewhere else.

The two of you need to agree to build together.
Wife, allow your husband to be the head that GOD assigned him to be. Just trust GOD with him. We are the weaker vessel and our high strung emotions prove it. I know that men can be impulsive creatures, making rash decisions, and causing unnecessary delays, but GOD made him in a way that he is to learn from his mistakes. If you are there constantly reminding him that he is a failure, how can you expect him to ever be the winner that you so want? There is life in your tongue. Use it to speak life over him. Use it to speak him into place.
Husband, listen to your wife. A good leader understands that he doesn't know everything. There were a lot of instances where I tried to warn Jean about something, but he didn't listen, and he found out that I was right all along. But I also learned to not beat him across the head with it. Just advise him and let him be. Your wives are called helpmates for a reason. Even though you are the head of that marriage, your wife is the neck and she can turn you in the right direction if you trust the GOD in her. A great leader pays attention to those he leads.

Control– Demons On the Freeway

All the control in the world could not control a person who wants to be free. Your questions won't change them; your tears won't change them; begging won't change them; your fist won't change them, and your gun won't change them. No matter what you do, if they have something in their sights that they want to go after, they were gifted with free-will, and they will utilize their free will because they can. You simply have a choice: Accept who and what they are, turn them completely over to the LORD, or walk away from them completely. GOD will deal with the spouse when they are wrong, and you have submitted them as a burden to HIM. *"Cast your burden upon the LORD, and he shall sustain you: he shall never permit the righteous to be moved" (Psalm 55:22).* We often look at that scripture religiously and associate the word "burden" with any non-human problem that we are having. When we have problems with our spouses, however, we often try to tear down the burden and then we wonder why our prayers are returning to us void. GOD said that HIS WORD would never return to HIM void. This means that if you want HIM to work out your issue, you have to submit it to HIS WORD, and let HIM work it out. Again, we often fail at this because when we are hurting, we want right-now solutions, and waiting on GOD does test our faith and long-suffering.

GOD hates a divorce so HE will deal with them as HE sees fit, but you have to submit to HIM to partake in HIS blessing. Again, HE has given them free-will, so after HE has warned them; they will then choose if they want to honor and do right by HIM, or if they choose to continue in their sin. HIS way has a 100% satisfaction guarantee for the believer. Even if they choose to continue sinning against you, HE has a special way to get their attention, and rip away whatever has been causing them to err. HE is the GOD of a second chance, and HE is a forgiving GOD; so if your mate is willing to change, honor your FATHER by giving them a second chance. Either way, you have to forgive them. Control won't control the issue because trying to control another human being is a blatant disregard for who HE is, and it is a form of witchcraft.

A controlling person is controlled by something evil. Maybe it's something in their past that hurt them, and they are steering the lives of others to make sure that they don't have to go through that again. But this is selfish behavior. They had to be hurt so they could learn to stop leaning to their own understanding. They had to learn to depend on GOD, and not their own wiles and devices. Trials and tribulations come to kill our flesh; not us. You are not that big chunk of meat that you see in the mirror. Your flesh is your earthly address, but when you change addresses your old location rots. And when it does, it stinks. This is just to help you understand that if you're being led by it and not GOD, you are walking in death and your actions stink to GOD.

I came to understand that when I was a controller, it was because my past was controlling me. I was trying so hard to defeat my demons by not allowing anyone else to lead me or hurt me, and this simply does not work. I needed deliverance, and when I got it, I began to fully understand just how messed up I was and what drove me there. The bible is a map, and those who refuse to pick it up will not know the **Way**. *"Jesus saith unto him, I am the way, the truth, and the life: no man cometh unto the Father, but by me"*

(John 14:6). Knowing **of** the Way and knowing the Way are two different things. I know of Albert Einstein and his reported brilliance, but I've never met the guy to make my own assessment. Therefore, I would have to gather a report on him and determine if what others are saying is believable, or if I deem it unbelievable. This works the same with GOD. Knowing *of* HIM is simply getting another person's account and opinion of HIM, but *knowing* HIM is having your own personal relationship with HIM and your own knowledge of HIM based on that relationship. Knowing HIM is intimacy. You cannot say you know the LORD if you don't know HIS ways. You cannot say that you know the LORD if all you know are a few bible scriptures and bible stories.

Behind every controlling person is the spirit of fear, a spirit of idolatry, or both. For example, men that are possessive and want to know their wives' every move often live in fear of being abandoned, and if they have ever had a taste of the power that comes with control, they are like animals that have tasted human blood. They will always come back for more. This also births a deadly chain reaction, because power is more addictive than any drug on the market. When one tries to remove it from a person who is accustomed to being drunk by it, they put themselves in danger because to the controller, whomever he or she controls is his or her piece of property.

Have you noticed that most women who were killed by their husbands were controlled by their husbands for most of their marriage? The moment she tried to free herself, she was killed. Why is that? Every demon that enters a person is standing on a foundation of disobedience. There was an access door open to his heart, and it served as a gateway for demonic activity. When someone begins to control and instill fear in another person, they become dependent upon that person. Because power is intoxicating. Power is addictive, and it is their drug of choice. It gives the person a false sense of security, and at the same time, it keeps them from ever wanting to come near deliverance. Fear of abandonment is gut-wrenching, and fear of uncertainty is overwhelming. A spouse does not have to hate you to want you dead. A person can love you, but his or her fear of losing control of you may be greater than their love for you. A lot of women put themselves in harm's way because they believe or believed their husband's controlling behavior to be evidence of his love when it is not. It is evidence of his pain; it is evidence of his self-worship, and it is evidence of the existence of fear in him. This is how two incomplete people break one another down. In this case, he becomes dependent upon her for power, and he begins to equate power with love. Anytime he feels himself losing control, he goes crazy and uses every device he can utilize to regain it. In the wife's case, she is now dependent upon him for what she perceives as love and direction. No matter what anyone says, or how much he beats her, in her understanding, he loves her, but she just needs to change.

In addition, there have been plenty of men who have lost their lives at the hands of their wives. In many cases, their deaths were the result of a power struggle or a transfer of power. The wives simply got used to ordering their husbands around, and they became dependent on this power to sustain a relaxed state of mind. They drew their strength from their husbands' weakness, and when he got tired of it and decided to leave, the controller did not know what to do to regain control.

Our heart is a freeway. Traffic comes in, and traffic goes out. We are instructed to guard our hearts to ward off every attempted attack or attachment by the enemy.
Your heart is protected or exposed by whatever is in it. If the WORD is in you, when a lie comes, the Truth will come forward to battle with and execute it. If evil is in you, when the Truth comes, evil will rise up to battle with HIM. One of the easiest ways to find out what is in you is to pay attention to how you feel, how you act, and how you react when trials and tribulations are upon you. Let me illustrate.

Those that have the Heart of GOD will have:	**Demonically Infected Heart**
WORD of GOD	Ungodliness
Long-Suffering	Short Tempered/ Little to No Patience
Truth	Lies
Knowledge	Lack of Knowledge
Prudence	Impulsiveness
Patience	Anxious/ Anxiety
Humble (Meekness)	Haughty (Prideful)
Virtuous	Immorality
Joyful	Anger/ Bitterness
Love	Hate

When we are born, we are like new iPods. As we begin to live, we will allow life to download new ways to view life. This is in addition to the generational curses or generational gifts that we have. For example, there are some families that have the gift of song. Everyone in that family can sing. That is their gift, and it is shared in their bloodline. Then again, there are the families where the individuals are born with generational curses. For example, you will see some families where everyone, or just about everyone in that family, has a chemical dependency. It is easier for the offspring of an alcoholic to become alcoholics because they are dealing with the very same demons that their parent(s) are dealing with or have dealt with. Again, the heart is like a freeway, and when it is not guarded by the WORD of GOD, it is open to all kinds of traffic. In addition, our environments play a major factor in what we trust to come in. So, if your mother loved to gossip, chances are you will become a gossip.

When we come to CHRIST, we come to HIM like a newborn baby.

We are born again in HIM. And we have to get the WORD of GOD in us so that we can begin to enjoy, explore, and apply the knowledge HE has availed to us. However, when there is little or no WORD in us, we allow replacements to come in and set up shop.

How is one set free from such a cursed spirit? *"If my people, which are called by my name, shall humble themselves, and pray, and seek my face, and turn from their wicked ways; then will I hear from heaven, and will forgive their sin, and will heal their land" (2 Chronicles 7:14).*
1. Humble Yourself.
2. Pray.
3. Seek the Face of the LORD.
4. Repent.
5. Receive your healing. (Believe to receive.)

First, you have to want to be free. Pride breeds quarrels. That's why you have to walk in lowliness.
Prayer works. Prayer is talking to the FATHER. HE wants to hear from you. What is your problem? What is your confession? Do you understand that you did wrong, or are you walking around in denial? Confession is important to HIM because this shows HIM that you acknowledge and understand your wrongs. Someone who does not confess does not always understand that they were wrong, or they are too proud to admit their faults. In this case, they will continue to commit these very same sins against the LORD. It's why our court systems give a lower sentence to someone who pleads guilty than someone who has to be found guilty.

Control is manipulation, and it roots itself in the most powerful form of witchcraft available to man. This is because the controller often has personal access to the person or people that they are controlling. When a person loses control of their life, they are like hungry souls without a vehicle. Because they have crashed their vehicle into their choices, they often try to hijack the vehicles of others. They do this by manipulating a person with kindness, using pity, intimidating a person, or threatening a person. This is done to gain access to that person's vehicle, and that vehicle is their heart.

When a person is controlling, their heart is rooted in a wicked place. This is a demonic place where their thoughts are steered, and their mind is constantly under attack as new demonic drivers attempt to get behind their life's wheel or will. GOD gave us free-will so that we can make our own choices, make our own mistakes, and become individually whole again. When someone tries to control another person, they are in the same trying to hijack the will of that person, so that they can get behind the wheel in that person's head. A spouse that is controlling is dangerous because they have continued access to the person or the people they are trying to control. They will often use differing devices of control and manipulation to try to get the person to relinquish their free-will to them. A controlling person doesn't care if you make a choice, as long as it lines up with the choices that they would have made or would want you to make. Their hearts are wicked because they are trying to steal something from you that GOD has given to you. Their life's vehicle is parked in the realm of devils where it is often taken for joy rides. Sure, they are allowed to make the choices that they make, but their belief system has been rewired. They believe that this person or that person is out to hurt them, or if allowed, will hurt them. They believe that their choices are better and safer than the choices of others. They believe that others are inferior to them. Even the most intelligent of their followers is redefined by them, and made to believe that they need them in order to gain access to happiness or the things they want in life.

What should you do if you are that controlling spouse?

1. Repent, and ask the LORD to change you.
2. Visit the root of that control, and ask the LORD to uproot it.
3. Be more conscious of the things you do and the things you say. When you see that you are being controlling,

apologize to the person whose mind you are trying to access, and tell them to make whatever choice they feel is better suited for them.

4. Ask your spouse and your children to make you aware of the times that you are being controlling, and when this happens, to come together with you in prayer. (P.S. Let them be the ones to pray for you because, until you are delivered, you may use prayer as a means of control, and this is undiluted wickedness. Don't play with GOD.)
5. Denounce the sin itself, and denounce every demon associated with the sin.
6. Ask your spouse if you can share the stories with them that have hurt you the most and made you who you are. Sometimes, you need to release before you receive.
7. Seek wise counsel from your Pastor or whomever GOD sends you to.
8. Never give in to the urge to control someone. Sometimes it will feel like certain situations need to be controlled, but life is not designed that way. People are given free-will for a reason. Let them utilize their own free-will.

What should you do if your spouse is controlling?

1. Make them aware of their controlling ways, tell them that you forgive them, and ask them to join you in prayer to come against it.
2. Develop a fun program that you and your spouse can participate in to come against those ways. For example, every time that spouse tries to control a situation after you have given your opinion, they have to give $20 to the charity of your choice. This way, they are being helped, all the while helping someone else.
3. Make them conscious about their controlling ways anytime they relapse, but don't do this in an angry fashion. You can buy some index cards and carry 10 of them (or more)

around on you. On these index cards, write the words, "You are being controlling again. It's time for prayer." Anytime they start attempting to control you or others, hand them this card and ask them to come into a quiet room with you to pray against you.

4. Confess your sins and repent of them as well. People tend to humble themselves faster around others who have humbled themselves.
5. When they tell you their stories of hurt and betrayal, encourage them and show them how they are victorious over these situations.
6. Seek wise counsel for them.
7. Never submit to their control because in doing so, you are feeding their demons. A demon needs a "yes" to proceed, but a "no" will cause it to puff up. When you see it start puffing up, deflate it with prayer.
8. Always make the controller positively aware of their progress. Celebrate them any and every time they walk away from situations (with a smile and no hard feelings) that they could not control.
9. Anoint the doors of your house and declare that every demonic force that has once had access to it is now bound and cast into the abyss to be held there until the day of Judgment. Your mouth has a sword in it, and that sword is called a tongue. It can be an evil sword when controlled by an evil heart, or it can be a yoke-destroying sword when controlled by a righteous heart.

The Voices of Contention

Our mind is a battlefield, where good and evil fight it out for control over our heart. What is in our heart stands its ground to wrestle with whatever has introduced itself to our minds. If there is no or little WORD in your heart, then you don't have a big army to fight with. You may overcome a few imps, but when the big boys come, you're in trouble.

Many souls have no unction to get up and read their bibles, and because of this, they keep getting beat on every side. Prayer requires faith, faith comes by hearing, and hearing by the WORD of GOD. Faith without works is dead. How can one have faith, or believe FATHER at what HE says, if they don't know what HE says? Again, when Satan tempted JESUS, JESUS answered him with, "It is written..." But, the sad part of this day is there are so many people who are not only married to their spouses, but they are married to their ignorance, and because they refuse to get a hold of knowledge and commit to it, they are perishing! *"My people are destroyed for lack of knowledge: because you have rejected knowledge, I will also reject you, that you shall be no priest to me: because you have forgotten the law of your God, I will also forget your children" (Hosea 4:6).* Knowledge is a necessity. Asking GOD to change your situation without any desire of knowing HIM is like asking your boss for a paycheck without you learning the tools at work. Sure, you may show up on time and when scheduled, but you don't know how to work the machinery, so your boss has to keep coming out to help you out. This wastes his time and the company's money.

Sometimes we wrestle with our thoughts and again, this is a process that has to be mastered before we even consider being someone's husband or wife. Nevertheless, there are many in marriages who married first, and now they are fighting with their thoughts and fighting with their spouses. Evil thoughts come to ALL of us; none of us are immune to them. Even King David had this issue and cried out to the LORD. *"How long must I wrestle with my thoughts and every day have sorrow in my heart? How long will my enemy triumph over me?" (Psalms 13:2-NIV)* FATHER instructed us in 2 Corinthians 10:5, *"Casting down imaginations, and every high thing that exalteth itself against the knowledge of God, and bringing into captivity every thought to the obedience of Christ."* You are the judge of your imagination, and there are many evils and goods that will come before you to audition for a role in your life. The bible tells us to cast down every high thing that **exalts itself against** the knowledge of GOD. What is the knowledge of GOD? The knowledge of GOD is the WORD of GOD. If you don't have the knowledge, how do you know how to judge what is good and what is evil? Evil doesn't always look, feel, or taste evil initially.

But, the thoughts do come, and sometimes they make sense. That's the reason you honor Proverbs 3:5, *"Trust in the LORD with all your heart; and lean not unto your own understanding."* Our understanding is rooted in our flesh, and our emotions are our flesh's response to what is in our imaginations or in our heart. When we challenge every thought with the WORD of GOD, anything not found to be from HIM will have to admit it is a lie.

But, when we challenge our spouse instead, we have chosen to go with our flesh and oppose our spouses. Chaos will then begin receiving mail at your address because it will be living there. You want to evict it? Evict the thoughts, purge your heart from all wickedness, and allow the LORD to transform you, instead of you being formed by every thought that proceeds past your imagination and straight into your heart. The problem isn't always your spouse; the problem many times is you choosing to fight against the person and not against your own personal thoughts.

Review this situation: Dan has been quiet lately, and he seems uninvolved and distant. Something is obviously wrong. Beth gets upset and begins to accuse Dan of wanting to get out of the marriage but just being afraid to tell her. She then goes on to tell Dan the scenario:
"You are coming home later! You haven't touched me in months! I have noticed that you don't want to eat my cooking too much anymore! You seem so inattentive to me, almost as if I am annoying you!
When I asked you if something was wrong, you said no, but I see that you're changing!"
What Beth didn't know was that for months, Dan had been on probation at his job because of a project his team failed to complete, and now they are talking about firing Dan. Dan has been working late hours to get everything back on track. He has been stressed, and even when he is at home, his mind is at the office. He didn't want Beth to know because he did not want to stress her out, and he did not want her to further stress him about the issue.

Do you see how an innocent situation became a full-blown crime scene in Beth's heart? Instead, Beth could have handled the situation like this: Dan comes home late often, and he is sad and depressed. He is inattentive and seemingly on the edge. He doesn't want to eat much and he's not touching her. Beth should have noticed that something is wrong. She should never allow the voices in her head to sit there and stagnate in her head. Beth

should have:
•Prayed with her husband.
•Prayed for her husband.
•Purchased a gift for her husband. Maybe his favorite shoes or a new watch.
•Taken Dan out to eat or out for a walk. Sometimes a change in the scenery will help us to unwind and release what is in our hearts. Avoid crowded places because a stressed out man or woman has a crowd of thoughts and will not do well in crowded places. Try a nice afternoon walk on the beach or a picnic at the park.
•When he shows annoyance, kiss him on the cheek, say "I love you," and leave him alone. He has a lot on his mind.
•Write Dan a love note. Do not write ANYTHING about his attitude or ways, but just a love note detailing how she loves him and how he has played a role in her life. Just write a short love letter or poem (original, please).
•Remind Dan that he can talk to her. "Dan, even if I don't have the answers to your problems, I could at least pray for you, and call those problems out by name and see you through."
•Invite laughter in. You don't realize how soothing laughter is.
•If Dan snarls, growls, or yells at Beth; she shouldn't take it personal. Instead, do something nice for him.

Why should you do something nice for him or her when they are acting like they don't have the sense the good LORD gave them? In the application of the knowledge of GOD, you will change the atmosphere and the situation. *"For where envying and strife is, there is confusion and every evil work" (James 3:16).*

The first step of course, is getting the strife out; don't let it in. Keep out confusion; these are intruders. Next, *"Submit yourselves therefore to God. Resist the devil, and he will flee from you" (James 4:7).* James is instructing us to submit; that is, adhere, obey, and will yourself to the will of GOD. Resisting the devil means to not be for him or his purpose, but to be against him. Don't act or react the way he wants you to do, instead, interact in love. In doing so, the devil will flee from you. When you do this, you are no longer turning to confront your spouse, but you are now confronting the instigator, the devil himself. When we bring love into an atmosphere where strife is, strife will attempt to war with it, but because love never fails, strife and its demons will flee. You break it in pieces by submitting to the will of GOD and not the will of your flesh or that devil that's trying to engage your flesh. Do you know how much power "I love you" has? Not just the words, but the actions? When a man or woman is **mad**, their mind is at war; don't you dare arm yourself to war with them as well. You become an enemy by doing so. Instead, join them on the battlefield by loving them, encouraging them, and being there for them despite how they act.

One such day for me came when Jean and I had been arguing. I was frustrated with him for being so engaged with his job. I felt that he was allowing them to make a fool out of him. I wasn't coming against what I thought or how I felt; instead, I challenged him. The argument intensified so much that he got his pillow and one of the comforters, and he went to sleep in our extra bedroom. This had never happened before, but that night, I was so upset that I was happy he didn't sleep in the same bed as me. The next morning, the atmosphere was still the same. When we were forced to interact for common things, he was being snippy and so was I. He even took his plate into the extra bedroom to avoid eating with me.

I decided to go into a different atmosphere (instead of changing the atmosphere in my home). So I went to Office Depot. I took my time carousing the aisles, looking at just about everything Office Depot was selling. As I passed down one aisle, I saw this typing software. It is an instruction program teaching people how to type. I remembered how Jean was always talking about how he wished he could type like me. The LORD told me to get the CD for HIM, and this is when the battle began in my heart. I thought to myself, "I'm not buying him nothing! He wants to act like that, and I'm supposed to reward his behavior?" I could hear the LORD nudging me to get it. HE said, "Get that CD for your husband. If you weren't mad at him, you'd get it. You shouldn't be mad at him anyway." So, I was in the middle of Office Depot in a spiritual battle because my flesh was telling me to drag this war out between me and Jean, but the LORD was telling me to get it. I stood there for a while, walked off, but kept coming back to it. I felt like a child in the store having a temper tantrum. "Why should I get this for him when he's at home acting like a three-year-old?" Nevertheless, I knew that with the LORD, one can't fall out in the middle of the store crying and kicking their feet, so I picked up the CD and headed for the register.

When I arrived home with the CD, I tried to open the bedroom door to give it to him, but he'd locked the door. I knocked on the door and he sternly asked me, "What do you want?!" I could feel my flesh wanting to answer him. I wanted to kick down the door in and cut him with the CD, but instead, I asked him to open the door. Now, again, my flesh was quaking, so I was in another mental war standing at that door. Again, he asked me what I wanted in an unfriendly tone. After convincing him to open the door, I handed him the software. The venom in his voice was still evident, "What is this?!" His accent made me think of how some cultures on his home continent oppressed women. Does he think I'm one of them? Does he think he can talk to me that way? I explained to him that the CD was software that teaches people how to type. I could still see the frown lines on his face as he stared at the box and asked me, "How much did this cost?!" I told him and he ferociously snarled that he would give me my money back. This was a moment that the flesh was screaming for me to handle him. I could hear my flesh screaming, "Don't let him talk to you like that! Who does he think he is? King? And I'm one of his royal and not so favored concubines who forgot to wipe the milk off his face during his morning cereal buffet? But I answered as the LORD would have me, resisting the devil and my flesh. "I don't want any money. I just bought it for you. I don't want anything." At that, he retreated back into the room for about 20 minutes; left to be indignant with himself. I wasn't arguing with him anymore. I wasn't going wit for wit with him. I was acting like a child of GOD. After about 20 minutes or less, I saw him coming out of the room, carrying his pillow back to our room and the atmosphere was so much better. Was I a fool? My pride said yes, but GOD said no. I was acting like a woman of the LORD. Less than an hour later, the atmosphere was peaceful enough where we had a talk about the issue and decided on a better way to handle it in the future.

This is a common scene amongst married folks. We get upset with one another and flesh brings pride to the mixer. The way to overcome pride is by simply doing opposite of what it says. When pride says one thing, we need to do the opposite. When hubby is puffy, I deflate him with a kiss to the forehead. You may not see immediate results, but you will feel an immediate shift in the atmosphere. Don't give way to the thoughts. When I'm rounding that 28 day corner of womanhood, Jean doesn't mind saying, "I'm not angry with you because I know it's almost time for your woman's thing. So, I love you and I forgive you."

Remember, don't entertain the thoughts! When something is entertained, it doesn't want to leave. You bore contention and every devil associated with it. Stop believing that by not arguing you are allowing the spouse to continue in their games. You can't control an adult, and you can't grow up a grown man or woman. Instead of using tactics, try communication. Communication is a sowing of a seed. You may not see the results immediately because the season has to come upon it, but you simply tell your spouse what it is that you want, do not want, and the reason why. **Why** is important in slaying other reasoning that may be plaguing the spouse's mind, in case they haven't learned to cast down evil thoughts.

Due Benevolence: Why 'No' Is Not a Bad Word

One of the reasons marriage is now being viewed as a death sentence is largely due to the fact that many women (and some men) get married and completely shut down in the lovemaking department. This implication obviously suggests that many couples engaged in a sexual relationship before marriage, but after the ceremony, one or both parties decided to become celibate and only save themselves for a happy day. Of course, you know that sex before marriage is sin, and it opens the door for Satan to enter the relationship. Nevertheless, many Christians engage in fornication because they believe that the person they are fornicating with will someday become their spouse. Once they are married, they decide to withhold themselves, and this is error.

Every one of us has a destination marked out in our minds. When we arrive at this place, we feel that we have really arrived at our life's purpose. Many people desire to become married, and they pursue this desire with vigor, but once they become married, they don't want to do the work of a marriage partner. They wanted the title of husband, wife, mother, and father, but they did not want the responsibility of either title. One of the reasons we have to consult the LORD about our potential marriage partner is we need to know if this is the person that GOD has chosen for us. If you wait until your feelings are involved to consult the LORD, you will not want to listen to HIM and end the relationshp.

There are many souls whose highest goal is to marry and have children. When they've arrived at this place, they are content. And this is when the sex stops. That partner's mental GPS is saying they have arrived at their destination. Of course, this is wrong, and it does lead to extra-marital affairs. 1 Corinthians 7:3-5 reads, *"Let the husband render unto the wife due benevolence: and likewise also the wife unto the husband. The wife hath not power of her own body, but the husband: and likewise also the husband hath not power of his own body, but the wife. Defraud ye not one the other, except it be with consent for a time, that ye may give yourselves to fasting and prayer; and come together again, that Satan tempt you not for your incontinency."*

The scriptures warn us that we do not have power over our own bodies, but our spouses do. The scriptures tells us to not defraud one another except it be with **consent** that you may fast and pray. Ladies, I have to take you off into this corner of conversation because, even though this does happen with men, this is a major problem for many of you. You're tired because you've been up all day helping the children with their homework, cooking breakfast, supper, and dinner, and so on. In a way, many of you have begun to inwardly resent your husbands because of this. You feel that you are not being fairly treated. So you decide to take away from him what you feel he has to earn. How can one earn wages that they have already worked for? This is where a breakdown of communication leads to other issues. Because you have the power to withhold yourself doesn't mean you should use it. Most men are very much like children to us because we are nurturers. And many of the same programs we initiate with our children to encourage good behavior are also effective with our husbands. For example, when our children do well, we reward them and when they are wrong, we discipline them. Now, discipline can be anything from a punishment to a spanking. Now, of course, we can't turn our husbands across our laps and spank them, and we can't take away their remote control, but we can discipline them by talking to them. To discipline means to correct. I know that many of you have already tried again and again to speak to your husbands, but to no avail, and this may have burned a hole in your marriage. But, having a sexless union won't solve the problem; it'll only create new ones. According to the scripture we just read, Satan tempts us because of our incontinency! So, you are being advised to fortify that area of your marriage so that Satan won't have that to use against you in a court of reason.

But, how do you get the husband to listen and make the necessary changes? The answer is in the WORD of GOD. *"Likewise, ye wives, be in subjection to your own husbands; that, if any obey not the word, they also may without the word be won by the conversation of the wives; While they behold your chaste conversation coupled with fear. Whose adorning let it not be that outward adorning of plaiting the hair, and of wearing of gold, or of putting on of apparel; But let it be the hidden man of the heart, in that which is not corruptible, even the ornament of a meek and quiet spirit, which is in the sight of God of great price. For after this manner in the old time the holy women also, who trusted in God, adorned themselves, being in subjection unto their own husbands: Even as Sara obeyed Abraham, calling him lord: whose daughters ye are, as long as ye do well, and are not afraid with any amazement" (1 Peter 3:1-6).* Be in subjection, and stop rebelling against GOD'S order. Your flesh will tell you that you **and** your husband are both the head of your house, but this is impossible; a two-headed man is divided in his thoughts. Man is the head of the home and the wife is the body. The head cannot operate with the body and likewise, the body cannot operate without the head. Subjection doesn't mean to kneel down and obey him like a happy canine at snack time. Subjection means to allow him to lead, and trust that CHRIST will lead him. Subjection is a word of will.

Let's say that you and the husband decide to write a book together. You agree that he'll come up with the book's name and topics, while you work on the content of the book. When he submits to you the book's title and topics, they are all wrong. They don't go with the content at all and he's insistent on keeping them. It took him a whole hour to come up with those topics, and another hour for the title of that book. After all, you both mutually agreed on which roles you would play in the book's making. Whatever should you do? Should you scream until you shatter his eardrums? Should you cry and throw a pity party for yourself until he sees how miserable you are? No. You simply add more details to fit his headers. Therefore, if you were writing a book on marriage, and he decided to give each chapter sports titles; why not try relating marriage to sports? That way you'd win over the male audience, and at the same time give your new book a unique edge. All too often, we have great opportunities to unite and create powerful products and services; but we get so caught up in what we want as an individual that we fail to see the big picture.

This concept is the same when being in subjection to our husbands. He wants to invite his friends over? Those same friends who you do not like and believe to be a bad influence on him? Why change his mind when you can change the atmosphere in your home? Invite your bible study friends over and turn it into a gathering of the saints. Of course, FATHER said where two are gathered in HIS Name, there HE is in the midst. Do you not understand that if FATHER is there, those devils will flee? It really works. When someone comes to your home that is not serving the LORD, simply invite GOD. Your atmosphere won't be an atmosphere that they are accustomed to; therefore, they will feel uncomfortable and leave. On a lighter note, you shouldn't be marrying a worldly man anyway or you WILL see issues where you want to serve the LORD, and he wants to serve himself.

One of the scriptures that you will find throughout this book is

James 4:7, *"Submit yourselves therefore to God. Resist the devil, and he will flee from you."* This is a key scripture in helping you to understand how to get the devil's hands off your marriage, and this scripture will teach you how to save time. As spouses, we spend too much time fighting one another and trying to change our situations, when all we had to do was to submit to GOD'S way and everything would have lined up perfectly.

If your husband has a habit of waking you up at three o'clock in the morning knowing that you have to go to work at seven in the morning; should you say no? Of course not. It is better to submit to your husband so he can go back to sleep than to withhold yourself from him. Another way to combat this is by coming to bed early and initiating the session before he goes to sleep, and if he's asleep, wake him up! You'd wake up an infant in midday to keep him or her from staying awake all night long, so it's not a bad idea to awaken a man who believes the midnight hour is mating season. You have to understand that his mind has to be changed. He may view midnight as a romantic time; nevertheless, you don't say no to your husband. It takes less time to submit willfully than it does to argue about being awakened.

Dear husband, never say no to your wife. Women aren't complex creatures; you simply have to learn how we view what we perceive to be the behaviors of love. Learn your wife. What offends her? What makes her happy? What makes her blush? Avoid barbed wire and spider web conversations and behaviors. And she should do the same for you. No more traps, just talk!
Your wife may be urging you to have intercourse with her for several reasons. Women don't necessarily have to be in the mood for sex to want it. It could be that she's feeling unloved, needs reassuring, or simply likes the romance of it all. She could have had a bad day at work, and this is her way of escaping it all. She could have had a great day, and this is her icing on today's slice of heaven. If she's coming after you, that's a good thing.

Pay attention to the behavior of your wife. If she's suddenly saying no a lot, get to the root of the issue. Both women and men tend to unconsciously carry problems from unresolved arguments, and these issues will cause you to pull away from one another physically. If there is a change in your home, find that scalable wall that the enemy has been entering through. Find where your marriage needs fortification. Sit down and talk with your wife. Put the children to bed and keep the atmosphere peaceful. Always make an agreement to discuss the issue without argument, voice raising, or sarcasm before the discussion begins. Make it a game. If wife doesn't get offended, yell, or display any vengeful behavior, you'll take her out to her favorite restaurant on a date chosen by her. And if you don't get offended, yell or display any revengeful behavior, she has to do something nice for you. Find the problem and get rid of it.

If she simply states that she's tired, offer to help out with some of her workload. Maybe you can pick the children up after school two or three days a week. Maybe you can cook two or three days out of the week. Maybe you can take on the task of helping the children with their homework. What she's sharing with you is that the atmosphere for her hasn't been one for cuddling. It's chaos, and when she has an opportunity to escape it all by going to sleep, she takes this opportunity without fail.

Never become monotone in your relationships. Simple gestures can change an atmosphere that would have been chaotic into a peaceful and love-filled atmosphere. The idea isn't just to try to play out a lovemaking scene that seems to be like driving down the same ole road for years. After a while, you could drive that road blindfolded. Remember this: When driving, if you become too familiar with a road, you have a higher risk of getting too relaxed and falling asleep on that road than you would on a highway that you had to remain alert on. That means you're bored! Keep the atmosphere peaceful and loving. You don't need a song about fornicating to set the mood, and if you do, you're in trouble. You simply need to learn your spouse. Also, do simple gestures like: Keeping the house clean, moving the furniture around sometimes, adding new art to the walls, changing the bedspread and curtains to another color, adding new lamps to the bedroom, trying a new fragrance to scent up your room, and so on.

GOD created sex as a way for man and woman to procreate. HE made it pleasurable for them to do so as a reward to the spouses. Don't steal the opportunity to enjoy being with you from your spouse. Sometimes, the act itself may change how the day is playing out for one or both of you. Even if your spouse has been upsetting you lately, you don't have the right to withhold yourself. You do have free-will, however, but if you use it to act like a single woman or a single man, you just may become that way.

Exercise or Exorcism?

The wealth of the wicked is laid up for the just. While this may be not be news to you, to someone else, this may be the highlight of their day. The world has discovered that regular diet and exercise promotes good moods. This is great news for the home front, because couples are often trying to find ways to get back to their happy places with one another.

As we gain weight, our health begins to deteriorate and our metabolism slows down. As a result, we become less interested in activities that involve body movement, and we become lovers of the couch and snacks. The man who once looked like a well sculpted statue now looks like a science project gone wrong. The wife now sports a ponytail every day, and sometimes the couch has given her an unfashionable Mohawk.

I was guilty of this crime, and so was Jean. Being from Mississippi, I thought I was supposed to feed him until he looked like a pot-bellied pig. I fried everything, had bread with everything, and sugar was our main dish, but exercise was not invited to the party. We sat in the house with the same routine. Husband would wake up to go to work, give his sleeping wife a kiss, and head out to work where he'd sit behind a desk for most of the day. I would wake up, complete the morning hygiene ritual, and then head to the computer to work. We both began to look like juice bars. Our energy levels declined. We were both beginning to morph into mountains of Jell-O, and we became **content** with that. Now, if you add 'ion' to content, you get contention. What is an ion? Merriam Webster defines an ion as *"an atom or group of atoms that carries a positive or negative electric charge as a result of having lost or gained one or more electrons."* Content is to be satisfied or fulfilled, but contention means to dispute.

When we become content, we stop moving towards progression. Yes, we should be content in our marriages, but we should always strive to better our marriages, better our relationship with the FATHER, and better our lives. The word content is tied to purpose. When we have reached our purpose or destination, we cease to live. We may exist, but we become nothing more than parked vehicles. You should always send a positive charge to your relationship first with the FATHER by continuing to gain more territory for HIM. When you begin to sit around and become complacent, you begin to become stagnant. Our minds are sponges that can hold immeasurable amounts of information. You would wow your spouse by exercising your mind and your body. Man of God, no matter how old you get, you're not supposed to have breasts. Woman of GOD, no matter how many children you have, you're not supposed to look pregnant unless you are pregnant. Now, this is a little humor for you, but it is the truth. Again, I was guilty of this. But, I have found with diet and exercise that Jean and I both are happier, and as the weight falls off, we are more energetic and we procrastinate less.

Weight gain in excess is unhealthy, and it does change the mood in your home. One of the things that has to change is how we start our relationships followed by how we live our relationships. Single people tend to take better care of their bodies, hoping to

find or be found by their future spouses, but once the vows are said and the rings are exchanged, we actually stop preparing for a life with one another and we start preparing to grow old together. This mindset sounds good, but if you are still young, you need to prepare to live and enjoy your life.
Women usually say, "He should walk with me sometimes."
Men usually say, "She should stop cooking all of that good food." As our bellies grow bigger, so does our pool of excuses and our attitudes. Isn't it funny how we never seem to have time to exercise, but we have plenty of time for arguing? Try this if you can: Buy two treadmills and place them side by side. Then when that great episode of 'it's time to talk' comes on in your marriage, meet up at the treadmills to discuss the issue.

Discover foods that are less fattening and have fewer calories. All it takes is trying new foods.

What about exercising our minds? The element of mystery is one that captivates and draws men and women into marriages. Our minds are funny because we tend to fill in the answers for any questions that go unanswered. As we go on in our marriages, we begin to discover more and more about our spouses until we feel that we know everything about them. Your spouse should never feel that they've reached the top floor in you; they should always want more. That's why we exercise our minds and keep learning. As a matter of fact, you should never feel like you've reached your highest point. You should always strive to know more, do more, and be more. This is what keeps you intriguing. Learn something new every day, and you should especially strive to learn the WORD of GOD more every day. Get the WORD in you in abundance; get knowledge; gain more understanding. Learn how to do something you've never known how to do. Travel more. Learn the laws in your state to find out ways you can help. Learn the statistics in your state and country, and apply yourself to helping to improve the stats in your area. If your conversation begins to become evidence of your excessive soap opera watching, or you know every new wrestler who graces the scene, you are investing your time and energy into something that will yield absolutely no return. Just like investing, your knowledge should yield a return, and when it does not, you are applying it into things and places that have no value. For example, learn about orphanages in your area and the conditions that caused those children to be given up or catapulted into the system. This is knowledge that yields a return when applied.

There is so much to learn. Just when your spouse thought he or she knew all there was too know about you, they discover that there is more to be learned. Do you see how this is blessing someone else, and at the same time, helping your marriage? If you happen to have one of those spouses who gets irritated with your unwillingness to stop learning and sit down, try to encourage that spouse to get involved. A lot of times our spouses may not know just how fulfilling it is to help someone else out or to learn a new trade. Invite them to come along, and speak well to them while they are with you.

What about the exorcism? A mind that is parked is usually parked by a devil. Procrastination and slothfulness aren't just flesh issues. In many cases, they are demonically inspired behaviors. Depression is linked to idleness. When we are outside of purpose, we find ourselves inside of the realm of depression, anxiety, hopelessness, and frustration. When we are idle or outside of purpose, we find ourselves getting into things we shouldn't. Sin will become the highlight of your life when you aren't seeing any fireworks elsewhere. Pray about what the LORD will have you to do. Renounce any and every demonic spirit, word, or power that may be hindering you. Even though you don't feel like moving, move anyway. What you are doing is telling that devil that he is a liar and he can't stop you from going forward, no matter how your flesh says you feel. You don't necessarily need someone to lay hands on you to remove that devil. You simply need to follow James 4:7, and that is, *"Submit yourself to GOD and resist the devil and he will flee from you."* Now, some devils don't go out straightway and do require fasting, as JESUS made evident to us in

Mark 9:29.

Exercise your way to a healthier mind, a healthier body, and a healthier marriage.

Married to An Unbeliever or Rebellious Spouse

I know your frustration; I was hard-headed too. We tend to do that when we are either young spiritually, or when we are just plain rebellious. Someone comes along and they seem to be perfect for you. Their rebellious nature does set off the alarm, but we punch the alarm out because we want to snooze a little more because our new love interest is so pleasing to the eyes. We tell ourselves that something so beautiful can't be so bad, or that we can change them with our love, loyalty, and long-suffering. That is until we get into the relationship and find out the true definition of long-suffering coupled with the torment that ensues when giving your heart to an unbeliever.

Funny thing is, we tend to believe that we can help them come to CHRIST. *(Don't act like I'm the only one Satan told that lie to.)* I used to think that a broken man can be healed by love, and he can; just not natural love. That man needs the love provided for HIM by GOD; he needs to repent, and he needs deliverance; and he needs it like yesterday.

Ladies: How shallow art we at times? We are emotional, and we have been watching FAR too many fairy tales. We have this happily-ever-after mapped out in our heads. We have bought into the media's lies. We watch movies where the bad guy was really good, but just a little misunderstood. Therefore, we go about trying to rescue grown men from their hurts and their sins. In addition, we have danced to too many songs that spoke to our right-now as opposed to our destined places because many of us don't yet understand that where we are today is not necessarily where we will be tomorrow. We tend to meet men who are not right for us because they are not right with GOD; nevertheless, because they look good, we try to fix them by taking them to church. When he says something Christian, we think that we've just gotten confirmation that our Christian words and ways are finally getting through to him. When he is his sinful self, we tend to write it off and continue planning the wedding. Either way, we will religiously quote Isaiah 55:11: *"So shall my word be that goes forth out of my mouth:* ***it shall not return unto me void****, but it shall accomplish that which I please, and it shall prosper in the thing for which I sent it."* Even after quoting it, the enemy convinces us that we are exempt from the WORD of GOD or that our situation is different, and the WORD does not apply to us because GOD knows our hearts.

Men: You aren't exactly the best at choosing mates yourselves because you are visual creatures. If you like what you see, you'll ignore what you hear. Sure, she's an exotic dancer, but she goes to church sometimes, right? Now, here you are a Pastor, and your wife is sitting in the front row wearing a spandex mini-skirt, four-inch fingernails, and blowing bubbles throughout your sermon. But, at least she does clap for you and she has never really given you a problem about coming to church. The ministry team keeps a special cloth to cover her thighs because she doesn't understand that her legs are supposed to be closed and her breasts were supposed to be hidden. Nevertheless, she still manages to give a peep show every Sunday when she dramatically heads to the front of the church to prostrate herself, or when she bends over to greet the children. There is a bright side to all of this; the collection plate seems to be getting some extra one-dollar bills and the youth thinks that you're cool.

We're human, and whatever our age is spiritually when we get married will determine the spiritual age of the person we marry. Some people were just patient enough to wait, and some people refuse to wait on their spouses; therefore, they often find themselves in bad relationships trying to pray their way out or beg to stay in. That's why GOD warns us in Matthew 6:33, *"But seek ye first the kingdom of God, and his righteousness; and all these things shall be added unto you."*
When this order is not followed, you are guaranteed to meet someone who is an unbeliever or a believer who is not in their season to marry. They can very well be a child of GOD, but they may be young spiritually, and because of this, they will do childish things.

When marrying an unbeliever, we often think that we've won. We've sinned our way in, and now we can repent and enjoy the benefits of serving the LORD. In reality, our win has been documented as a loss because GOD will never let you sin your way to a blessing. As you continue to grow in the LORD, you have to witness their baby antics. To top it off, you have to take your place and try to win that soul without becoming too parent-like.

As a woman, I found that my behavior was more mature than the man I'd chosen for myself. I would be all about GOD, and he would be all about himself. When we were around others, they thought that he was a nice guy with a motherly wife. I spent years trying to figure out if I was in error because my personality was more dominant than his. When it came to the things of GOD, I stood my ground; but because he did not know GOD, he was open to any and everything. Therefore, I was the one aggressively having to fend off attempted attacks on my home. I was the one having to explain why we couldn't hang around certain people. Again, I thought I was too aggressive and I often repented of this.

I would even continually war against the spirit of Jezebel because I felt like it was trying to attach itself to me. That was until the LORD explained to me what was going on. I'd married a man that was not dominant at all; he was passive, but I'm not passive. I love the LORD with all my heart, but he didn't know GOD. He knew HIS Name and he could even quote a few scriptures, but he did not really know GOD. I gave him the right to play grown-up when he wasn't even born again yet. He hadn't started his journey to even be named as a babe in CHRIST. Therefore, the disorder I was witnessing wasn't me not submitting myself because I consciously made sure that I was in submission to my husband. The disorder I was witnessing was what it was like to be unequally yoked with an unbeliever. I am sure that any and every one who married an unbeliever or a rebellious individual can testify, it is a TRYING (I wish I could put animated fire around that word) experience.

It's not the end of the world for you. I used to cry and pray that the LORD would remove me from my marriage. I literally found myself wanting to throw tantrums because I wanted more than anything to be free to do right the next time. I just wanted to be free to serve the LORD, do HIS will, and eventually GOD would send me the man HE anointed for me. I thought Jean was like a bad computer program that did not live up to my expectations. I thought I could just delete him and move on. I even proclaimed my willingness to just live single and celibate for the rest of my life and just dedicate my life to serving FATHER. However, there is no turning back. The only person that is allowed to retreat from an unequally yoked union is the unbeliever. 1 Kings 7:10-15 reads:

"And unto the married I command, yet not I, but the Lord, Let not the wife depart from her husband:
But if she depart, let her remain unmarried, or be reconciled to her husband: and let not the husband put away his wife.
But to the rest speak I, not the Lord: If any brother has a wife that believes not, and she be pleased to dwell with him, let him not put her away.
And the woman who has a husband that believes not, and if he be

pleased to dwell with her, let her not leave him.
For the unbelieving husband is sanctified by the wife, and the unbelieving wife is sanctified by the husband: else were your children unclean; but now are they holy.
But if the unbelieving depart, let him depart*. A brother or a sister is not under bondage in such cases: but* ***God has called us to peace****."*

I've met many men and women who have married unbelievers, and we've all shared a laugh because we all thought the same thing. We thought that we could repent, divorce our spouses, and get it right the next time; but we could not legally do this in CHRIST. So, we tried to pray our spouses away from us. I even tried praying that he would run off. The more I wanted out of the marriage, the more my husband seemed to want the marriage. I realized later that it was because I was running from him. Men are hunters, so I became a challenge to him; nevertheless, when he felt like he'd caught me, he'd go back to acting simple.

How does one continue in an unequally yoked marriage? By following the WORD of GOD. Here are a few tips that should help you get through the hard parts.

Key word here is roles.

1. Pride stirs up contention. Humble yourself. Even when you want to try to educate them and change them, humble yourself and let GOD be GOD. You just play your role.
2. Don't compare them to believers. Sure, you want to tell them how this person or that person is always at church with their spouse, and they serve the LORD together, but this won't draw them in. Ladies, your chaste behavior, coupled with your fear of the LORD will draw in an unbelieving man. Fellows, just stay in place with CHRIST as your head. By doing so, you will cause GOD to always dwell in your home.
3. Don't force them to come to church. A person battling a spirit of rebellion is going to do just that....rebel. Get up

and go alone, but ask them if they are coming. If they say no, kiss them and head out the door. If you beat them over the head about going to church, they'll avoid it at all costs. They need to feel like it was their decision, not yours. So, trying to convince them or force them into going will only back-fire.

4. Don't feed demons or any evil in the spouse. If the spouse begins to act negatively towards you, don't react in the flesh; react with kindness. Oftentimes, people have addictive personalities and some are addicted to attention. Whether it's good or bad attention, they just want attention. What I have found is the best route to take is to carry on in your day just like you would any other day. Clean the house, cook, sing, exercise, or whatever you normally do. Enjoy your day. This leaves them with their issues because you are refusing to be a part of the problem, but you have availed yourself for a solution, should they reach for it.
5. Keep them away from prideful or negative believers. What you don't want is for them to get a bad taste in their mouth about being a part of the church. If you take your wife, for example, around Evangelist Edward's wife and she keeps going on and on about herself and her walk with the LORD, it may make your wife uncomfortable. Pray that the LORD sends friends around the two of you who will understand where you are and know how to come out, because they were once there.
6. Always celebrate progress, but never criticize their falls. When the spouse falls, just think of them as an 11-month old baby who's learning to walk. Sure, they may stumble and fall from time to time, but as they grow, they'll begin to walk without using you as a wall to hold them up. Trying to bash your spouse over the head about their descent will only cause them to descend further. Just say, "It's okay, baby. I love you still and GOD still loves you even more than I do. It'll come together; just keep moving forward. You have my support."
7. If your spouse is an unbeliever or is rebellious, chances are

they have unbelieving or rebellious friends. It goes without say that you want that friendship over...finito! But, the more you try to drive away their friends, the more they want to hang with them. Have you not learned from your dating years that if you try to keep someone away from another person, they will unite against you? If you keep encouraging their growth, they will eventually walk away from those friends because they won't have anything in common anymore. Be truthful with them about their friends, but don't turn it into a lecture. Just tell the truth and let the truth take root in their hearts. Most believers who have been elevated know that in elevation, you tend to lose a lot of friends because they can't go where you are going. Therefore, encourage growth.

8. Get them to help out in things that they are mature enough to help out in. Often times, people in purpose stay out of trouble because they are so occupied. Find out what they are passionate about. Try going down to some nursing homes and visiting some of the patients whose families have abandoned them. (Now, if you are dealing with a rebellious spouse, it is not a good idea to take them to a prison, since they may begin to relate and try to establish friendships with the prisoners rather than rehabilitate them. Be wise and prayerful about what activities they can and should be involved in and vice versa.)
9. If you treat a child like a child, he or she will grow up to be a big child. Don't exalt yourself over the spouse and **definitely** do not follow his or her advice for you to stop going to church or serving the LORD. If it's the woman who is an unbeliever, treat her like a woman of GOD. Wives, if your husband is an unbeliever, treat him like a king and remain in subjection to him. Acting like Vashti will not make him change; instead, it'll make him go on the hunt for an Esther.
10. Prayer works. Remember to pray for the unbelieving or rebellious spouse, and don't be afraid to ask the LORD that HIS will be done. Oftentimes, believers try to control the

LORD'S Hands by telling HIM what to do and what not to do. As a designer, I have found that people who tell me how to design their websites, seals, logos, or whatever I'm designing for them aren't my favorite clients. They are attempting to control my anointing, and this is frustrating. I can only imagine how GOD must feel when we are trying to control HIS hands. HE knows what situations will bear fruit and which ones will not. Remember, FATHER knows best. You just have to trust HIM.

11. When strife presents itself, always remember to keep your eyes focused on GOD and not the person. Stay focused on winning the soul, not the fight.

Your First Love

You've probably gone deep into your imagination and imagined the first man or woman who stole your heart; nevertheless, we're not talking about who your first love was; we are going to discuss who your first love should be.

There is an order in the Kingdom of GOD. When the proper order is followed, everything else falls into place. When we deviate, things fall into the wrong places and react. That's like if you were working at a chemical factory, and on one side there were bottles being filled with bleach, and on the other side there were bottles being filled with ammonia. The machine that fills the bleach bottles malfunctions, so you have to manually fill it again until the machine starts working again. But there's a mix up. You use the fork-lift to tip a big canister of bleach into what you thought was bleach, but it turns out that you've just poured ammonia into the canister of bleach. A deadly reaction will ensue undoubtedly. That's because the wrong thing went into the wrong place and caused a reaction. Or a more subtle example would be a glass falling off the counter and shattering on the floor. The glass's reaction to the force was to shatter.

So are the things of CHRIST. Everything that we do, speak, or touch ignites a reaction. Whatever we communicate with will communicate back to us. Whenever we do right, right things will follow us; but whenever we do wrong, wrong things will chase us.

In learning the scriptures, you will find that GOD likes HIS right off the top. HE requires the tithes upfront, and HE requires that we have a relationship with HIM before we seek relationships with men and women. *"But seek you first the kingdom of God, and his righteousness; and all these things shall be added unto you (Matthew 6:33)."* This should tell you something about our LORD. HE is the first to bless you to wake up, so HE should be the first you speak to in the morning. HE is the first and only to give you life, so HE should be the first and only One we give glory, praise and honor to. HE should be our first love.

Many teachers, when speaking of marriage, speak of the three-fold cord. Of course, FATHER has to be in that cord, but one thing many fail to teach is the positioning. GOD is before your spouse and not the other way around. If a cord is not knotted correctly, it is weak. But, if it is intertwined in order, it will make a strong rope. Therefore, a lot of strife that happens in the home is a direct result of something or someone else being our first love. Maybe your love for your wife outweighs your love for GOD. If this is the case, you are out of order, and because of this your home will be a home of discord, disorder and dysfunction until you place GOD where HE belongs. Or maybe your husband is your everything. This is out of order, and until you realize that GOD is your everything, you will witness Satan's order unfolding in your home. If you want it right, make it right. Put everything and everyone where they belong.

Think about your head. If your head was placed on your thighs, you'd fall for any and everything. Everything on your body has placement and that placement has purpose. You are the body of

CHRIST and everyone in HIS body has placement and that placement has purpose. CHRIST is the head of man and husband is the head of the wife. When the wife turns and tries to be the head or walk side-by-side with the head, she is refusing him the leadership position given to him by GOD. In doing so, she picks up a witchcraft spirit because she has uncovered her head to follow her own devices. CHRIST is the husband's head, and when she refuses to submit to her husband, she is in the same refusing to submit to CHRIST. She chooses to do it her way because she believes that she can produce better results for herself, and she does not want to wait on GOD to give her what she wants. Her way isn't GOD'S way; therefore, she has exchanged her lovely crown of submission for a crown of thorns. CHRIST suffered this crown for her, but because she refuses to submit to HIM, she has chosen to bare her own sin. She feels justified in this because some man hurt her before or because she was taught to be independent.

How do you know when you have placed the husband or the wife above the LORD? The way the LORD revealed my heart's location to me was through trial by fire. When I was married the first time, I would go through extreme emotions and I would react in a like manner. I would first start off by trying to do things GOD'S way. I would try to initiate a talk, but when that was rebutted, I would start to argue. Finally, I would get frustrated and start cursing and screaming. I felt like rage was the language he understood the most. In my reactions, I was sinning against GOD. My words weren't holy when I was upset because I loved the man more than I loved GOD. Again, GOD began to reveal this to me at the end of the marriage, and this is when I made the decision to re-order my life. Therefore, you will know if you have placed your spouse above the LORD when you are tried by fire with this spouse. Sometimes, these situations come upon us just to show us where we are. The same thing happened with Jean. In the beginning, he knew the right and wrong buttons to push with me. I was a lot stronger, but if he pushed that button hard enough, I wouldn't act like a woman of GOD; I would act like a mad woman.

When I saw this in me, I began to pray it out of me because I knew that this meant that GOD was showing me ways that were still in me that were not of HIM. It took a while for the transition to fully complete itself, but what I learned was I didn't need to educate myself on how to be a better wife; I needed to learn how to become a better daughter to GOD. The wife part will automatically fall in line when you fall in line.

A lot of women do not understand that submission is not obedience; submission means to follow the lead of whomever you are in submission to. If you are a praying woman of faith, you will know that you can trust GOD to lead your husband. If your husband rebels, you are a gap-stander and GOD will honor your home because you stood in the gap for him, just as Moses' wife did when she circumcised their son. But, again, that's why you should be patient and marry the man GOD has for you, so you can trust him to follow the LORD. The LORD will not release you to a man who is being led by something or someone else. In addition, a man cannot be your equal because he is called into a role of leadership. Could you imagine a head with arms coming from the ears, and the hands were holding the nose; the torso stuck out sideways from the nose, and the feet sideways from the torso? That's out of order. The order of GOD is: GOD is the head of CHRIST, CHRIST is the head of man, and man is the head of woman. No matter how hard I have tried to refute this truth in my years of not understanding what head was, I could not.

Again, submission does not mean that the husband commands you around; to submit to your husband means that you trust CHRIST to head him up. When you see that he is being led by something other than CHRIST, go to his head (CHRIST) about him. Submit yourself to GOD and resist the devil and he will flee from you! You do the will of GOD, and you win your husband back for the LORD. In submission, you are allowing GOD to move in and through your husband, and to correct your husband without your interference. You are demonstrating a living ministry in yourself by refusing to follow behind the flesh of your husband or yourself and continuing to honor the LORD. And when your husband witnesses this, he will be convicted. He may respond angrily to that conviction or lovingly to it, but no matter how he responds; GOD is speaking to him through your actions. If he doesn't want to listen, allow GOD to deal with him, for you are not his head. GOD knows how to lead him and HE knows how to correct HIS leaders. Your role is to simply be who GOD has called you to be, and that is HIS daughter first and that man's wife second.

Numbers represent order. One represents first, two represents second, three represents third, and so on. When we number it 3, 2, 1, we call the numbers backwards because they are. When the order of GOD is not followed, your home is backwards and out of order. As such, you will witness countdowns to heartache because anything that is not ascending in GOD is descending into darkness.

In all things, give thanks unto the LORD. When you wake up in the morning, your first words should be to praise the LORD for waking you up. Before you eat, you should thank the LORD for the food you are about to receive. GOD has to be first in order for your house to be in HIS order. Anything that is set up in any other arrangement is disorderly, deformed, and dangerous.

In addition, your children do not come before your spouse; they come after the spouse. This is the GOD-given order that, when exercised, forms a greater love and a greater protective barrier around the children. We are to protect our children, and of course, you should never allow your spouse to harm your children in any way. In blended families, it's relatively hard to discipline children that are not your own because you have to worry about the opinions of both natural parents and their families. I have found that if you want your spouse to love your child as if it were his or her own, allow them to parent the child without interference. A house divided cannot stand, and if you place the children in the wrong order, your house will be divided. Therefore, if you end up divorcing because of the children's inability to get along with their step-parent, your divorce won't be the result of your spouse not liking your child; it came as a result of you not liking the WORD of GOD. You had your own edited version of the truth and you forgot to read the book in its entirety. In the end, the relationship ends because GOD was not in it. Mom and Dad, be they biological or step parents, should be one in their decisions. When your children come to you about something, your spouse should be speaking the same thing as you. If the child becomes angry, it is often because they are challenging your spouse's role and trying to place themselves above your spouse, which is NOT the order of GOD. If you do the will of GOD, HE will cause your children to be at peace with your spouse eventually. They just have to see that their attempts to divide are not working.

Remember, if the order of GOD is there, everything will fall into place. GOD is number one; HE'S first and foremost, and above all. After all, HE gave HIS first and only Begotten Son for you. How dare you try to give HIM any other place in your life than first place. When HE'S first, a lot of what lines up to attack you will never come up against you because JESUS is on the front line. Now, if you place HIM behind your spouse, children, job or anything or anyone in your life, you will be con<u>front</u>ed by the enemy and you will have no protection. Remember, obedience is better than sacrifice. A home that stands on the WORD cannot be destroyed because the foundation is indestructible.

Compare Me To No One Please

When I was a teenager, my parents used to compare me to their friend's daughter. She got better grades, seemed more mature, and she dressed like a young adult. I, on the other hand, made all A's, B's, C's and D's, but not because I didn't understand the lesson; truth was, I needed glasses and my parents couldn't afford them. I played a lot because I was still a child, and I was in no hurry to grow up. After all, I was around 13 years old. I wasn't so intrigued with boys, and I liked to dress like a business woman slash tomboy. They couldn't understand why I preferred to hang out with the little sister of their friend's daughter rather than her. So, they would give me this verbal lashing and praise her in my presence, and all the while I kept thinking how they didn't really know the real her. When I did hang out with her, she wanted to dress sexy and go boy hunting. We'd even heard of marijuana being referred to as grass, so we went into her little sister's playhouse and rolled up some brown, freshly picked grass into some typing paper and tried to smoke it. This wasn't my thing, and this wasn't my character. I liked playing clubhouse and beating up boys rather than playing house and trying to romance boys. I liked digging in mud and pulling out earthworms. I liked climbing trees, even if I was wearing a skirt. I didn't mind the occasional bout with poison ivy, and I loved the feel of a frog in my hand. Plus, I was trying to wear makeup at this stage (when Daddy didn't see me), so I was between the stages of wanting to be a professional woman and a child. But, my parents' pressure pushed me to hang out with older, more mature girls who were sexually active. Of course, they didn't know the girls were sexually active, but I did. And you know what happened next. I didn't want to hold frogs anymore; I wanted to hold a man.

The purpose of that testimony is to illustrate to you the danger behind comparing your spouse or children, for that matter, to another human being. Many times, you don't know the whole story behind that other person's life. Example: You see Jason's wife. She loves to dress up, keeps her hair primped, she exercises daily, cooks for Jason every day, and she and Jason seem to have the perfect relationship. But your wife sits around the house, hair being formed by the elements, weight spawning out of control, and she sees McDonald's as her personal cook. What you didn't know: Jason's wife is having an affair with Jason's best friend, so that's why she dresses up so often and exercises to keep in shape. Her excessive lingerie spending isn't for her husband, it is for his friend. She cooks for Jason daily because she knows that after Jason eats, he usually falls asleep in an hour or so. It is during this time that she kisses him and says she's heading out for her daily workout. She didn't lie. Jason's friend has been giving her a powerhouse of a workout. But, you are pushing your wife to be more like her. The character was comparing his wife to Jason's wife. His wife was out of order because she was not taking care of her home or herself, but remember, there is a root to everything. Nothing grows without a root. She may be depressed; she may have a demon attached to her; she may have a lot on her mind, or her husband may be out of order. When the head is out of order, the body will not function correctly. He should have been coming against whatever was challenging your wife. Maybe she grew up in a home where the lead woman (her mother or step-mother) was lazy and this has trickled down to her. This is a stronghold that needs to be broken. All too often, people try to break the spouse, when it is not the spouse that needs breaking; it is the stronghold that needs breaking.

How do you do this? One thing is by not comparing your spouse to someone else. Another tip is to pray for your spouse and encourage them to do right. Don't yell at them when they do wrong; only celebrate them when they do right. When she gets up on Sunday to cook, talk about how good the food is and make the moment memorable for her. Don't talk about how salty the chicken is and how your mother cooks better potatoes. You'll only discourage her. If the food isn't good, you don't have to say it's good, but eat what you can and thank her for the food. When you get the chance, cook that very same meal again and show her the way that it should be cooked. Ask her to join you in the kitchen, and show her how much salt should be added. If she insists on adding more, simply tell her that you don't like yours to be that salty; you like the salt to be mild.

Pray with your spouse, and encourage them to want to change; don't discourage them by trying to change them into what you want them to be. They only need to change into what GOD wants them to be. The shoes that GOD created for someone else may be too small for us and hurt our feet, or may be too big for us and cause us to trip often.

You should both read the bible together and agree on being who GOD called you to be. In doing so, your spouse will evolve into the man or woman of your dreams, even if the LORD has to change your original dreams; which by the way, were probably shaped by a period of sinful thinking.

Your spouse cannot be who you want them to be because they were called by another name. When Peter acknowledged JESUS as the CHRIST, how did JESUS respond to him? *"And Jesus answered and said unto him, Blessed are you, Simon Barjona: for flesh and blood has not revealed it unto you, but my Father who is in heaven. And I say also unto you, That you are Peter, and upon this rock I will build my church; and the gates of Hades shall not prevail against it. And I will give unto you the keys of the kingdom of heaven: and whatsoever you shall bind on earth shall be what has been bound in heaven: and whatsoever you shall loose on earth shall be what has been loosed in heaven" (Matthew 16:17-19).*

When Peter acknowledged who JESUS was and is, JESUS revealed who Peter was. Every person who has not found revelation is still searching for it. Many people try to steer us into being who we are not, and if we never know who we are; how can we inherit the Kingdom of GOD, being that we never followed the path of GOD? Even if your spouse knows who they are, they are still searching (purpose) for who they are. That means the journey does not end as long as they are alive. Through trials, tribulations and revelations, we come to be who we are chosen to be. Trials are meant to convict the guilty part of us, and free us from the bondage of sin. If your spouse is not allowed to take this journey and make their own mistakes, how can they learn?

Do you truly believe that in comparing them to someone else, they will find who they are in that person? Do you understand that if they begin to mimic that person, they will eventually go mad because they are warring internally with themselves? The mind is the real battlefield. Instead of comparing, you should try to help them discover who they are in CHRIST. You do this by discovering who *you* are in CHRIST. How can you lead someone when you are still following dreams that are not your own? Your purpose is not tied to the things of this earth; it has a direct connection to heaven, and purpose is discovered in obedience. Purpose is revealed to us as we arrive at checkpoints that GOD has set up for us.

Your spouse is treasured in the eyes of the LORD, but they have to discover who they are, even when they think they know the answer. We never stop searching if we want to stay alive. A man who has served his purpose has no reason to live. His assignment is finished. That's why you see people who retire at the age of 80, and their health begins to rapidly decline. They had a sense of purpose when they were working, but now that they are sitting at home, they begin to lose momentum.

As GOD reveals to you and your spouse who you are, you will continue to wow one another. You will never truly discover everything about your spouse, and they will never truly discover all of you because the depth of you cannot be reached in this lifetime. You are your FATHER'S child and you are made in HIS image. Don't compare your spouse; prepare your spouse for the journey ahead. It is then that you will get the blessed opportunity to watch their transformation and they can witness yours as well.

Chiseling Away Layers

There is so much to you that is waiting to be revealed, but before a jewel reveals its beauty, its surface has to be chiseled, buffed, and cleaned. As we go through the changes associated by our great revealing, we cry out in pain. That's normal because we are taught that laughter and smiles are good things, and anything that hurts is bad; but that's not always true. Labor pains are pains that come before a child is born. Those pains signify that the body is trying to push the child out because it is the child's time to come forth. Drunken laughter is a false sense of joy that comes about when the poison of alcohol has tossed our inhibitions to the wind. That's not real joy; that's pain drowned so deep that it doesn't have enough sense to call itself what it is: misery.

In many cases, revelation is waiting on us; we simply need to step into obedience and put on the fear of the LORD. It is then that we would discover that in our absence, FATHER has left quite a few messages for us. We needed to be in the right place to play them. And that's why we should allow HIM to chisel away layers that have come upon us through our hardships, cultures, and habits.

These are layers of flesh and demonically crafted ways that have taken their places in our lives.

GOD did not send you a spouse according to where you were; HE sends them according to where HE has called you to be. That is, even though they may be on your level today, they are called to a higher place with you. Men: That's why you shouldn't search for a wife until you have been released as a husband. If you don't wait, you'll find a woman in the realm that you are, and when you're elevated; she'll still be in that place. This will cause the two of you to grow apart. Women: That's why you shouldn't be out watering anyone's mule, hoping to be picked up by your Romeo. The place where you may be spiritually does not house the type of man who GOD has chosen to be where you are heading. And if you take a man from that realm; as cute as he may be, he is going to want to stay there, and he will want you to stay there with him. When you continue elevating in the LORD, he will begin to lose interest in you because you are moving so far away from where he resides. You don't have the same conversations anymore. He can't relate to you because you want to talk about the LORD, and he wants to talk about some rapper's new album and how it relates to him. You may be hip today, but GOD has called you to a different place. It is your GOD-appointed place that <u>your</u> husband will find you. That way, you will grow together and not apart. GOD has to chisel away those layers of foolishness that have kept you bound for so many years.

Even if you are already married, and you married the wrong person, or you married the right person in the wrong season, you still have an obligation to the LORD to elevate. Your spouse's deliverance may very well be found in your obedience. GOD has a plan for you, and no man or woman will halt that plan when you stay in HIM. Each day of doing right by HIM pulls down layers of dark covering that pretended to shield us from harm, when it was really shielding us from the light of truth. Just because they don't serve HIM doesn't mean they won't serve HIM.

Pay attention to your actions. Every act is a reaction. You eat because you're hungry; you simply reacted to your hunger. The message here is: every act that surfaces has a stem or root. If the reaction is not a good one, the root wasn't good or it was placed in the wrong soil.

The brain is a sponge and the older it gets, the harder that sponge gets. That's why we say a lot of older people are stuck in their ways. They can change, but they are less likely to change than a younger person who is absorbing more. Here are some tips to help exercise your spirit and soul and get you into spiritual shape.

1. Learn something. Never ever allow your brain to sit like stagnant waters. Every day and every chance you get, you need to learn something new. A scripture, a new word, a new recipe, and so on. Anything that stays in the same place is dead because living things move. Isn't it a catastrophe to see someone you were friends with twenty years ago still in the same mind frame that they were in when you last saw them? It's because their brain has been churning that same information for years. If you don't eat, you don't grow. You need to feed your mind and spirit with new information daily. More than anything, learn those scriptures. You can't fight the devil with your fist.
2. Pray and praise. This communication sets the pace for other communications. Talk to the LORD and don't be ashamed to tell HIM what you wrestle with. It's not like HE can't see it. Praise HIM every day, for HE is worthy to be praised. Don't just say that religiously; understand that it is true.
3. Help others. In our helping others, things that have been anchoring us often fall off. Ask any leader who speaks to the brokenhearted. Many times the LORD will minister to you while ministering through you. This is a beautiful cycle indeed!
4. Change your language. There is truth, and there are lies. Some of what you say was learned in your life of sin. “She's killing me!” “He makes me sick!” These are not

words that should leave your mouth, since we have life-giving power in our tongues. Instead, learn the WORD so you can speak the language of faith. This way, you will give life to what you want to give life to and take life away from anything that's not supposed to have it.

5. Break and build habits. Pay attention to your habits. The bad ones have to be destroyed and new ones need to be established. Bad habits are strongholds, or ways that hold you captive to sin and sin's residue. Every choice you make is an investment, and it will yield a return.
6. Get skilled. The more skills you have, the more skills you'll use, and the more beneficial you will be to yourself and others. Men, if you don't know how to fix a car; take some classes. If you don't know how to sing, but you want to, take singing lessons. Ladies, if you don't know how to cook, take cooking classes or ask a friend to teach you. Or, if you don't know how to swim, take swimming lessons.

What you are doing is refusing to become predictable, repetitious, and simple.

Fact: Elephants in captivity rock side to side because they are stressed and the rocking is their coping mechanism. Trainers try to reduce the stress because as time passes, the elephants become more and more aggressive. Does this sound familiar? Park a man or woman and don't feed them information, and <u>they will become aggressive</u>. Chisel those layers away; start feeding the good and tearing down the bad. If you are rocking side to side, chewing straws up beyond recognition, eating ice habitually, and pulling at your ears; these are signs of stress. Don't be like that elephant. You can't hide from stress; you have to come against it. It's time to chisel.

Changing Your Atmosphere

Your atmosphere affects and infects your mood, and your atmosphere can be changed by anyone in your household. Have you ever witnessed this with yourself or a friend? The baby is screaming, children are arguing, mother is frustrated and snippy, and dad can't bolt off to work fast enough? Then, in the evening, Mom doesn't really want to come home and neither does Dad. As they pull into the driveway, they stare at what now feels like a haunted house. They sit in their car as long as they can because they do not want to come in because they've grown tired of the chaotic atmosphere. In a situation like this, the marriage is undoubtedly in danger. It's a bad sign when one can find a more peaceful atmosphere at work, and many go looking for a more peaceful setting in extra-marital affairs. This gives the intruder the opportunity to hide their fangs and pretend to be what this stray spouse does not have at home as they begin to cultivate a more peaceful atmosphere for that person.

Think about what's happening to the ozone layer as we speak. All of the pollution is slowly ripping away at the ozone layer, and scientists believe that if this does not stop, we will eventually burn to death. Personally, I think hell is a peeping Tom and it's getting more brazen. The more pollution that is in the air, the more the atmosphere changes. During the summer, the temperatures escalate higher than the previous year because of the damage done to the ozone layer.

Your marriage has an ozone layer. Every time you fail to listen to the LORD in your marriage, a layer is ripped off, and your marriage comes closer and closer to destruction. It may start off with small problems that come infrequently, but as the years pass, those problems become larger and more frequent. In such cases, both spouses are looking for one another to change because they believe that if the other spouse would just submit to marriage their way, that the marriage will be saved. They continue these prideful sieges against one another over the course of their marriage until one or both parties decide that divorce is the only option. The problem isn't that the marriage could not be changed; the problem is you have two prideful people who have hardened their hearts to change. You have to agree that you are not right, your spouse is not right; but GOD is always right. Do things HIS way.

During labor, a woman's contractions will become more frequent as she nears the hour of delivery. The only time a woman is silent during delivery is when she is drugged with anesthesia and she is asleep. Marriage works the same way. The closer you get towards your breaking points in the marriage, the more you will fight with one another, or the more silent you will become with one another. Everything that we do gives birth to consequence. Ephesians 4:26-27 warns us this way, *"Be ye angry, and sin not: let not the sun go down upon your wrath: Neither give place to the devil."* When divorce is in the midst, it's because we slept on our problems, we gave the devil a knapsack to sleep in our homes, and we did not honor the WORD. If every issue is settled the day it presents itself, both parties will always go to bed happy, and Satan will have no place in their home. Bringing GOD into the midst is key to solving every problem that presents itself. HE has the final word.

Feelings are tied to flesh, and flesh is temporary.

Your atmosphere can be created by what is around you. A dirty house creates a bad atmosphere. Let's take me, for example. I would clean the house every morning. I would cook in the evening, so Jean would have something to eat when he came home. But once we ate, I would put the dishes in the sink, and they'd stay there until morning and sometimes evening. I'd make sure they were clean before he came home, so I felt like a super wife. On the weekend, when he was off, the dishes would sit for more than 24 hours sometimes, and during those times, we argued more. It was never about the dishes, but just general arguments about any minute thing. I can remember waking up on Saturday morning to a sink full of dishes, shoes thrown across the living room, papers stacked up on the ottoman. Hubby and I had argued Friday night, and we woke up in the same realm we went to bed in. The LORD began to minister to me about this. I had to evaluate myself. What you allow to fester around you represents what you allow to fester in you. I had a tendency to procrastinate on cleaning the house because I had a tendency to procrastinate on getting clean on the inside. I had an attitude problem. I didn't like the word no, and I felt like I couldn't be wrong. I needed to clean up my heart and stop procrastinating on doing so. I could not continue to be the wife that I was; I had to change, and fast. *"And be not conformed to this world: but be ye transformed by the renewing of your mind, that ye may prove what is that good, and acceptable, and perfect, will of God" (Romans 12:2).* I had to learn how to humble myself. Pride says you're right all the time because pride is a liar. I had to learn that arguing didn't fix anything; only the WORD of GOD does.

I had to learn to wash dishes when they got dirty. I had to learn to ask the hubby to pick up behind himself immediately, and to ask him to do so in a polite tone. You can speak in a joking and loving way and still convey the same point without the prick that comes with sarcasm or a direct verbal lashing. The idea is to make sure that your atmosphere is one that GOD can come into. There are certain atmospheres that house demons and the works of evil. *"For where envying and strife is, there is confusion and every evil work" (James 3:16).* But, there is also an atmosphere that invites GOD in. *"For where two or three are gathered together in my name, there am I in the midst of them" (Matthew 18:20).* Which environment do you prefer?

GOD is a GOD of order. As procrastination fell off of me, I found that when Jean and I did disagree, we were more likely to sit down and reconcile before the night was finished. We never let the sun set on our anger anymore. Nowadays, when he is frustrated, I set the mood by setting the atmosphere. First, I call upon the LORD, and I come against any and every spirit that is not of GOD. After that, I may reorganize or rearrange the room that we are in to make it more inviting. This brings about a calm, because the mind tends to associate a certain setting with negativity, and this is why people often leave their homes when they are frustrated. Nevertheless, you live at home, and if you have come out of a rough time with your spouse, it is always good to rearrange your home so that you and your spouse can focus on something positive instead of revisiting the negative. It could be that lamp that sits in your living room that has a bad memory attached to it. Maybe you picked it up in a threatening way during an argument, and now that lamp has a negative feel to it with your spouse. Anytime the spouse sees it, they remember how you were ready to sling it at them. Because of this, they often, and for no apparent reason, develop a negative attitude towards you.

I try to use happy colors or romantic colors in my home because colors do affect mood. Black and red are depressing colors and should never been the main colors of a room. They make great accent colors, but a room painted black or red will be one that is depressing to be in. Blues are calming, and white is peaceful. Now, this information was found in many case studies, but their studies usually record what affects the majority of people that were tested.

Let's say your husband has been frustrated. He's frustrated with work, home, and just people in general, but he doesn't want to talk about it. You're sitting and watching him deteriorate into an angry and depressed state, and you don't know how to bring him back into the realm of peace. First understand that his body is with you, but his mind is in a different place. You love the man, but you do not understand why he's been so agitated and negative lately. What can you do? First off, don't argue with him. You cannot cure a disease with a disease. You have to help bring your husband back into the realm of peace. If it'll help, think of the two of you on the war-front. He's wounded. Do you place his arm around your neck and help him to safety, or do you finish him off? Unfortunately, many spouses choose to further frustrate the spouse because they don't like the atmosphere being generated by the spouse. The correct way is to rescue your loved ones and change the atmosphere.

Here are a few tips that may work for you:

1. While hubby is at work, take time out to talk to the LORD. Really talk to HIM and tell HIM what's going on. Yes, HE sees it, but HE wants to hear from you. Instead of asking HIM up front to change the situation, ask HIM to help you to understand the situation for what is really is. Sometimes, our spouses' decline is a direct result of where we keep taking them, and GOD not only wants your spouse to change, but you may be required to change as well. Don't always see the one suited up for war as the problem. Sometimes, we throw so many warring words at them, and then we wonder why they walk around on the offensive.
2. Pray over your house. Some people have demonic attachments and when you welcome them in your home, you give their demons a house key. If you notice that after a visit of a certain friend or family member that you and your spouse tend to fight more, you may want to stop those visits. Cast down every demon, power and stronghold that may be looming in or over your home.

3. Next, be sure your house is clean. Not just straightened up, but clean. Get rid of anything that has a negative attachment or memory to it. For example, any clothes that you had during fornication should be destroyed. If you or your spouse had an extra-marital affair, whatever clothes they wore during this affair should be destroyed because they have a negative energy and memory attached to them. Doing this not only helps to remove all of the negativity from your atmosphere, but it teaches you to remain positive in all that you do. For example, if you are a swearer and you've cursed your spouse out a few times, you should agree to throw out any and everything that you were wearing when you did this. This will teach you not to curse or to curse your spouse out because before you think to do so, you will become more conscious of what you are wearing, and this may serve as a deterrent.

4. Speak peace into your home every day. *"And when you come into a house, greet it. And if the house be worthy, let your peace come upon it: but if it be not worthy, let your peace return to you"* (Matthew 10:12-13).

5. Invite laughter and positivity into your home, but lock out negative emotions. Don't watch negative movies or listen to songs that are condescending. Look for the spirit behind everything that you listen to or watch.

6. Pay attention to the vibes or energy on others. A person's energy will radiate from them and contaminate or bless whatever place they are sitting in. Their energy tells you what spirit is in operation in them. If a demon is in or attached to them, they will display negative energy, and this energy is contagious. This is why you feel drained after being around certain people. They are draining because negative energy sucks away at positive energy to try and charge itself. Energy represents power. Don't let negative people come and suck the life out of your home, your marriage, or your children. It's okay; if they are negative, they are speaking negatively about you anyway, because

this is the power that is in operation within them.

When You Need to Be Quarantined

Hubby and I were arguing one day and I was furious. Being that he is not American, of course we have a difference of culture. Well, in his culture family can call or visit every day, all day with no regard to your plans. Of course, most of us Americans enjoy our peaceful romantic days with our spouses....alone, with no phone calls or visits. *(Thankfully, we stay far away from his friends and family, otherwise, I'd probably be writing this book leaving bloody fingerprints, but I digress.)* Anyhow, hubby had just started his vacation, and I was excited about being able to spend some quality time with him. Suddenly, his phone rang, and I could hear the yelling from the other end of the phone. Here we go again; somebody has a problem in his family, and now it's supposed to be our problem. I could also feel the atmosphere changing in my little humble abode as he yelled into the phone line, pacing back and forth. So, I decided to talk to him once the call ended, hoping for a positive response. Maybe he'll understand that I want some time with him without his phone ringing, and I definitely don't want anyone calling here dropping off their problems. I made my plea and was met with an aggressive tone. He instead became aggressive in his tone towards me, accusing me of not wanting him to talk to his family. His response and his tone caught me off guard. I wasn't guarded, and I wasn't hostile. But, I knew what it was: He'd just gotten a frustrating call, someone's negative energy was transferred to him, and he turned and transferred it to me and I didn't receive it well. Before I knew it, I was ready to call him everything but a child of GOD, but I could feel the LORD pulling me. I tried to take off my ring, but I hurt my finger. I was upset, so I went into our bedroom and closed the door to keep myself from speaking because I understood that I was about to pour out something that should be cast down. As I was lying on the bed, I had all kinds of thoughts flooding my head and they weren't good thoughts. All of a sudden, I was reminded to cast down the thoughts; nevertheless, I wanted to go out of the room and tell him a piece of my mind. Then I heard the LORD say, "Quarantine." I was being quarantined because of the infectious anger that I was displaying; I had to be quarantined so that I would not further contaminate the atmosphere. It started with the phone call. Someone called and poured out their negativity into him, and he turned and poured it into me. For some, the flu gives them nothing more than a slight cough, but when they give it to someone else, that person's body doesn't handle it well. They become gravely sick and have to be hospitalized. This is what happened on that phone call. When the negativity was dumped on him, he had a slight attitude, but when he gave it to me, my anger became highly infectious. Because of this, I had to be quarantined. So, I decided to take a walk to calm myself down.

While I was walking, I could feel the anger subsiding. I walked, and I talked to the LORD and made a commitment to HIM that when I arrived home, I wouldn't say anything out of anger to Jean. I would wait to calm down, and we would have one of those family meetings that he detests. Not because he hates them, but because this is what we agreed to in times of peace. When problems arise, once we're calm, we have to talk about them.

Anger is contagious, and it can sometimes be deadly. In the fury of anger, we have to be mature enough to quarantine ourselves until the anger subsides. That way, we can communicate in love and not say the things that we have to apologize for later. When negative energy is transferred from one person to another, its friction often draws a bigger spark when it hits the surface of their heart. As human beings, we like our heads to be left alone so we can think clearly, and when something invades it, we tend to overreact. Especially women. Many women like to see their husbands waving in surrender so that a treaty of communication can be set in place, whereas men tend to stab and retreat. That is, men like to throw a few hard words and then try to flee the argument by withdrawing into their imaginations or by going into another room. If it gets too bad, men tend to leave the house to avoid further confrontation. In arguments, men often avoid eye contact by focusing on something close to their wives' eyes so that they can pretend to be listening. The nose and teeth are favorite focal points as well, and if there is a pimple somewhere on the wife's face, it's now getting more attention than she is. Of course, this is not all men....just a large number of them.

Please keep in mind the next time that you are upset with your spouse that anger is an infectious disease that doesn't have to be heard in order to spread. There are better ways to resolve issues than to resort to verbally attacking one another. The correct way to argue is to not argue at all.

Fellows: I know that talking about problems isn't always welcome. You hate 'the talk.' Nevertheless; most women aren't complicated, but they seem complicated to your own understanding because you believe you have to assert your position and diffuse your wife of whatever power you perceive she's carrying. This is because of the warrior that is built in you. You have to learn when to unleash the warrior, and when to embrace your wife. Most decent women tend to speak truthfully, without having some off-the-wall motives. Listen to your wife without allowing the devil to convince you that she's trying to take over. She may have a real problem in real time and want real solutions. If you don't do this, you may have to quarantine your wife.

Ladies: Get to the point. Being a woman, I understand that we like to present exhibit A through Z before making our case, but this isn't necessary. With a lot of men, you have two minutes to make your point. After that, he's watching cartoons in his imagination, or he may get defensive, and you may end up having to quarantine him.

Stop regurgitating issues from the past. You were cured of that mess long ago, so why is it still in your blood? That's easy. Because you keep allowing your mind to have relations with it, and every time you do, you get infected again. The infection sits and stews until the next argument, and then it pours out in your spouse's ears. Ask yourself this, "What am I hoping to gain by constantly bringing up things of the past?" If your answer is, "So history doesn't repeat itself," then you need to go and pick up the bible and study Isaiah 43:25, *"I, even I, am he that blotteth out thy transgressions for mine own sake, and will not remember thy sins."* You cannot stop history from repeating itself by constantly repeating history. Some things are better left in the past. If GOD will forgive us, who are we that we can't forgive one another? If GOD will forget our sins, why do we remember the sins of others?

Remember, the next time you feel angry, go someplace where you can wrestle with yourself. Explain this to your spouse in times of peace, so that they will understand what you are doing when you go off into another room when you are upset. This is an agreement that the both of you should have. The angriest spouse needs to be quarantined. The provoking spouse needs to be quarantined and during these times, you have to search the WORD of GOD for a cure. Treatments are only good for a little time, but cures last forever.

When we allow ourselves to pour out the venom that we have allowed to enter us, we bring about plagues of hurt that our spouses have to recover from. Walking around your own home, not speaking isn't an option because you are not supposed to let the sun go down on your anger. Instead, the two of you should go into separate rooms to cool down when anger is present. DO NOT ALLOW WICKED THOUGHTS TO FOLLOW YOU INTO THE ROOM. Instead, think of the peace that you want and make your planned discussion with your spouse goal-oriented at reaching that peaceful place. Write down your notes for the family meeting, and your spouse should do the same. It is better to look past the problem than to look at the problem.

Release Date

Marriage can be very much like a lengthy prison sentence if it isn't cultivated and pruned daily. It has to constantly be shaped, and every thorn in it has to be snipped; otherwise, we begin to prick one another often. And when we think we are serving time with our spouse, many times it's not the marriage that is in bondage, but it is our minds that are in bondage. Just because your marriage is a struggle doesn't mean you are married to the wrong person. It could very well be that you are married to the wrong kind of person, meaning the season wasn't right; you picked that plum a little too soon and now, while it's bitter, you think the devil is in it. But in truth, we all had to and continue to mature in the things of GOD. Then again, you may just be the bitter fruit. You could possibly be married to the individual who GOD had just for you, but he or she is struggling through a jungle of flesh. You don't send divorce papers into the jungle to rid yourself of the problem. If you've come out of that jungle, then you know the way...lead the way. Even when they don't want to follow, you should lead by example. Sometimes leading is following. Don't follow the mate into sin, but there are some things that you can compromise on;

nevertheless, you refuse to because your pride says no. A good example would be a wife wanting to spend Saturday mornings with her friends. The husband objects to his wife's desire to hang out with the girls, and this has brought a rift between them. One or both of them has to compromise, but many times an issue as small as this will serve as the foundation for other issues to come. Should she listen to her husband or should he honor his wife's request? Yes. Yes to what? She should listen to her husband and he should honor his wife's request. How so? They should sit down and try to figure out how to merge their wishes by detailing what they feel and why they feel that way. If insecurity is on the back burner, you do not feed that issue; you check the root so the both of you can team up to pull it up. The problem is people are blind and see their spouses as the problem. If the two would truly open their eyes and see Satan as the problem, they could form a big fist in unity; but blind people fight the wind.

Betty was born blind and she met and married Bob, who was also born blind. One day, Betty's sister, Myra, who doesn't like Bob, came to the house and began pushing Bob into Betty. In Betty's anger, she starts to attack Bob, while Myra stands by laughing inwardly. Bob gets tired of being attacked, so he lashes out as well. In the end, Bob files for divorce, citing irreconcilable differences, and Betty goes on to meet another man who Myra picked out for her.

Who's the devil here? Myra, of course, but at the same time, both Betty and Bob were foolish for not communicating. Should they have talked, they would have found out how evil and divisive Myra was, and they could have banded together against her. Instead, they gave Myra what she wanted, and Myra continues to make plans for Betty's life by setting her up with someone who she handpicked. Isn't this what Satan does to us? He shoves us into one another in misunderstandings, miscommunication, and pride so that we can fight one another and eventually divorce one another. Afterward, he sets the men and women both up with his own children so that their walk will continually be hindered, all the way to the grave.

Ladies: Do you know how powerful your home would be if you stopped resisting your husband's attempt to be the head and you stood in position, ready to be the strong Proverbs 31 woman that you claim to be?
Fellows: Do you know how powerful your home would be if you stopped being so forceful and stubborn and you did what GOD commanded Abraham to do? HE commanded Abraham to hearken or listen to the voice of his wife.

The two of you wouldn't have to separate and reconcile if you would only learn to sit down and reconcile your answers. For example: Your husband wants new shoes, but you don't like them. What should you do? Deal with it. Let him be his unique self and stop trying to form him into being your idea of what you want your husband to be. Your wife wants to cook beef stew her own way, but you prefer your Mom's way. What should you do? Marry your Mom or learn to love your wife's cooking. Stop trying to get your mom to teach her how to cook it "her" way. In this, the answer will always present itself in a way that supersedes what you initially wanted. You wanted Mama's beef stew, but you got wife's beef stew. As time goes on, your wife will get better at it, and she will begin to find her own unique recipe that you and the children will learn to love.

Never put your spouse in bondage. Please know that when a prisoner gets released from prison, oftentimes they go out and commit the same crimes because there was no rehabilitation in the prison. They were punished, but not corrected. Corrected would imply that they were shown the right way. When you try to imprison your spouse by attempting to tell them what to do, you have become their warden. When they do get some time away from you, oftentimes they repeat the crime or commit other marriage crimes because they weren't rehabilitated; they were simply punished. If your spouse, for example, has been unfaithful to you before, you should not try to control their time away from you to ensure that it doesn't happen again. You communicate what you want from your spouse, what you expect from your spouse, and the consequences they may face should they re-offend. You leave it at that for the spouse to decide whether the risk is worth it or not. No matter what you do or say, if a person wills themselves into the arms of another, they have made a choice, and you can't stop them from following through with that choice. You simply decide if this is what you want for you or not. You cannot make them serve time in your prison of hurt and emotion, hoping that if they see how hurt you are, they'll stop.

If you are the binding spouse, you yourself are in bondage. This is why you want to imprison your spouse. Rather than working on your relationship, try working on you, and it'll trickle down into your relationship. If you don't think you are wrong, simply pray this prayer (Talk to the LORD first and be honest with HIM, and then you can follow it by saying the following):
LORD, you see everything. You know that I love (insert spouse's name here), but I have been feeling (insert your feelings here) about him or her. I have been bothered and I felt like I needed to keep my eyes on him or her to make sure that it doesn't happen again, but LORD, you are GOD of all. I don't want to lord myself over your creation. LORD, I ask that you search out my heart and my spouse's heart and remove every demonic seed, every rebellious root, and every idolatrous way from us and cause us to love and trust you more. FATHER, feed us with wisdom, knowledge and understanding and keep us even when we don't want to be kept. Give us peace and change the both of us that we may better serve you and in doing so, I know that we will automatically begin to be the couple who you have called us to be, unified and true. In JESUS Name, we pray...Amen.

Freedom To Make Mistakes

Almost every married person strives to be perfect until they realize that being perfect isn't possible or necessary. But, isn't it amazing that we place standards on our spouses that we can't live by ourselves? For example, hubby is chewed up and spit out because he forgot to let the toilet seat down. That is not the way to handle a person who loves you. The wife is making those irritating popping sounds with her teeth again, and you think it's a plot to destroy your sanity. Now, you're not speaking to her in an attempt to break her habit for her. One thing about being married is you get the opportunity to see your spouse fully naked. Not just without clothing, but without the outdoor face that we tend to put on for the world. You have the blessed opportunity and the wrenching disgust of seeing your spouse's flaws. Even if your husband turns out to be a Pastor; only you and GOD get the chance to see him as he is: full of flaws. But, in giving your hand to him in holy matrimony, you are committing to never expose his flaws to the outside world, but to help him become as flawless as possible, and he must do the same thing for you.

When your spouse's flaws are before you, how do you react? You should always empathize and understand that we tend to deal with one another according to where we are. Therefore, your spouse's flaws are simply a reflection of where they are spiritually. Let them grow up in CHRIST, and don't try to force feed them, hoping to speed up the process. A baby cries because crying is an instinct that he or she is born with. This is the baby's only means of communication, and it lets the parent know that something is wrong. Maybe the baby is hungry, or the baby has soiled himself or herself. Maybe the infant is not feeling well. A child's cries are his or her alarm system.

What about the grown-up you? You have your very own reaction that lets others know when you are not happy. It's your alarm system, and depending on how sensitive that system is, it goes off rarely or regularly. With a baby, this is a coping mechanism until the baby learns how to speak and communicate through speech. That is why a good parent should always encourage verbal communication. If you can speak it, you'd better say it; but if you cry it, you're too young to have it.

Even though we are adults, we are still GOD'S children and we still have to mature in some area of our lives. Just when we think we're grown up, GOD will allow a storm to come into our lives to show us how old we really are. The same goes for your spouse. As their dark places are exposed to them, they are exposed to you. But, as their spouse, you are called to help them to come out of those dark places, not to further expose them. The bible calls Satan the great accuser, so if you are acting as an accuser, you have allowed Satan to adopt you.

When I was younger spiritually, I wanted to tear down my husband as he was, and rebuild him the way I wanted him to be. I tried every tantrum a child throws. I tried tears, screaming, threatening, and even cursing at him. Now, of course, some of the things he was doing were wrong, but he didn't understand that because a lot of it was learned behavior. He couldn't see his own wrongs because my reaction acted as a distraction. GOD often wants us to be silent so that HE can show our spouses what they need to change. This requires our silence, love, patience, and most of all our trust in GOD. I even cried to the LORD and asked to be released from my marriage, but GOD wasn't listening to my flesh. HE had to work on me before HE would even touch Jean. There was so much flesh on me that was still alive and functioning, and it had to be killed. GOD broke it down to me; cursed words come from cursed people. You can't speak a curse and not expect a curse. Of course, that was enough to stop me from cursing. Temper tantrums are for babies, and babies are often chastened. GOD chastens (corrects) those HE loves. Hebrews 12:7 reads: *"If ye endure chastening, God dealeth with you as with sons; for what son is he whom the father chasteneth not?"* Therefore, many storms aren't demonic attacks; they are flesh-killing floods sent to cause you to stop defaulting to sin. They are sent to grow you up, purge you of wickedness, and send you out as a new man or woman in CHRIST.

The best thing I could do for Jean was to let him make his own mistakes. I was to tell him that what he's doing is not a good move, but when he didn't listen; my role was to take it to JESUS. The LORD would then chasten him and make him face the truth. Experience is a much better teacher than an argument.

After all of the layers of punishment that I tried to bring upon Jean, GOD dealt with me. How can he ever grow up to be discerning and wise if you are always in front of him badgering him like a mother? No one goes straight into walking. They fall a few times and even when they are older, sometimes they trip. What I was doing was hindering his growth. Dear women of GOD: No matter what you say, every individual will go their own way, but in the end if you let him see for himself, life will utter to him the same words that you spoke to him and he will begin to trust you more and more. Force feeding a man is never a good way to get him to eat, but setting a plate before him is a meal that, even if he doesn't want to eat it now, he will come back to eventually.

The lesson here is clear. Your husband may have a friend who you KNOW is bad, but he doesn't see it. Or your wife may be hanging with a woman who you know is immoral, but she doesn't want to accept the truth. Don't be so afraid that these people will change the character of your spouse. Only lay the foundation of truth for them to walk on and let them stumble when and where they need to stumble. But, always be there to pick them up when they do. After a while, you won't have to say a word.

Trying to stop your spouse from making a mistake is a mistake in itself. I had a cousin who had a one-year-old baby boy. I was 15-years-old at the time, and of course, I knew little about children. Anyhow, the little boy was extremely curious, which of course is normal behavior for an infant. One day, I was curling my hair, and he kept trying to reach and grab the curling iron off the dresser as I would lay it down. I kept picking it up and repeating no, and telling him that it was hot. But, no matter how many times I said those words, he would get on his tip-toes and try to reach the curling iron. His mother kept yelling at me from the bathroom, "Tiffany, stop telling him not to touch it, and let him see for himself. He doesn't want to listen, so let him grab it. After that, he'll learn what hot means." I thought she was a horrible mother to make such a request. But, after her yelling that at me a few times, I finally gave in and when he stood on those tips again trying to reach the curling iron, I just stood there and watched him. Those little fingers stretched wide open as he fumbled around to find the object of his affection. He finally found it, and he gripped the curling iron in a way that only a one-year-old could grip it. He closed his whole hand on it, before those neurons told him to let go. That only took a half a second and he was screaming and squealing as he snatched his hand back to check for damage. Besides a bright red palm, he was okay. He cried and ran to his mother, who verbally scalded him some more about not listening. After that, he never reached for that curling iron again, and when someone told him something was hot, he'd withdraw his hand, step back, and repeat those words.

Sometimes, you have to let your spouse 'burn their hands.' You can scream and holler, beg and plea and they still won't listen. But, if you stand by and just watch them as they do what they want to do, you may just be in the right place at the right time to comfort them when they get burned. You don't have to rub it in their face. Experience is GOD'S belt carrier. Experience will beat a grown man into a snotty pulp. All you have to do is continue to be GOD'S star child, so that they can see how HE blesses you, even from within the same house. Ministry isn't always spoken, but it is lived and demonstrated.

A man or woman refusing to listen to your guidance isn't always a foolish person. Sometimes, it's a wise man or woman searching for their own way. Every teacher starts off as a student and oftentimes, your spouse is not called to be in your classroom because you'll either be too hard on them or too lenient.

You have to learn to stop arguing and just learn to build up the man or woman who GOD has loaned you. When a brick falls out of your wife, that isn't a good time to run and show her how unbalanced and destructible she is. That's a good time to pick up that brick and hand it back to her. She has eyes to see and ears to hear. Let her learn to use them. And every time your husband falls down, you shouldn't be there to stand over him and remind him of what you said. Because, in doing so, you are trying to lord yourself over him. This isn't the place that GOD has carved out for you. A Jezebel spirit comes into operation when the head (man) operates as a body and the body (woman) operates as the head. The correct order is GOD--> CHRIST--> Man--> Woman. Circumstances set climates, and there are some climates and atmospheres that demonic spirits thrive in. When you allow this atmosphere into your marriage, you are living amongst demons.

Let everyone make their own mistakes so they can learn from them. Have you ever seen a little boy whose mother shielded him from everything? He has absolutely no experience in life and is just as naïve and shallow at 25 as he was at two. In her shielding him, his mother didn't warn him that one day he would be without his shield. When battles arrived in his life, it didn't take much to bring him down because he didn't know how to fight after his mother passed. Little things in life were enough to break him. Men who were shielded don't handle break-ups well, even the ones from women that they barely knew. Nevertheless, that experienced little boy who has fallen off his bike a few times, made many mistakes, gotten many whoopings, and has experienced being broken up with a few times, tends to do okay once his mother is no longer with him because she let GOD be his shield. She simply prayed that his life and his health were kept and that GOD would turn him around, should he stray. He dealt with the immoral woman, he has lost a few jobs, he may have even gone into the extremes of sin, but one day he woke up a man. Strong, wise, and able to bear long-suffering, he presses forward as a soldier. Hard times don't scratch him, they buffer him. This man is wife-ready. He knows that no matter what storm comes upon his home, it too shall pass. He knows that no matter how many times he and his wife argue, he can still take his place under CHRIST and make it right again.

Marriage Is Not All About You

One trait that does not belong in a marriage is selfishness. Selfishness is a surefire way to destroy a union and cause it to end bitterly. The truth is that we are all selfish beings, but this is why we are called to first seek out GOD and let HIM appoint the season for us to get married and the person that we are to marry. During the seasons before you are to meet your spouse, "me" is slowly being scraped away from you. This means you are dying to yourself and learning to be selfless. Our selfish self wants to be married because we want someone to come and serve as tools to make us happy or happier. In other words, the average person's reason for even wanting to be married in the first place is rooted in pure selfishness. As we go forth in CHRIST, the selfish man begins to perish and shed away from us. Then, we are clothed with knowledge, wisdom, understanding and righteousness. We absolutely must have these blessings in order to survive a marriage or for our marriages to survive. Without wisdom, knowledge, understanding, and righteousness; the selfish man thrives and goes into marriage seeking a god or to be a god. When the spouse does not serve to fill the void of the natural man, contention will always follow.

But, what if you are already married and the selfish man just didn't die before you got married? Now, there are plenty of problems arising in your union and not enough solutions. The best thing that you can do is stop trying to resuscitate the marriage and start trying to resuscitate your faith. Ask GOD to change you and your spouse, and then you have to be willing to let HIM kill your flesh. The issue is that you are not in order when you are trying to revive a relationship with a person without first reviving your relationship with the LORD. Sure, you may be praying to HIM every day, but that doesn't mean that you are in good standing with HIM. That simply means that you are on speaking terms with HIM, but is HE speaking back to you? Are you not hearing back from HIM in relation to your marriage? The distance between you and GOD is always created by you, not GOD. Your sin will drive you from HIS presence. Maybe you have someone that you have not yet forgiven. Maybe that person is your spouse. Maybe you're the type of spouse that holds grudges because you believe that the longer you hold that grudge, the more you'll break your spouse down and teach them a lesson. When you think like this, it's because you are still wrapped up in yourself, and therefore, you are still trying to get your spouse to serve your hurt, unforgiveness, need for power, void, and so on. If selfishness is not in a union, neither spouse will hold a grudge. A grudge is born of selfishness and it only dies when wisdom lives in you.

What's the shelf life of your problems? Are there issues from years ago still sitting on your heart's shelves that you have stored away from some time? Just like food, every issue in your marriage has an expiration date, and anytime you let them sit past that expiration date, you cause what is in your heart to send its foul vapors from your mouth. Every problem that you have or have had with your spouse should be already dead. In order to move to the next level in your marriage, you must bury the problems of old in order to birth the blessings of new. You can never get to a blessing by acting as a curse.

It's easy to tell which spouse has issues with selfishness. It's always the one who is the moodiest. Moody people are that way because they think things should play out a certain way for them, and when they don't, what's on the shelves on their hearts begin to release its fumes. Maybe you hurt your spouse at some time in the marriage, and now that spouse is trying to get you to serve their hurt by reminding you of what you've done. This is an issue that has to be removed from the marriage immediately in order for it to continue. Serving one's hurt is serving time in a mental prison, and such a prison can open up the doors for many additional problems to enter a marriage. For example, let's say that you are a husband and you're still angry with your wife for talking to her ex-boyfriend last year. She felt neglected by you and she was angry at you for your indiscretions in the marriage, so she chose to tell him about what you did. In her mind, she thought she could exchange numbers with him and just catch up on things, get his perspective on things, and she simply didn't have a plan as to where she'd go from there. This has served as a point of hurt and heartache for you, and you can't seem to escape it. Your wife has assured you that her intentions, while unwise, were innocent, and she has reassured you over and over again that she will never make this mistake again. Nevertheless, you can't seem to fully get past the betrayal. After all, this is the same man who got in your face about her when you were dating. So, nowadays, you take it day by day. Some days are good, and you are able to provide your wife a steady flow of happiness that day. Some days are not so good, and you prefer to be alone on those days to wallow in your hurt. Now, you want her to serve your hurt, and she's not doing a great job at it anymore. Do you see how the disease of "me" can spread from partner to partner and kill a marriage? Situations like that not only destroy a marriage, but they cause the marriage to suffer a slow and agonizing death where the corpses of trust, understanding, and respect sit and rot away.

"Me" is a disease; let's see it that way. "We," however, is the cure. Selflessness doesn't taste so good when you're used to dining on selfishness, but it is an acquired taste that you can and will adjust to if you want to.

Your marriage has an atmosphere that it thrives in, and this is the temperature that you need to keep it at. Anytime either one of you is selfish in your demands, actions, or words; you will find that the temperature of that marriage will begin to drop, and if you don't stop, that marriage will slowly die. Rather than talking about how you feel all the time, try considering how your spouse feels. Marriage was not created to serve you; marriage was created to mimic our relationship with GOD and help us to understand our relationship with HIM. Marriage always fails when there are two selfish individuals trying to head it up. If you want a near perfect marriage, you and your spouse must try to make the marriage better than good for one another. In doing so, the both of you will learn to love, trust, and respect each other at such a capacity that can only be accomplished in GOD. Anytime two people try to please one another, they experience a better marriage; but anytime there is a selfish stow-away in the marriage, the union will slowly lose its life.

How do you remove selfishness from your union?

1. Wake up every day with your mind on pleasing GOD. Do HIS will at all times.
2. Always be pleasant to your spouse...even when they don't deserve it.
3. Seek ways to please your spouse daily. Little gestures mean a lot. For example, try bringing in the newspaper and sitting it on the kitchen table in the morning. (Please note that this is not to be done with expectation of gain. Instead, do it from your heart and your spouse's selfishness will slowly fade away. You don't have to correct your spouse; GOD will do it through you when you obey HIM.)
4. Do the opposite of what you want sometimes. If you hate fishing, but your spouse loves to fish, go fishing with him or her sometimes. Make it 50/50. One week, your spouse

does what you want, and the next week, you should do what he or she wants. Don't just act like you are enjoying yourself; find ways to enjoy yourself. Your spouse will not have a good time if you're moping along, making him or her feel as if he or she has dragged you there. You don't have to touch the fish, for example...learn to identify them. This could serve as a hobby for you and help to unite you with your spouse even more.

5. Say the opposite of what you want to say when you're upset. When you want to tell your spouse how terrible they are, try telling them some of the things about them that are good. You have no idea how powerful this weapon is! In doing so, you will cause the atmosphere to break, demons to flee, and the blessings of GOD to shut the door behind them.

6. Spend time alone with yourself to see how well you get along with yourself. Wait until the spouse goes to work and just find a comfortable spot and sit there. Can you handle your thoughts at this time, or are they bothering you? If your thoughts are bothering you; your words are bothering your spouse. If you will, go out to eat alone...maybe when the spouse is away. Are you picking up that cell phone constantly to call your spouse or someone else to rescue you from yourself? If so, you need to work more on yourself until you love being with you. Nobody else will like to be around you if you can't stand to be around yourself.

7. Sow a seed into your marriage. Money tends to rise in power in many Christian homes, and for this power to be demolished, you need to sow a seed. How do you sow a seed into your marriage? By putting a certain amount of money into a savings account every week or month. This money is stored up for a vacation to be taken once a year. You can also buy things that your spouse needs.

8. Simply do the opposite of selfishness by consciously taking

notes of your actions and moving immediately to change them.

Creating an Itch For the Spouse to Scratch

As spouses, we sometimes have days when we are not the happiest or we simply want something to occur that day. So we create conversations, arguments, and scenes just so we can play out this situation that has been looming over us.

Have you ever taken a thread and ran it across your skin to create an itch just so you can scratch it? Have you ever taken your fingers and gently rubbed them across your arm until it itched? Believe it or not, many people do this; not just with thread, but in their marriages. We do this when we are bored, and our minds start acting like a dead battery. It'll engage many thoughts until it finds one that has enough spark in it to crank us up, and this is when trouble starts roaring its engine.

It goes without saying; every day isn't always a fun day for us. Some days are great, and we'd love to go back and relive them, and then there are the not so great days. In many cases, you will find that your worst days aren't necessarily the days where trouble met you at your bedside, but these are the days when you were simply idle and went looking for trouble. When we are idle, we start looking for itches to scratch. Many people would argue that much of what they dig up are unresolved issues that have been pressing them for a while. This is how they justify creating chaos in their homes. Chaos, however, starts in the heart and rips its way out. So, whenever you are feeling the need to start a fight, or have that talk that you know is going to lead to a fight, you need to take the time out to address yourself. Ask yourself what it is that you are searching for in this re-match that you are trying to call. Be honest with yourself. Let's take it up a notch. Go into a room alone, get a piece of paper, and write a note to yourself. Describe what you are feeling and why you are feeling that way. If that doesn't calm you down, write a note to your spouse and detail how you feel in the note. Once you're done, tear the note up and you will more than likely find that the desire to confront the spouse is no longer there. Oftentimes, the issue does not need to be taken up with the spouse; the issue is coming from within the spouse who is carrying the problem. Rather than taking it to the spouse, take it to JESUS.

The best thing to do is to stay busy. A busy mind doesn't have time to wander. If you find that your mind is traveling down dark roads looking for trouble, it's time to step back and pray yourself back into the driver's seat. Remember, the best thing that you can do is go and confront the issue...not your spouse. If there is an old issue that has been looming over your mind and you have already talked with your spouse about it, yet you haven't received any resolution of the issue, it may be a good idea to seek Christian counseling. Sometimes, a mediator can help your spouse AND you see things from a better perspective. Never go to a personal friend of yours unless GOD leads you to speak with them. Oftentimes, our friends will take our side and they may truly agree with our way of thinking...after all, they are our friends, and that's why we hang around them. Like minds think alike. Occasionally, you may find that one friend who is completely honest with you...whether you like it or not. But that doesn't mean they will always give you the best advice. The advice you get needs to be in line with the WORD of GOD.

The best thing to do for self is to draw up a plan to discipline yourself. If you find that you are being argumentative and cranky, go into a secluded room and deal with yourself until your attitude has been corrected. Go somewhere and get busy. Tell yourself the truth without taking your own side. Would you want to live with you or deal with your attitude? If you answer is no, then don't make someone else deal with it. There is no need to create an argument just to scratch your boredom or your guilt. Instead, always seek to keep peace in your home. Every day, you need to consciously pay attention to your marriage so that you can recognize anything that's out of place. When you find something out of place, simply adjust it in love and get back to living.

Adultery Prevention

What if there was an issue where your spouse hasn't been completely honest with you, and you can't seem to find any peace? You want the truth so that you can start the healing process and the two of you can move forward with your lives. One thing that I found to be an effective way of getting Jean to be completely honest with me is by not getting mad when he tells me something, and by not bringing it back up in later arguments. Thankfully, I haven't had any known issues of infidelity in my current marriage, but there are many issues that people try to hide because they are afraid of how you (the spouse) will react. What I did from the beginning of our marriage was to talk to Jean about minor things, and I would ask him to be honest with me. I told him that I wouldn't get mad, and I didn't. Over the years, I have made it a point to show myself faithfully calm, loving, and understanding about the issues that my husband would have ordinarily tried to keep under wraps from me. This has proven to be very effective because he now feels and knows that he can tell me anything and I won't get upset. My goal was to show him that I would not and could not in good conscious let him carry around a burden in our home and not share it with me. Ladies, you will find that men tend to keep more secrets than women do. They worry about how they will be seen by their wives. For example, if your husband isn't performing his best at work, he may not tell you because he's afraid of how you will view him. It is always a great idea to keep the lines of communication open, and for your spouse to know that if he or she was to access a line that you'd never want to answer, that you would handle the communications with love and with understanding. In doing so, you will find that a lot of marriages that ended because of an adulterous affair could have been saved should those lines of communication had been opened. This isn't to justify the adulterer because they bore more of the responsibility of that failed marriage if the spouse was submitting (physically) to them. Everyone's marriage is different, and I understand that everyone won't have the same lines of communication open in their homes as others have. Honestly, it will depend on the individuals involved and what they can and cannot handle.

After having one marriage end because of adultery, I decided to speak with Jean about adultery before we said our nuptials. I decided not to leave any rock unturned, so I was honest with him about my previous marriage. I'd committed adultery in my previous marriage trying to take revenge against my previous partner because of his indiscretions. I admitted to Jean that I'd regretted the choice to commit adultery from the moment I acted it out; not just because it was wrong morally, but I was more torn up that I had hurt GOD and threw away my virtue. Knowing that I'd went against GOD ripped at me more than anything, and that punishment was too great for me. I told him that I would never and could never hurt GOD again because I love HIM too much now, and because adultery is not a cure for adultery. After my testimony, I thought that Jean would judge me and wouldn't trust me, but instead he shocked me by telling me that he understood that I was just hurting and wasn't thinking clearly. After opening up to him, he began to open up to me, and soon this became the norm for us. We learned to be best friends, and we learned that we could trust one another with our thoughts. So, we opened the door for truth and I told Jean that there were a lot of women in this world who'd happily throw themselves at him. I asked him to tell me about any incidents where he was tempted or any incidents that seemed weird to him, and I in turn agreed to do the same with him. Do you know what that did? Because pride didn't come in and close the door of truth, truth came in and opened up a line of communication. When that line opened, not only did it close many doors of temptation that could have come open, but it also opened up a line of comfort and compatibility. Jean and I are comfortable with one another, and we don't worry about one another having an affair. That fear is not there! This is amazing to me because I was once imprisoned and tortured by that fear, but now I know what peace feels like. Am I saying that my husband could never and has never had an affair? No, I will never say what a person will, can, and cannot do. What I am saying is that I know that if it ever happened, he wouldn't be afraid to tell me because as he states, he loves and appreciates not just our relationship, but our friendship. Many couples forget to have that friendship in their marriages. Instead, many have romantic expectations of one another.

Woman of GOD, let me tell you that there are times when other women will try to seduce your husband and he won't recognize what is happening. Men don't think like women, and they don't see all situations the way that we see them. Therefore, flirtation sometimes doesn't look like flirtation to many men. They simply see an overly friendly woman, but you will see the truth because you are a woman. A lot of times these women can be your husband's co-workers. Having that line of communication open allows him to tell you about incidents that were strange to him, and you can explain her behavior to him and tell him how to prevent anything from happening. Please understand that if he does not know, he may very well not have any intentions to commit adultery against you, but that woman could easily go and say that he made advancements at her. This has happened a lot! There were many cases where, for example, a man would let his co-worker come and sit in his office on her break. To him, she was just being friendly and wanted to tell him about the issues she was having with her husband...but, in truth, she was trying to open a door to have an affair with him. After he didn't make a move on her, she decided to make one on him. When that didn't work, she went to the office and lied on him because she was too humiliated to look in his face another day, she was angry that he'd turned her down, she was upset that she'd wasted so much unfruitful time flirting with him, and she did not know how to handle rejection. You warn your sons about these types of women, so warn your husbands as well. If the lines of communication are opened between the two of you, and he knows that he can come to you about her without you getting upset, such an incident can be prevented. That's why GOD calls you the help-mates.

In addition, let's be honest with ourselves; our mates are human beings wrapped in flesh. To tell yourself that your spouse could never and would never be attracted to another human being is to lie to yourself and to set yourself up to be hurt. There are many people in this world who your spouse will find attractive. After all, they've got eyes to see. One of the worst things you could do in your marriage is to compare yourself to or compete with another human being. As beautiful as that woman is, she does not have what you have....your spouse. And don't forget.... you are beautiful as well. I never look at another woman and compare myself to her because I think I'm beautiful, just like I may see her as beautiful. Her beauty does not discount mine. Instead, there is one who will behold her beauty and he may not see me as beautiful, and there is someone who will see me as attractive that does not find her attractive. That's just how it works. I don't worry that Jean would think another woman is prettier than me because men don't think that way, so I don't subject him to such foolish questions. A man will see a woman that is attractive to him, and he will decide what he wants to do about it. That's it. She doesn't have to be prettier than his wife for him to decide to have an affair. In many cases, the mistress (by the standards of many) isn't as pretty as the wife...but, this did not matter to the man because beauty is irrelevant when it comes to sex, and beauty is irrelevant when it comes to matters of the heart. Therefore, woman of GOD...never act or be insecure around other women. It is absolutely disgusting to come across a woman who tries to tear other women down because she is intimidated by them. Instead, always be attractively yourself...confident, intelligent, and loving. Jean tells me all the time that there is nothing more attractive than a confident woman. He always says that if there was a room filled with beautiful women, and there is one woman there that is not as attractive as the rest of the women, but she is more confident than they are, she will be the one who gets the most attention. I've been around women who have folded their arms and pouted when other women were around. They snarled at their husband for even communicating with these women. This makes them stick out like a sore thumb, and it makes those other women look even better.

Man of GOD, your wife is a treasure that many men wish they could have. You know that there are many men out there that will flirt with your wife, hoping to ignite an affair. They don't necessarily want to marry your wife, but just like women, men can be competitive. He just wants to win...that's it. Sometimes, he just wants to play hero if he finds that your wife needs rescuing. One of the worst things you can ever do to your wife is to put her in a position where she needs to be rescued. Not just from you, but from any pain that is lingering on the inside of her. Women are fragile creatures who love to feel understood, protected, and most of all loved. Nevertheless, women can be challenging because each woman has her own definition and understanding as to what love is and what love does. Your challenge is to find out how your wife defines love, and if her definition is wrong, redefine it for her so that she can experience real love. You too have to close any doors that temptation can enter in through. Unlike men, women can carry on affairs for years undetected. Is it because men aren't as intelligent as women? I don't think that's the case; I believe it's because the outside man may not want to have your wife on a permanent basis, he just wants to continue having sex with her with no strings attached. So, he'll happily hide out and help her to keep her secret under wraps. Women aren't the same, however. Most women who sleep with a married man have every intention of taking him for themselves; therefore, women don't hide out well. Women will hide out for a little while, because women are creatures of organization. We like to organize things, schedules, and our discussions. So, many times the mistress will give the man a certain amount of time to leave his wife, but she won't always tell him that he's on a time frame. She just believes that, for example, in a year's time, the husband should have left his wife and come to her. When that time comes and goes, many mistresses will come out of hiding and either confront the wife, threaten the wife, or begin to leave obvious clues for the wife to find. If the husband won't leave the wife, she'll try to make the wife leave the husband. Anyhow, back to the message. Temptation will come at your wife; don't think otherwise. But, women aren't so easily tempted into adulterous affairs. You will find that many women come home and tell their husbands about, for example, that flirting co-worker. That's because women try to show their husbands that they can be trusted, and they hope the husband will reciprocate.

Women are tempted the most when they are starving emotionally. Let's say that your wife came to you and wanted to talk about your marriage. She's been feeling neglected lately, and she wants to know what is wrong. This is irritating to you because, in your mind, there is nothing wrong. Instead, the stability of the marriage is scaring her because she is used to the highs of being on cloud nine, but now that you are at cruising altitude, she is panicking. Anyhow, you send her away because her conversation is stupid to you, and you think that she's just trying to start an argument. That's not always the case. Women sometimes have to be reassured because women go through hormonal fluctuations that tend to affect their moods. There will be a time where she doesn't need much reassuring because she's full of estrogen and the sun is shining. Then, there are the times when those estrogen levels may not be so high and she may be feeling gloomy. That's not her fault; we have Eve to thank for that. The best way to handle a gloomy wife is to be her sunshine. Think about it this way. How long does an argument generally last in your home? On average, an argument lasts about thirty minutes. How long would it have taken you to reassure your wife? On average, a loving gesture could take as little as a minute, and up to five minutes. Jean found a loving way to deal with my "bad" days. If I'm acting cranky, he will simply turn and look at the calendar. If "woman's day" is close, he will look back at me and say, "I'm not even mad at you. I understand that you are about to go through that woman's thing and your hormones are making your crazy." He says this with a smile on his face that can only make me laugh, and then I look at the calendar and apologize. Anyhow, when a woman is feeling neglected, the best thing you can do is look for a way to solve the problem with her. If she feels neglected, and she brings the issue to you only to have it thrown back at her, she may try to talk to another man about the problem. BELIEVE IT OR NOT...THIS IS COMMON WITH WOMEN. It's not that the woman is looking to have an affair, it's just that she's trying to understand you and feels that a woman can't give her the answers that she needs. This isn't a wise move because it does give that man an edge over the husband because he gives her something that she needs...a listening ear. Women tend to be attracted to men that listen; ask any woman that. Therefore, you need to make sure that your wife remains attracted to you.

If your wife is a talker and you know she'll go on and on for days on end, try buying her a tape recorder. It's a funny gesture that just might work. (Now, if she's the explosive type, don't do that.) Give her the tape recorder and tell her to record messages for you to listen to. Tell her that you will listen to the messages and respond face to face or via recorder. Open up the lines of face to face communication as well, but for those days when she's long-winded, give her the recorder. Women feel awkward talking into a machine, but women like to communicate what's wrong...so, it's a double-edged sword. She'll likely use the machine to communicate if you ACTUALLY listen to the message and respond. At the same time, she won't talk as much as she ordinarily would because she's talking into a machine and a machine doesn't have facial expressions or body language. With you, however, she can see when you don't agree through your body language and this would cause her to talk a little bit longer.

In the same, there will be men who will flirt with your wife and she may not necessarily recognize their advancements initially. Especially if she's the type of woman that tries to see the good in everyone. That's why it is a great idea to open up the lines of communication with her and let her know that she can trust you with whatever she gives you. In addition, never ever get angry about anything she tells you, or you'll close that line of communication. Always communicate what you want and what you do not want. In addition, always be honest with her. When she sees that you tell her things that a man would ordinarily be afraid to tell a woman, she will feel at peace and confident with you.

Lastly, please understand (wives and husbands) that there are some spouses who are just not marriage material, and for such, there isn't much affair prevention. The only thing you can and should do is be the best spouse that you can be so that if the marriage ends, you can walk away without the weight of guilt on your back. Guilt will always anchor the guilty to the past.

Towers of Reception

Remember the towers of reception. We know the limit of our spouse's reception, and we know when we've gone too far. The worst thing to do is to try to build more towers by going out of your spouse's range constantly, thinking that they will learn to pick up your signal eventually. This mentality is really common in failed marriages, and it is rooted in pride coupled with an unwillingness to do the work that marriage requires. This is why we should always wait for GOD to send us our spouses. The spouse that GOD has for you has been tried, refined and approved to be a spouse, and they have been conditioned to be your spouse. Without this refining process, the person that you choose won't be able to endure the ups and downs of who you are. Instead, you will end up with a seasonal partner who loves you during the happy times, but detests you during the not so happy times.

Oftentimes, disagreements start with you. We look at what is happening on the outside that triggered the reaction on the inside, when we should always come at problems from the inside out. We need to check our feelings at the front door, so that when we enter our homes, we are giving our spouses a fair shot at happy matrimony. When GOD challenged me, I found that a lot of what I felt came from past experiences. Not with Jean, but with people from my past who hurt me at some point in my life. That meant that I was out of season when I chose to get married. I wasn't ready yet, and any fruit that's not ready will be bitter. As human beings, we often make our spouses pay for the crimes of others, and this just isn't fair to them. Let's be honest with ourselves for a change...many times, it's not so much that we were hurt by others, we hurt ourselves by going out of the will of GOD to get into relationships that GOD did not call together. We fornicate, we date, and sometimes we marry the wrong people. Then when a devil acts like a devil, we want to confront the LORD to find out where HE is in all this. But, you didn't invite HIM to your courtship, you didn't ask HIM if this was the one for you, and you didn't ask HIM if HE approved of the relationship. You didn't even invite HIM to the wedding because deep down you knew HE wouldn't approve. You just thought that you'd get married and then invite the LORD into your marriage. Then come the challenges that you weren't seasoned for. You're going through stormy weather with a person, when you are conditioned to be receiving the winds of change. This was not a season you were called to endure, but because of your rebellion, you have to weather it. After the relationship ends, you walk around with a new rule and a new bruise, added to the old rules and bruises that were the result of other relationships. And the sad part is you expect your spouse to fix you.

This is where we have to build some brand new towers of reception and get rid of its two evil sisters: perception and deception.

Perception is how we perceive someone. What we perceive is not always based on truth or even facts, for that matter. Perception stems from where we are at the moment. If we're in a place of hurt, our perception stems from hurt, and we will view and respond to what we perceive as opposed to what is actually happening.

Your husband could be an action movie junkie, love to wear suits, love to wear sunglasses, and love to travel; but that doesn't mean he's a spy for the Secret Service. You shouldn't always believe what you perceive because perception is self-deception. Of course one plus one is two, but sometimes we add things together that aren't really a part of the problem.

Deception comes from two directions but is received by one tower, and that tower is your marriage. People don't deceive us when we are adults, since we are creatures of will. Instead, we are seduced by lies and by our own desire to stay within the happy zone of our emotions. Deception has to be believed to be received. When someone brings a lie to you, they can't force it into you; therefore, they deliver it with compliments or a bad attitude. People will always try to manipulate you into receiving a lie because the way GOD designed you is to only receive the truth. To manipulate is to move some things around in your mind so that they can get that lie in. Nevertheless, no person can get into your mind without you first allowing them in there, and even when they dance around the outskirts of your mind, there is an alarm built inside of you that will signal to you that something is wrong. If you push snooze on this alarm because the lies taste good, the deceiver isn't the only guilty party in your deception since you willed that lie in. You self deceived you.

In our marriages, we are the greatest self-deceivers, believing that we are right and our spouse is wrong. You have to agree that GOD is right and both you and your spouse are wrong. That is the only way to resolve a dispute. But pride is self-deception manifested in arrogance. Pride spawns contention.

To kill deception, you must first attack perception. To attack perception, you have to cure your heart by applying the WORD to it daily. You have to become brand new again. That's why a virgin makes for a better spouse, because oftentimes they are innocent to the harmful effects of a soul tie, whereas someone still bound rarely knows that they are bound. Pride guards the heart from receiving the truth, and offense stands hand-in-hand with pride to form a deceptive circle around any tower that it is guarding. Since you are no virgin, you have to be restored. This is where prayer and faith comes in. Faith comes by hearing and hearing by the WORD of GOD. You have to hear HIM. And you have to talk to HIM and listen to HIM.

I have found in listening to GOD that HE has me doing and saying things that my flesh does not want to do or say. When I'm angry with Jean, GOD will tell me to go and tell him that I love him. Do you know how that feels? To be angry and be told to go and apologize and or say "I love you" to the person you feel has made you angry? It's no easy task until you understand why GOD has you doing it. Pride breeds contention, so in your arguments, pride is the culprit or the instigator. Therefore, instead of going up against one another, GOD will have you (if you will only listen) to come against pride. How do you know when pride is there? You will know that pride is there when it hurts you tremendously to check yourself.

In being obedient to GOD, you'll find that the atmosphere almost always breaks and peace takes its rightful place. It's not about winning the fight; it's about building towers of reception. It's all about unity. Satan hates unity because it strips him of his power. This is why he comes against a marriage so fiercely. *"And if one prevails against him, two shall withstand him; and a threefold cord is not quickly broken" (Ecclesiastes 4:12).*

Here are a few tips to guide you along:
1. Pray and ask the LORD to stand in the midst of you and your spouse's communication.
2. Come together with your spouse and agree beforehand that you won't argue about the issue or manipulate one another, and you won't avoid the tough questions. You will simply talk and, if need be, laugh to lighten up the atmosphere.
3. Talk about the issue.
4. Don't leave the conversation until you have penned out a

resolution. Pen it on paper. If you can't come to a resolution, pray about it or seek Christian counseling.
5. Search the scriptures and see what GOD has to say. Oftentimes, your own personal solutions are your enemies. They come in looking peaceful, but they leave out with your wedding rings.
6. If your spouse is uncooperative, don't let your flesh drive you down. Pray for the spouse and ask the LORD to let HIS will be done, and not your own or your spouse's. (Sometimes, the LORD will take away the very things we are fighting about. If you can't play nice with it, neither of you will have it. It's a humbling experience, but one purposed in getting you both on the right track with HIM.)
7. Remain humble and let GOD be GOD. If you're anything like me, you may be a little on the inpatient side. You want to see results and now! But, the spouse is being stubborn and uncompromising. Needless to say, the problem isn't that the spouse is unyielding in this situation. The problem is that you are unyielding and you are anxious. When we are anxious, we experience anxiety, since anxiety is a symptom of anxiousness. *"Be anxious for nothing; but in everything by prayer and supplication with thanksgiving let your requests be made known unto God" (Philippians 4:6).*

Your tower of reception is communication with one another. It is better for the two of you, during times of peace, to sit down and discuss the issues that may challenge the marriage and draw up a solution immediately. That way, when one spouse steps on the battlefield of flesh, you can bring out the resolution. (Note: Make copies, some angry people like to tear paper).

Draw up a bonus for the winner in times of peace. The winner is the one who remains calm, doesn't use manipulation, and listens. The winner is the one who takes it to GOD. The winner should say something like, "Let's see what GOD has to say about it and agree that we will do what HE wants and not what we want." You can both agree that the winner will receive something special for their behavior. For example, you could say, "If I win, you are responsible for all household chores for one week, and you have to tell me that you love me every time I blink at you." It may sound silly, but adding humor to it will lighten up the situation. Don't say, for example: "If I win, you have to take me out to eat at _____________ restaurant every weekend for 4 weeks." This is not a punishment, and sometimes your spouse will purposely argue with you because they want to take you out and get some alone time with you. But a week's worth of household chores and the ability to slap pride in its face does a little something to one's schedule and their ego.

Crying is not communicating. So ladies, let's put away this emotional weapon for the sake of correcting the problem, rather than having an emotional tantrum. Men usually don't respond well to tears. On television, they feel bad, get up, and comfort their sobbing wife. In real life, most men get upset and try to escape because men associate crying with manipulation. Some women do use it as a tool of manipulation, but oftentimes women cry when all other forms of communication fail. But, if you feel the need to cry, it is better to go into a room and do it without his knowledge, so that he won't come into the discussion feeling pressured to escape it.

Grunting is not communication. Don't make sounds while your spouse is speaking. You may want them to know that you don't believe them, you don't receive what they are saying, and you could care less about how they feel. Direct communication without the use of games is the more effective communication.

Silence is not communication. You may be that spouse who figured it out. A silent spouse carries the bigger weapon. After years of arguing and yelling, I dabbled around in silence and found I got a better response. My argument success rates went up more than 50% and I (in my head) won the argument almost every time. The emotional spouse is always the one who comes up with the short end of it all. I tried it once and saw that the man I was married to could not take my silence. He was used to me being dramatic, but here I was saying nothing, and he went that extra mile to get an argument out of me. Nevertheless, I wouldn't give it to him because I was enjoying watching him be the emotional ruin that I usually was. Once I witnessed the power of silence, I used that as a tool of manipulation, and this was wrong. No matter what, there is no game that will help you win in marriage. Simply tell the truth to your spouse, and tell it in love. If they continue to be argumentative and refuse to compromise, that's when it's a good idea to be silent.

Remaining innocent will help you to remain focused on what is important. If the spouse is an unbeliever or a backslider who decides to leave the marriage despite your efforts, grieve and let GOD be GOD. You will heal a lot faster if you just forgive because you have remained innocent and have not lowered your self value. So if GOD allows them to divorce you, HE will know that you did your best and will send you the spouse who HE sees is a better fit for you.

Decide where your towers are and what your limits are. Try to stretch a little more than what you feel you can. If you can't stay within your own limits, don't restrict someone else to them.

With your marriage towers, you will sometimes receive mixed signals or no signals at all. The key isn't to tear down the tower and rebuild it when the signal isn't strong; again, the key is to build new towers. You have to communicate with one another during times of peace to establish new towers and get a broader range of communications. The more you broaden your range, the less you will fight.

In addition, don't control communication and don't tamper with the results using seduction or sex. That's not a tower of communication; that's a tower of witchcraft. Sex feeds the problem and then puts it to bed. You need to starve the problem and evict it. Some people like to control their spouses using sex, and some spouses like to start arguments for the sake of making up. Of course, to do so is perversion, and perversion means to turn away from GOD'S design for your life, your body and your mind. Your body will only engage in perversion when your heart is perverted, or better yet, when your heart is turned away from GOD. Control is manipulation, just as manipulation is witchcraft. To control someone is to move around the furniture in their head in order for you to feel comfortable there. The problem with this is that GOD arranged our minds to think a certain way and to follow a certain pattern. When you begin to mess around in someone's head, you are using witchcraft because once their mind has been reformatted, they will not be stable. Instead, they will become a vehicle for devils to drive. People sometimes make others unstable for their own comfort. This means they reprogram the man to serve them and to act in a way to suits their brokenness rather than being who they are or who they have learned to be. It is not uncommon for a man or a woman to believe that their way of thinking is far better than their spouse's way of thinking; therefore, they will attempt to rearrange the spouse's thoughts. This is when you will experience your spouse being at his or her most aggressive state or most passive state, because you are now crossing into forbidden territories trying to build an altar of yourself and your needs in that person's head.

We judge others based on where we are. A man has to absolutely have a sane and stable mind to provide, protect, and cover his wife. Take this from him and you've just allowed a devil to use you to break him. A woman has to absolutely have a sane and stable mind to help her husband, submit to her husband, protect her children, love her children, and keep a stable home. Take this from her, and you put your very kids in danger because you are basically telling her that the way that GOD has designed her is all wrong in your eyes. When we do this to one another, we cause one another to become unstable, not trustworthy, and most of all dangerous. Let a man (or woman) make their own mistakes, and use each mistake to build a new tower of reception. One of the best lessons I learned in being a wife was to allow Jean to trip whenever he went in the wrong direction, but to tell him beforehand that he was heading in the wrong direction. If he listened....great, he avoided the pitfall that I saw ahead. If he went forward anyway...great, he fell in the pitfall that I saw ahead, and he got up with experience, and experience yields knowledge just as listening to wise counsel yields it. In doing so, he learned that he could trust me to be his help-mate because he saw that I was not trying to be his controller or his mother. His falls opened up new lines of communication with us because the knowledge he gained on the way down became a testimony. I don't rub it in his face and remind him that I told him so. I learned that such communications will ultimately backfire because pride only engages pride. Instead, I listen intently as he shares the lesson with me, and I then share more of what GOD has given me with him. And guess what....after that fall, he listens because he knows that he can trust me to be his wife, his help-mate, and he can trust me to tell him the truth.

Remember, selfishness is not a tower; it is a hurricane that will sweep away all of the towers of communication that you have open. In a marriage, both lines have to be open for communication to be a success. You should never try to get your spouse to serve your hurts or your selfish needs. Instead, ask them to help you to heal from whatever is stirring you up on the inside. Ask them to pray for you and just be there for you when you are going through deliverance from such issues. But remember, you can't let these issues become hungry whales that swallow up your time and your joy. Any problem you find needs to be evicted from your marriage and never brought up again. If the problem visits your mind, rather than confronting the spouse, confront the problem.

When the towers of reception are many, you will find more peaceful days in your marriage, and Satan won't find a signal anywhere near your union. Take it day by day. Don't try to think ahead because such thinking breeds anxiousness, and anxiousness breeds anxiety, expectation, and yokes. Today, make it a point to be the best spouse that you can be and ask your spouse to do the same. Better yet, make it a point to be the best child of GOD that you both can be, and in doing so, everything else will fall in order.

Your spouse is not your enemy and should never be seen as such. Let's refocus our attention on the real enemy (Satan), and let's refocus our hearts on our first love (JEHOVAH).

Get your pen and paper out and start creating towers. Review the example below.

From me to hubby. Here are a few towers that I am asking to establish in our marriage.

1. When I am upset about something, please try to understand me and don't get angry with me. Instead, please take your role as the head of the house and communicate with me or set up a time to communicate with me. Understand that this time has to be before we go to bed. I agree to listen to you and not use anger, tears, or resurrect old issues in our communications, and I agree that the meeting will take no longer than 30 minutes. After the meeting, I won't bring up the issues again.
2. If I say something hurtful, I agree to pay you a settlement of $100 and you can do what you want with it. I agree to keep all of our communications respectful, and I will not engage in name-calling, cursing, ridiculing, or any speech about separation or divorce.
3. Hey baby. I like going to ________________ church, but you refuse to come with me. Why is that? Can we agree to pray on it, and if GOD gives us the green light, we will visit the church as much as GOD tells us to? Will you agree to be open to listen to GOD?

From me to the wife. Here are a few towers that I am asking to establish in our marriage.

1. Sweetie, sometimes you get angry and you won't leave a situation alone, and this is tiring to my soul. Sometimes I just want to go back to peace, but you insist on war. I would like you to take about 30 minutes to yourself when

you are angry. During these episodes, I ask that you write a note to me or record what you want to say to me and then reread or listen to what you have said or written down. If you still don't feel too good about the situation, I will agree to speak with you for 30 minutes about the issue. I agree not to get angry, raise my voice, show any signs of negative emotion, laugh at your pain, or close the discussion early. Please understand that even during the discussion, you may not get your way, and a meeting doesn't automatically mean that you will get your way. Instead, I am agreeing to us coming together to explore the issue and then explore what GOD has to say about the issue.

2. If I say something hurtful or disrespect you in any way, I will agree to pay you $100 and you can post a photo of me wearing a clown costume in the hall of shame. I agree to keep all of our communications respectful, and I will not engage in name-calling, cursing, ridiculing, or any speech about separation or divorce.
3. Hello darling, I know you like going to that church, but I'm not comfortable there. Please understand that as the head of the house, I have a responsibility to protect you and my children and if I feel something is not right, please trust the GOD in me. I cannot agree to go to that church because I feel that the place is not in order. Instead, let us come together and ask the LORD to share us where HE'D like us to place our feet. Will you agree to be open to listen to GOD?

As you can see from the above examples, husband and wife are creating a dialogue that will continue throughout the course of their marriage. They are learning one another and agreeing to respect the fact that they won't always agree. Create some towers like this for you and your spouse. Create as many as you can, because the more towers that the two of you agree to build, the better reception you will have in your marriage.

25 Tips For Married Couples

1. Kill any problem in your marriage by starving it, and anything that you want to grow, you sustain it by feeding it.
2. An angry spouse doesn't need to be corrected; they need to be covered. Stop exposing one another.
3. Love is not an emotion. Love is spirit. Just as hatred is not an emotion, it's a spiritual condition. You can't turn love on or off. You can only feed someone's wholeness or contribute to their brokenness. Never choose to break what GOD has handed you. If you saw a crack in your fine china, you'd try to fix it, right? Your spouse is worth more than fiberglass.
4. Babies don't fix marriages. Be fruitful and multiply, but never use a child as a way to hold on to one another.
5. No one can destroy your marriage unless you or your spouse gives them permission to do so. Therefore the problem didn't come from the outside, but from the Benedict on the inside.
6. Never pray and ask the LORD to make you into what your spouse needs. He or she may be broken and need to be

rescued. Instead ask the LORD to make the both of you into what HE has created you to be. That way, you meet at the altar again and again.

7. When raising children who are biologically not your own, it is better to love, discipline, and guide them. When married to someone who is not the parent of your child or children, it is better to let them love, discipline, and guide them. Children sometimes sit in divided places in your marriage and push the gap open a little wider; not because they are bad, but because they are children.
8. Crushes do crush marriages. That is adultery viewing the empty place in your heart to see if there's enough room for it to move in. Never engage in mental adultery, for it is a sin, and it is a prelude to physical adultery. Pray it off of you, and cast down all evil imagination.
9. Some friendships have to end for the sake of maintaining your marriage. There is simply no way around it.
10. Never remind your spouse of how right you are and how wrong they are. You'll turn what would have been them learning to trust the GOD in you into them continuing in their rebellion.
11. Let that man fall down so that he can learn to stand on his own. We sometimes act as a crutch to prevent our husbands from hitting a low in their lives, but didn't those lows bring you into a place of wisdom and awareness? If you carry him over the hole in the ground, he's going to fall in it one day when he tries to cross without you. It is better to let him learn to walk on his own. That's when you'll see growth. Growth doesn't come from your nagging him.
12. Let your wife see that she can trust you with the lead. You do this by basing your decisions on what the WORD of GOD says and not what you think.
13. Change atmospheres. Demons thrive in strife. Contending with the spouse and then praying for peace is like creating a dark, damp place, and asking mold not to grow. But, demons can't survive where the WORD is. Get into your closet and begin to pray and speak the WORD over your

home, spouse, and children. And then walk in forgiveness and watch that atmosphere shift.

14. Job's friends sounded wise to the untrained ear, but GOD said they darkened HIS counsel. Meaning, they took HIS advice and added evil to it. Do you know that there are plenty of people who are friendly enough to destroy your marriage with a smile? Be careful who you let speak into your marriage, because once you receive their advice, they have become a part of your union.
15. If a husband does not cover his wife's head, she will be in a constant battle with a Jezebel spirit. Cover her! You may never have to protect her physically, but you always have to protect her spiritually. Remember, GOD is the head of CHRIST, CHRIST is the head of man, and man is the head of the wife. If the order isn't followed, you leave your home open for attack.
16. Never underestimate the responsibility of your spouse. Appreciate them even for the little things.
17. Don't allow (in your home and presence) anything that you wouldn't want for your marriage. Do you have a brother who likes to cheat on his wife, for example? That's not your problem, but deliverance should be your prayer. Don't let him come in your home with that mess. Do you have a cousin that is not married, but she wants to visit your home with her boyfriend? Don't let her! When you allow people to sin in your home, you not only welcome them, but their demons as well. Guard your heart and your home. If that demon came in, it's because it bound the strong man first.
18. Watch your mouth. Sometimes we curse one another intentionally or out of ignorance. Be careful what you say. Don't tell your husband he makes you sick, and don't tell your wife that you love her to death. You are in your own land; develop your own language, and get rid of demon dialect.
19. Jealousy never stopped a man or woman from cheating. Do you see a cheating heart on your spouse? Talk to them and then go into warfare. Start binding up devils and

loosing warring angels. Anoint your home and drive that devil out. Anoint his or her shoes and decree: You will not step into the home or any place near a woman or man that is lusting after you. Anoint his head when he sleeps and decree that his thoughts will be pure and all evil thoughts are brought into captivity. Anoint her hands and decree that she will not touch any other man (or woman these days) in a lustful way. Anoint his eyes and decree that they are eyes for you and they will not look upon another woman (or man these days) lustfully. Anoint her ears and decree that she will hear the truth and not be deceived by a lie. You'd be amazed at how much power is in you!

20. Agree to argue less and pray more.
21. Love your spouse in spite of their imperfections. No one is perfect. Never put the responsibility and the yoke of expectation on your spouse to be error free when you yourself can't even pull off that feat.
22. Bury the past and impregnate the future. Stop exhuming foolishness. What's done is done, but to move forward, both of your feet have to take steps in the same direction, or you'll keep falling. Instead work on and towards what you want to see.
23. Get a hobby together. Sharing a like interest brings couples close to one another.
24. Study each other. Sometimes you will find things about your spouse that even they didn't know about themselves. Be a pioneer for change and not an engineer for strife.
25. Don't rearrange the furniture in your spouse's heart. Love the mess that they are and let the LORD clean them up. After all, your streets aren't without debris.

www.ingramcontent.com/pod-product-compliance
Lightning Source LLC
Chambersburg PA
CBHW051943090426
42741CB00008B/1248

* 9 7 8 0 9 8 5 4 1 0 6 0 5 *